The Ferns of Florida

The Ferns of Florida

A Reference and Field Guide

Gil Nelson

Drawings and Photographs by
the Author

Pineapple Press, Inc.
Sarasota, Florida

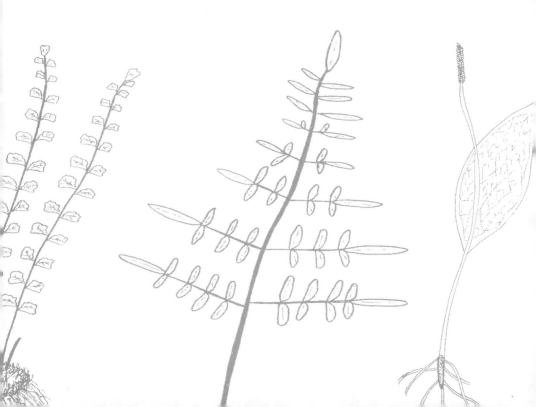

Dedicated to

Angus K. Gholson Jr. and W. Wilson Baker,
mentors, field companions, friends
in anticipation of our continued quest for the "little people."

Inquiries should be addressed to:

Pineapple Press, Inc.
P.O. Box 3899
Sarasota, Florida 34230
www.pineapplepress.com.

Library of Congress Cataloging in Publication Data

Nelson, Gil, 1949–
    The ferns of Florida / Gil Nelson.—1st ed.
        p. cm.
    Includes bibliographical references (p.).
    ISBN 1-56164-193-6 (hb : alk. paper) — ISBN 1-56164-197-9 (pb : alk. paper)
        1. Ferns—Florida—Identification. 2. Ferns—Florida—Pictorial works. I. Title.
QK525.5.F6 N46 2000
587'.3'09759-dc21   99-042528

First Edition
10 9 8 7 6 5 4 3 2 1

Composition by Shé Sicks
Printed and bound by Edwards Brothers, Ann Arbor, Michigan

TABLE OF CONTENTS

ACKNOWLEDGMENTS

No book of this type is written alone. Many individuals, both professional and amateur, lent their technical expertise and assistance to help me insure that the content that follows is as accurate as possible and reflects the current status of Florida's ferns and fern allies. As important as the technical help, however, was the understanding, encouragement, and spiritual support provided by my wife, Brenda, and daughter, Hope. Both have been consistent sources of inspiration. They have also been sympathetic supporters and patiently tolerant and accepting of my often overwhelming preoccupation with ferns and writing about ferns. They provide the strength in whatever I do and accomplish.

Chief among those who provided technical help include my good friends and field companions, W. Wilson Baker and Angus K. Gholson Jr., to whom this volume is dedicated. I have spent numerous hours afield with both of these gentlemen (including many occasions close to the ground in search of the Little People), and many more in discussion about our native flora. Both have freely shared their expertise and knowledge with me, often challenged my assumptions, and even more often led me to sites with rare or hard-to-find species. In addition to our regular field time, Wilson eagerly volunteered to read and comment on the manuscript, and Angus allowed me open use of his extensive private herbarium. Much of what might be considered the best of this book can be attributed to their encouragement and help. They have been both friends and mentors.

I also owe a great debt to Keith Bradley of Homestead, who corresponded with me regularly and who spent much time in the field with me, both in south and central Florida. Keith led me to, and helped me get photographs of, several of the state's rarest ferns and kept me updated on his botanical discoveries as they related to the state's pteridophyte flora. He read and commented on the manuscript and straightened me out on a number of misconceptions. His company, assistance, and expansive knowledge are greatly appreciated.

Dr. Loran Anderson, professor of botany and curator of the Florida State University herbarium, was an early and enthusiastic supporter of my research and this project. His invitation led to a courtesy appointment on the biological sciences faculty at FSU, which allowed me unrestricted access to the herbarium as well as other often-used and much-needed university resources. In addition, he corresponded and conversed with me regularly and made numerous contributions to my knowledge. His assistance made my research both easier and more efficient.

I would also like to thank Dr. Richard Wunderlin, professor of botany and curator of the herbarium at the University of South Florida. Dick welcomed my use of his outstanding herbarium, regularly corresponded with me about nomenclature and the status of certain of Florida's fern species, and allowed me the opportunity to read and critique the pteridophyte portion of the *Flora of Florida* project. He has also offered much encouragement for my work. Dick also introduced me to Drs. Rolla and Alice Tryon, two well-known figures in pteridology, both of whom have offered me encouragement as well as access to their extensive knowledge.

Also among the top contributors to my knowledge were Roger Hammer, Mike Owen, and Dr. Bobby Hattaway. Together, these three gentlemen took me to some of the

Fakahatchee Strand's most difficult-to-access and most beautiful natural gardens. On one of these occasions, and in only two days, I photographed over 30 species of ferns, including some of our state's rarest and most restricted species; catalogued at least 25 native orchids; and saw a host of magnificent epiphytes, which adorn the Strand's pond apple, cypress, and popash trees. Roger also introduced me to Don Keller, whose knowledge of south Florida pteridophytes is immense and whose willingness to share it was much appreciated. Don's personal fern garden is an outstanding laboratory for learning our fern flora, and his lists of endangered, extant, and extinct species of the southern peninsula became important resources in my research. My visits with him were both enjoyable and educational. Bobby Hattaway also reviewed the manuscript and made numerous helpful suggestions and criticisms.

Dr. Herb Wagner Jr., professor of botany at the University of Michigan and one of the world's leading pteridologists, also read and commented on the manuscript and made many helpful suggestions that strengthened its content. His willingness to review the work, our several phone conversations, and his encouragement of the project are greatly appreciated, as well as is the huge quantity of work that he has contributed to our knowledge of North America's, and especially Florida's, ferns and fern allies.

Dr. David Lellinger, curator of ferns at the U.S. National Herbarium of the Smithsonian Institution, was also extremely helpful. Dave's *A Field Manual of the Ferns and Fern Allies of the United States and Canada* proved an excellent reference and starting point for my research and his personal assistance with a variety of issues on numerous occasions have been much appreciated.

The treatment of the quillwort family is due in large part to the assistance of Dan Brunton of Ottawa, Ontario. Dan was an enthusiastic supporter and provided numerous resources that were essential for understanding the changing taxonomic landscape in the Isoetaceae. Dan also procured and contributed the fine scanning electron micrographs of the megaspores of Florida's three species of *Isoetes,* which are a welcome addition to the book.

I also owe a debt to Kent Perkins, manager of the herbarium of the Florida State Museum at the University of Florida, and Rufino Osorio. Kent was most supportive in allowing my use of the herbarium and responded to several inquiries for herbarium label data, and Rufino contributed the excellent color photograph of the sori of *Neurodium lanceolatum.*

In addition to those above, numerous others also helped in various ways. To this end, I would also like to thank Alan Cressler, Judith Garrison, Bruce Hansen, Carol Lippincott, Bruce McAlpin, Richard Moyroud, Rev. and Mrs. Charles Roesel, Cole Skinner, and Bill Thomas.

All of this help notwithstanding, any errors in the current volume should be attributed to me and me alone.

INTRODUCTION

Florida has the richest fern flora of any state in the continental United States; among U.S. territories, only Hawaii and Puerto Rico have greater numbers of fern species. Depending upon the authority used, at least 164 spontaneously occurring taxa (including species and varieties) have been recorded within the state's borders, 123 of which are considered native. Even if we discount the handful of very rare species that have not been reported in many years and may actually no longer be extant in the state, Florida's fern list is still larger by far than any like-size region of North America.

The Sunshine State's expansive fern flora is accounted for by at least three related factors. Perhaps foremost is the state's geographic location in the region of overlap between two climatic zones. At its northern edge, Florida is primarily temperate, while its southern extremity is distinctly subtropical. This results in a mingling of species from both zones. Some ferns that are typically more northern in distribution find the southern limits of their ranges in the northern panhandle, while some of tropical origin barely make it into the state at the southernmost tip of the peninsula. Secondly, and again at least partly because of its geographic position, Florida leads the nation in habitat diversity. Tropical forests, mesic slopes, riverine wetlands, rocky hammocks, steep-sided ravines, and limestone-studded sinkholes provide suitable growing conditions for a wide assortment of fern species. Third, the Florida peninsula is regularly and significantly impacted by storms and winds that originate in the tropics. Since ferns reproduce by microscopic spores that are easily carried great distances by air currents, at least some of our populations probably got their start by spores that were swept away from tropical climes and deposited in Florida.

How to Use This Book

This book is divided into two parts. The introduction offers a brief history of fern study in Florida, a note about the importance of fern conservation, a discussion of fern classification, a treatment of botanical nomenclature and descriptive vocabulary, an explanation of the fern life cycle, a brief discussion of fern hybridization, and a glossary. This is followed by a field guide to all of Florida's known native and naturalized ferns and is illustrated with 204 color photographs, as well as several black and white photographs and line drawings. It is this latter section that will provide the most help in identifying specimens found in the field.

Modern botanical manuals and floras, including *Flora of North America,* Volume 2 and Wunderlin's *Guide to the Vascular Plants of Florida,* are commonly arranged in phylogenetic order. Such organization is useful and scientifically defensible, and encourages readers to learn evolutionary relationships as they learn families, genera, and species. Nevertheless, I have chosen, not without some degree of misgiving, to arrange the current volume alphabetically by family, genus, and species. Though this arrangement somewhat obscures phylogenetic relationships, it facilitates use by making it easy to quickly look up a family, and to find a particular genus or species within the family. Since the volume is designed primarily as a field guide, it seems reasonable to forego phylogenetic organization in deference to handiness. For those interested in taxonomy, figure 3, on page 10, displays a phylogenetic treatment of the included taxa.

1

The first part of the book ends with a standard botanical key, which may be thought of as a word map that leads to the included species. The initial key is an artificial dichotomous key designed to lead readers to a particular family, genus, or in some cases a particular species. The key is composed of a series of paired statements or couplets composed of two leads, each of which offers an opposing condition. Armed with the key and a particular fern specimen, the reader first determines the lead that best fits the plant at hand, then follows that lead to the next opposing couplet. Carefully following the leads will most commonly lead the reader to a particular family or genus, though in a few cases it will lead directly to a particular species. In some instances, especially with large genera or families, the introduction to the genus or family will offer an additional key to its member genera or species. In small families, or in genera with only a few species, the keys are sometimes dispensed with and the reader need merely compare the specimen with the several descriptions and their illustrations to determine the specimen's identity.

In most cases, the species descriptions follow the same format, which begins with the common and scientific names, followed, where appropriate, by descriptions of the species' form, fronds, petiole, rachis, blade, pinnae, sori, habitat, and distribution. The distribution statement is sometimes followed by remarks about the species, which often include tips for identifying the species in the field as well as specialized notes regarding the species name, its scientific discovery and taxonomic history, or its use in the garden. Species remarks are followed by a list of the more common scientific synonyms by which a plant may also be listed in both professional and popular botanical texts. These synonyms are scientific names that have been applied to the species by previous, or sometimes current, taxonomists and will help the reader cross-reference this book with other field guides.

Many ferns have several common names by which they are known in different parts of the state or country. Where possible I have attempted to include all of those relevant to Florida. When a species has more than one common name, the first one listed has been determined as the most common or best. This is purely subjective on the part of the author and may be subject to differing opinion.

Some species are described as evergreen. In some cases this is true only for those plants growing in central or southern Florida. In others, such as for the Christmas fern *(Polystichum acrostichoides)*, it is true for north Florida as well. An attempt has been made to make this clear in the text.

Accompanying each description is a range map showing the general region of Florida in which the plant is found. These maps divide the state into four geographical sections as detailed in the state map located immediately following the table of contents. It should be noted that these maps are presented only as guides and are intended solely to show at a glance in which parts of the state a particular species might be expected. The maps are most helpful for the more common or widely distributed species. For rare species, or those with discontinuous ranges, use of the maps alone can be misleading since a plant shown as occurring in a particular region may actually only occur in one or a few counties in the region. Thus, for a more complete discussion of each species' range, readers are directed to the distribution statements.

In addition, I have also attempted to include in the distribution statements all counties in which particular species have been documented by scientific collections. Since some of these collections were made many years ago, certain species may not be currently present, or at least known to be present, in a particular region. Including these old records is intended to motivate readers to rediscover some of the state's lost populations.

In addition to a statement about range, the distribution statements also often indicate whether the species is native or alien to the state, and whether it is listed as endangered in the state. The six species that are listed as Category I and Category II pest plants for Florida are also noted. This same information is provided in checklist form in appendix 1.

Each family and most genera are introduced by a description which includes such information as the derivation of the family or genus name, its taxonomic history, and its salient morphological characters, as well as useful information common to its constituent species. Since botany is often as much about the people of botany as the plants, I have included the birth/death dates of many of the botanists who are mentioned in these family and genus introductions, as well as in other parts of the text.

A Brief History of Fern Study in Florida

It is not surprising that pteridology—the study of the ferns and fern allies—has enjoyed a rich and colorful history in Florida. Beginning at least as early as the mid-1800s, a cortege of botanists and fern enthusiasts has visited the state, collecting, recording, and mapping both common and elusive species and describing the habitats and natural areas in which they grow. Even today, new species are occasionally found, new sites for rare and threatened species uncovered, or old, once-lost sites rediscovered.

Three of the earliest chroniclers of Florida's ferns include Lucien Marcus Underwood (1853-1907), Alvah Augustus Eaton (1865-1908), and Allen H. Curtiss (1845-1907). Curtiss, the earliest of these three collectors, was an avid fern enthusiast and collector in the 1880s and early 1890s, as reported in his 1902 review for *The Plant World,* in which he noted that Florida was credited with 54 species and varieties of ferns. He is also recognized as the discoverer of the legendary "Citrus County fern grottoes" which were later explored and reported upon by numerous Florida botanists and pteridologists from the time of Roland Harper and John K. Small to the present. These fern grottoes, the most important of which was located near Pineola, were limestone sinkholes and chasms that supported an extensive array of ferns. The most important of these are now in private hands and have been destroyed through misuse, abuse, and the encroachment of nonnative plant species. *Asplenium* X *curtissii,* one of Florida's four endemic ferns from this region, was named for Curtiss by Underwood.

Underwood, a well-known pteridologist, professor of botany at Columbia University, and author of several editions of *Our Native Ferns and Their Allies with Synoptical Descriptions of the American Pteridophyta North of Mexico,* reported on a collecting trip to Florida in 1890-1891 (Underwood, 1891 [1892], 1906), and Eaton (1906) reported on three excursions to Florida that began in 1903. Underwood's 1891 report attributed 43 fern species to Florida, 24 of which were found in no other state. Underwood also suggested four regions in Florida worthy of further pteridophyte exploration: the river regions of west central Florida, the interior lake region of south Florida, the Keys, and the Biscayne Bay region. His 1906 article in the *Bulletin of the Torrey Botanical Club* included four newly described fern taxa from Florida, including *Asplenium verecundum, Asplenium* X *curtissii, Stenochlaena kunzeana* (now known as *Lomariopsis kunzeana*), and *Tectaria minima* (now known as *T. fimbriata*).

Eaton's report outlined a rambling adventure through many of Underwood's central and southern Florida destinations, including stops in Tampa, Bradenton, Ft. Myers, Key Largo, Miami, the Ten Thousand Islands, Flamingo, the Everglades, and numerous of the so-called Homestead hammocks. Several of the hammocks described by Eaton are now part of the Dade County park system. Others, such as Brickell Hammock, are now mostly or entirely gone.

The end of Underwood's and Eaton's careers with their deaths in 1907 and 1908 ushered in a period dominated by the explorations and writings of John Kunkel Small. Arguably the best-known name in Florida botany, Small's work includes nearly 100 articles detailing botanical explorations in Florida, several of which focus on the state's ferns, as well as a wide array of important botanical guides. His *Manual of the Southeastern Flora,* published in 1933, has long been out of print but is still a sought-after and frequently consulted reference. In 1918 he published *Ferns of Tropical Florida* and *Ferns of Royal Palm Hammock,* the first of Florida's fern guides, and in 1931 Science Press published his more comprehensive *Ferns of Florida.* Small's 1931 work listed 107 fern species in 14 families and 48 genera as occurring in Florida. He listed only three naturalized nonnative species, a much smaller number than our current 34 alien species. In 1938, the year of his death, he published the lavishly illustrated *Ferns of the Southeastern States* (reprinted in 1964 by Hafner but now long out of print), which included updates to his earlier Florida works, as well as a few species not then known to occur in Florida but that were later discovered in the state.

Figure 1. John K. Small and his fern hounds, left to right: Small, E.P. St. John, William Knight, and R. St. John

During Small's time, and at least partly due to his influence, the first four decades of the twentieth century constituted an active period for fern enthusiasts in the state, especially in the southern and central regions. Many visitors reported on their finds and adventures. Pember (1911), Smith (1911), Noble (1916), Satchwell (1916), Knappen (1929), Spurr (1941), and naturalist and ornithologist Maurice Broun (1936b) are some of the lesser-known names, while Roland Harper, Edward and Robert St. John, Donovan Correll, and Mary Diddell are some of the better known.

In one of his wide-ranging explorations across Florida, Harper (1916) visited and described *The Fern Grottoes of Citrus County, Florida.* These grottoes were first discovered by A. H. Curtiss in April 1881 but were not described by him until 1902. Mary Noble, a fern enthusiast who lived in Inverness, visited the site of these grottoes in 1908 and later corresponded with Harper about her findings in anticipation of his own visit in 1915. Harper's description of this remarkable location describes a 2- to 3-acre hammock at the edge of a river swamp where "cliffs, chasms, and grottoes" supported a profusion of rare ferns growing on soft, moist limestone in the dense shade of an overstory of ironwood, swamp chestnut oak, sugarberry, sweetgum, red maple, bald cypress, flowering dogwood, live oak, and red bay.

The St. John brothers, in particular, followed Harper in Citrus, Sumter, and Hernando Counties and were leaders in exploring the limestone-studded hammocks of west central Florida. Considered by Small to be part of what he dubbed his "fern hounds" (figure 1), Robert P. and Edward P. St. John wintered in the village of Floral City, in present-day Citrus County, and spent many hours investigating and reporting on explorations into the sinkholes and grottoes that dotted the region. Their reports (1935, 1936) described a fern paradise replete with delicate spleenworts, maiden hairs, filmy ferns, marsh ferns, and adder's-tongues, many of which were hidden among the crevices and recesses of ancient limerock or in the moist woodlands along the Withlacoochee River.

In 1938 Donovan Correll produced one of the state's first county checklists of ferns. Correll's list included 119 species and 3 varieties and offered a map showing the distribution of fern collections in the state. Sixty-one of Correll's 122 taxa were found in Dade County; another 30 in Alachua, Citrus, Hernando, Highlands, Polk, and Seminole Counties; and a still lesser number in the central panhandle. Correll attributes the sparse fern distribution in other parts of the state to a lack of botanical activity. While it is true that certain areas had received more botanical exploration than other parts of Florida, it is equally true that the three centers of distribution shown on Correll's map, namely the southern Florida peninsula, the west central peninsula, and the central panhandle, still encompass some of the state's richest natural ferneries.

Correll's map also shows a number of collections from Duval and St. John's County. These are likely attributed to Mary Diddell, a resident of Jacksonville and one of Small's correspondents. Diddell was a fern gardener and collector who wrote several papers for the *American Fern Journal* (Diddell, 1936, 1941, 1956) and was an early avid fern enthusiast. Many of her specimens are now on deposit in the herbarium of the Florida State Museum at the University of Florida in Gainesville.

The more recent history of fern botany in Florida begins with Olga Lakela and Robert W. Long, who produced the second statewide guide to Florida ferns (Lakela and Long, 1976) as well as *A Flora of Tropical Florida* (Long and Lakela, 1971), the latter of which included a treatment of the ferns of the southernmost peninsula. Their *Ferns of Florida* included 135 species and 11 varieties or subspecies in 21 families and 52 genera, a significant increase from Small's earlier work. Long and Lakela made pteridophyte collections throughout Florida, many of which are on deposit in the herbarium of the University of South Florida.

Long and Lakela have been followed by Warren H. Wagner Jr., Clifton Nauman, and Richard P. Wunderlin, among many others. Wagner and Nauman have both been active in Florida pteridology and have published many scientific articles in a variety of professional journals. Wagner and Alan R. Smith wrote the section on pteridophytes for *The Flora of North America,* Volume 1, and Wagner, Nauman, and Smith figured heavily in *The Flora of North America,* Volume 2, which includes treatment of nearly all of Florida's ferns. The two volumes of the *Flora of North America* provide the taxonomic underpinning for this book.

The latest treatment of Florida's ferns is provided by Wunderlin (1998) in his *Guide to the Vascular Plants of Florida.* Wunderlin's treatment is included within a technical botanical manual to the state's flora. Though it does not parallel in all respects the taxonomy followed in the *Flora of North America,* it does include an excellent phylogenetic overview of Florida's pteridophytes, as well as keys to families, genera, and species.

A Note about Fern Conservation

Forty-three of Florida's native pteridophytes are listed as endangered, seven as threatened, and three as commercially exploited (see appendix 3). Seven additional taxa are tracked by the Florida Natural Areas Inventory because they are sufficiently uncommon or their occurrences so poorly documented as to warrant concern about their status. This brings the total number of threatened species to 58, or about 47 percent of the 123 species that are known to occur (or in a few cases to once have occurred) naturally in the state.

Much of the loss of Florida's fern flora may be attributed to habitat destruction, first for agriculture and later to accommodate the state's rapid and massive growth. J. K. Small's 1926 treatise *From Eden to Sahara: Florida's Tragedy* reports on some of the earliest of this destruction and ominously foretells much of what was to come. His little volume shows photograph after photograph of destroyed natural areas, among them some of the state's finest natural ferneries. Others that he mentions, such as the grottoes described by Harper in 1916, have now been all but destroyed, and the territory surrounding them has been radically altered. Sumter County, the home of these magnificent fern showplaces, has recently been named as the state's fastest-growing county, an accolade surely to put even more pressure on the few sites left that harbor some of our more rare and singular fern species.

Small's book offers convincing evidence that those things we now view as abundant may one day be counted among the rare. Hence, it is imperative that those of us who cherish our natural flora learn to appreciate it where it is and not try to bring it home with us. This is especially true for fern enthusiasts. Since many fern species occur in large populations and are readily transplanted, it is easy to persuade ourselves that taking just a few will not do appreciable damage to natural populations. This is not true. Given the number of responsible native nurseries that propagate and sell native fern species, coupled with the relatively low cost of such nursery-grown specimens, there is neither need nor justification for taking specimens from the wild. It should be noted that collecting any plants on public lands, whether for scientific or nonscientific reasons, is expressly forbidden by state law without the proper permit, and the collection of any listed species on any land, public or private, is also governed by statute and also requires a permit.

As Florida's growth continues to accelerate, it will become even more important that citizens become diligent conservationists by acting responsibly to protect our natural gardens and to speak out on their behalf. It will also become more important for our state to continue its practice of buying and preserving public lands that protect our most endangered communities, including those that harbor our rarest ferns.

Fern Gardening

Gardening with ferns is an interesting and relatively easy adventure that yields immensely pleasing results, even for those of us who lack significant gardening experience or skill. Whether massed in mixed plantings, trailing along foundations or shrubbery beds, or used to accent naturalistic settings, their soothing form and pleasing textures lend a charming aspect to the home landscape.

As might be expected in a state so rich in natural ferneries, fern gardening in Florida has enjoyed a long history. Early editions of the *American Fern Journal* regularly mention some of the state's earliest fern gardening enthusiasts, with some reports even going so far as to provide home addresses of particularly active gardeners and encouraging readers to visit them. Others are written by the gardeners themselves and detail the number and kinds of ferns that can be effectively grown in Florida's subtropical environs.

As with all gardening, the primary considerations for establishing ferns in the home garden are air, light, and moisture. While a few species will tolerate relatively open light and somewhat dry soil, most require shade or dappled sun and moist conditions. A few species require generous calcium in the soil and do well in rock gardens composed of limestone chips or boulders. In the central and southern parts of Florida, ferns can be planted and tended nearly year-round. In the state's more northern climes, the best time to prepare beds is in the spring, since all but the hardiest species die back during the region's cold winter temperatures. Fertilizing is typically not required in the fern garden and, in fact, may be detrimental to a number of the more tender species. During rainy seasons normal precipitation will keep ferns damp, though supplemental watering may be required during dry periods or seasonal droughts. Insect control is also typically not a problem with ferns, since only a few species are bothered by insect pests.

The desire to grow ferns is sometimes coupled with the desire to dig them from the wild. As noted earlier in the discussion of fern conservation, this should never be done. Many of Florida's native nurseries carry excellent and reasonably priced selections of native species which have been grown from spores or propagated vegetatively from spore-grown plants.

In addition, two statewide organizations provide information about using Florida's native plants in landscaping and gardening. These include the Association of Florida Native Plant Nurseries and the Florida Native Plant Society. The first of these, which can be reached by writing AFNN, P.O. Box 434, Melrose, FL 32666-0434, produces a catalog detailing the offerings of its more than 80 members as well as sponsors its own web page (http://members.aol.com/afnn/). The Florida Native Plant Society, which can be reached by writing FNPS, P.O. Box 690278, Vero Beach, FL 32969-0278, also sponsors a Web page (www.fnps.org) and publishes a quarterly journal that focuses on native plants. Both are excellent sources of information for acquiring native ferns without taking them from the wild.

Many fern enthusiasts learn to grow their own specimens from spores, an exciting and rewarding undertaking. Several good fern gardening books, such as those by F. Gordon Foster and John Mickel, both of which are listed in the bibliography, provide excellent information about how to do this.

In addition to not taking ferns from the wild, care should also be taken when gardening with nonnative species. Avid gardeners—fern gardeners, in particular—are often drawn to exotic plants from faraway places to add to their own manicured landscapes. Often, especially in Florida, these plants do not stay where they are planted but spread into nearby natural areas, where they compete with and sometimes displace native species. Since ferns disperse by tiny spores that are easily carried by the wind to distant locations, nonnative ferns planted in a single garden might produce spores that find suitable conditions for development many miles from the original planting. The Japanese climbing fern *(Lygodium japonicum)*, one of the state's more notorious invasive weeds, likely got its start from home gardens and is an excellent case in point. Hence, before using nonnative ferns in your garden, check them out carefully to insure that they are not considered invasive and are not listed as such by the Exotic Pest Plant Council (see appendix 1). Better yet, limit your gardening to some of the more than 100 species that occur naturally in Florida.

Plant Classification

The classification of vascular plants involves arranging species into a systematic and logical sequence. Throughout the history of botany, many systems have been developed for organizing our understanding of the world's flora.

The earliest recorded classification schemes categorized species by their form or habit. For example, the ancient Greek philosopher Theophrastus (370-285 b.c.), a student of Aristotle who is often credited as the father of scientific classification, divided all plant species into trees, shrubs, undershrubs, and herbs. Such concepts dominated the science of classification into the 1500s and are still quite handy in field botany and horticulture.

Later schemes, most notably that of Carolus Linnaeus (1707-1778), used what are often called mechanical or artificial systems. Such systems take into account observable morphological differences between groups, rather than their genetic or evolutionary relationships involving all types of characters. Linnaeus, for example, used what has been called a "sexual system," in which plants were divided into classes based upon the number, arrangement, and morphology of their flower parts. Linnaeus's system dominated systematic botany throughout the 1700s. However, his continued influence on modern botany rests mostly with his system of botanical nomenclature which is outlined on page 16.

Mechanical systems were followed by the development of so-called natural systems in which species were categorized by their relationships rather than by artificial characters. Classifying plants by natural affinities was probably first conceived by the English naturalist John Ray (1628-1705) in the late 1600s, but was only fully appreciated after its further development and more widespread publication by the French botanists Bernard de Jussieu (1699-1766)

Figure 2. Taxonomic Levels* Using Resurrection Fern (*Pleopeltis polypodioides* var. *michauxiana*) as a Sample

Level	Scientific name	Common name/meaning
Subkingdom	Embryobionta	Spore-bearing Plants
Division	Polypodiophyta	True Ferns
Class	Polypodiatae	Polypody Class
Order	Polypodiales	Polypody Order
Family	Polypodiaceae	Polypody Family
Genus	Pleopeltis	Mock Polypody Genus
Species	polypodioides	Specific Epithet
Variety	michauxiana	Variety Name

*Based on Cronquist, Takhtajan, and Zimmermann (1966), and Wagner and Smith (1993)

and Antoine Laurent de Jussieu (1748-1836), and the English botanists George Bentham (1800-1884) and Sir Joseph Hooker (1817-1911). Bentham and Hooker's three volume *Genera Plantarum* (1862-1883) was for many years the standard reference for botanical classification.

Since the publication of Darwin's *On the Origin of Species* in 1859, classification schemes have increasingly emphasized a phylogenetic arrangement of species. Such arrangement is based largely on evolutionary lines and relationships, with the earliest-known and more "primitive" species listed first, followed in order by those that are presumed to have developed later or that are thought to have been derived from the more primitive forms. The best-known and earliest of the phylogenetic systems include those of the German botanist Adolph Engler (1845-1930) and the American botanist and former head of the botany department at the University of Nebraska, Charles Bessey (1845-1915). The systems proposed by Robert Thorne (1968, 1992) and Arthur Cronquist (1981, 1988), both of which are based on Bessey's work, are two of the best developed and most widely used in current botanical classification.

These modern classification schemes place species into a hierarchical format, in which each level in the hierarchy is inclusive of more diversity and variation than the level immediately below it but less diversity and variation than the level above it. Each level or rank in this hierarchy is referred to by a commonly accepted, though somewhat varying, label or name. The name associated with each level or rank is known as a taxon (taxa, plural), which is sometimes confusing to beginning plant enthusiasts. In botanical parlance, it is equally correct to use the term "taxon" to refer to the fern genus *Asplenium* as it is to refer to the species *Asplenium monanthes,* or to the family Aspleniaceae. Figure 2 illustrates these levels.

The Classification of the Pteridophytes

The classification of the ferns and fern allies is a somewhat unsettled science that continues to produce a variety of interpretations. Various modern authors treat the group in varying ways (Lellinger, 1985; Mickel, 1979; Tryon and Tryon, 1982; Wagner and Smith, 1993; Wunderlin, 1998). Most disagreement seems to be at the family and higher levels, but there is also some disagreement at the genus and even species levels, particularly with the treatment of hybrids, varieties, and subspecies.

Figure 3. Phylogenetic Summary of the Pteridophyte Divisions, Families, Genera, Species (varieties*), and Hybrids that Occur in Florida

Division	Family	Genera	Species	Hybrids
Psilotophyta	Psilotaceae	1	1	
Lycopodiophyta	Lycopodiaceae	4	6	2
	Selaginellaceae	1	6	
	Isotaceae	1	4	
Equisetophyta	Equisetaceae	1	2	
Polypodiophyta	Ophioglossaceae	4	11	
	Osmundaceae	1	2	
	Gleicheniaceae	1	1	
	Schizaeaceae	1	1	
	Lygodiaceae	1	3	
	Anemiaceae	1	2	
	Parkeriaceae	1	2	
	Pteridaceae	6	22	1
	Vittariaceae	1	1	
	Hymenophyllaceae	1	5	
	Dennstaedtiaceae	4	4 (2)	
	Thelypteridaceae	3	18	
	Blechnaceae	3	6	
	Aspleniaceae	1	12	4
	Dryopteridaceae	15	22	2
	Polypodiaceae	8	14	
	Marsileaceae	1	5	
	Salviniaceae	1	2	
	Azollaceae	1	1	
Totals	24	63	153 (2)	9

*Note: Several taxa counted at the species level are species that are represented in Florida by only a single variety or subspecies. In contrast, the number in parentheses represents the single species *(Pteridium aquilinum)* represented in Florida by three varieties.

I have chosen in this volume to follow the work of Wagner and Smith (1993) and the *Flora of North America,* Volume 2. According to this system, which is founded at the higher levels on the work of Cronquist, Takhtajan, and Zimmerman (1966), all fern taxa, as well as the so-called fern allies, are included within the divisions Psilotophyta, Lycopodiophyta, Equisetophyta, and Polypodiophyta. Each of these divisions (which are cited by varying names at the class level by some authors) includes one or more extant taxa. Figure 3 lists these divisions, and summarizes the constituent families and number of genera and species that occur in Florida.

Accepting the classification proposed in the *Flora of North America* results in this volume being a departure from the treatment of the pteridophytes presented in Wunderlin's (1998) work on the flora of Florida. Most differences between Wunderlin and this volume are found at the family level. Wunderlin, for example, treats the genera *Actinostachys, Anemia,* and *Lygodium* in the family Schizaeaceae, whereas this volume assigns them to three separate families. The same is true for several other genera.

With two notable exceptions, the treatment of genera and their constituent species in this volume agrees well with the treatments in Wunderlin. The exceptions include *Phlegmariurus dichotomus,* which Wunderlin treats as *Huperzia dichotoma,* and *Cheiroglossa palmata,* which Wunderlin treats as *Ophioglossum palmatum.* Appendix 2 contains Wunderlin's treatment, organized alphabetically by family, genus, and species. Appendix 1 includes a similarly arranged list of the species included within this volume.

Close observers will note that 13 species that appear on the list in appendix 1 are not reported in the *Flora of North America,* Volume 2 as occurring in Florida. One of these species, *Ophioderma pendula,* was left out of the flora because it was not discovered in Florida (or in North America) until 1998, while two others were included in the flora but were not shown as being distributed in Florida. The other ten taxa, which include a variety of rare, uncommon, or newly naturalized species, were apparently overlooked by the editorial committee and were not treated as occurring in North America. In addition, two species listed in the *Flora of North America* as occurring in Florida—*Diplazium pycnocarpon* (Sprengel) M. Broun and *Ophioglossum vulgatum* Linnaeus—were apparently included inadvertently and are not known to occur in the state.

The Language of Botany

As with most sciences, botany is equipped with its own technical language. Though this language can seem daunting to beginners, learning its fundamentals is an important endeavor. For professionals, the use of standard botanical language is a necessity. For amateurs, it enhances the enjoyment, fulfillment, and sense of accomplishment associated with their hobby and makes professional literature accessible, readable, and exciting as well. Though the descriptions and discussions that follow use only the most common technical terms, becoming proficient in the language of botany should not be ignored. The following discussion and the glossary that follows will be helpful in understanding any standard resources about ferns and their allies.

Botanical parlance may be divided into two parts: morphology and nomenclature. Each of these categories has its own lexicon of frequently used vocabulary. Morphology refers to the parts of a plant, each of which has a specific name that is used in the plant's description. Morphology also includes terms that are used to convey the appearance or habit of a plant,

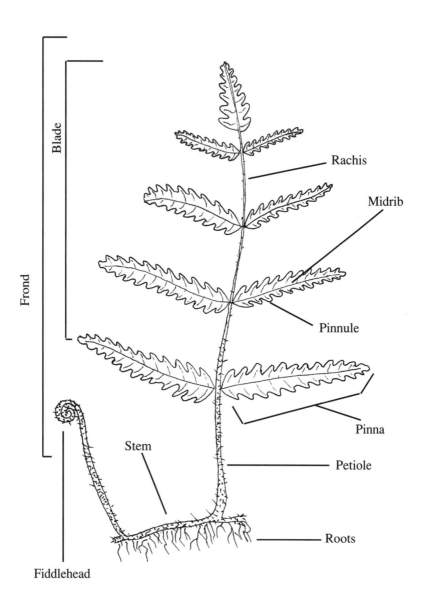

Figure 4. Parts of a Fern Frond

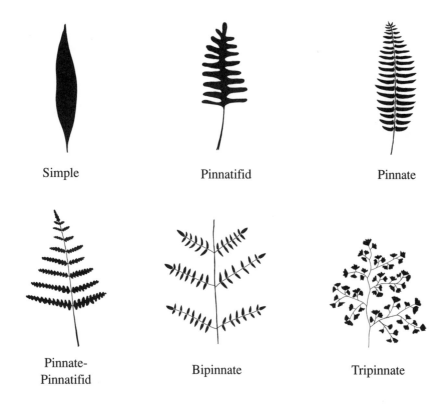

Figure 5. Typical Shapes of Fern Fronds

its outline, and the shape, texture, vestiture, and technical details of its parts. Nomenclature refers to the scientifically accepted conventions used in naming each species.

Fern Morphology

Those new to fern study should begin by learning to identify the major parts of a fern (see figure 4). As outlined later in the section on the fern life cycle, most of us are familiar with ferns only during their sporophytic, or frond-bearing phase. During other parts of their life cycles most ferns are so small or inconspicuous that they escape our notice.

The "frond" or "leaf" is that portion of a fern that typically grows above the ground and gives the plant its typical fernlike appearance. It includes both the petiole (also called the stalk or stipe) and the blade. The "petiole," which may be long and conspicuous, short and inconspicuous, or absent, is that portion of the frond that connects the stem to the blade. It may be rounded, flattened, or angled in cross-section, and it may be smooth, hairy, scaly, variously longitudinally grooved, or some combination of all of these.

The "blade" is the expanded portion of the frond that arises at the apex of the petiole or, occasionally, directly from the stem without a petiole. Blades can be undivided (simple), once-divided (pinnate), or multiply divided (bipinnate, tripinnate, or more). Figure 5 illustrates the typical blade divisions found in the ferns.

As might be expected, the divisions of the blade also have names. In divided blades, the first division is called a "pinna" (plural, pinnae). Pinnae arise from the rachis, or central axis of the blade. The rachis typically appears as an extension of the petiole and is often, but by no means always, similar to it in color, grooving, scaliness, and hairiness. Pinnae are also sometimes called "segments" or "leaflets," though the latter is discouraged by some pteridologists, as it might be confused with the same term used for describing the segments of compound leaves in the flowering plants. Divisions of the pinna are called "segments" or "pinnules," the latter of which is ordinarily applied only to a pinna's first division. The last division of a multiply divided blade is typically referred to as the "ultimate segment."

In many ferns, especially those species that occur in Florida, the stem is underground and seldom seen. Occasionally it extends slightly above the ground, as in the Florida tree fern *(Ctenitis sloanei)* or grid-scale maiden fern *(Thelypteris patens)*, or grows along the surfaces of limestone or tree trunks, as with the goldfoot fern *(Phlebodium aureum)*.

Below ground stems, which are also called "rhizomes" (and sometimes, though not preferably, "rootstock"), may be described as hard and knotty, in which case the fronds are usually bunched together at the ground surface, or they may be described as short- or long-creeping, in which cases the fronds may arise at intervals along the ground surface. A few species, such as the several members of the highly specialized family Ophioglossaceae, have short, erect, or bulbous stems with fleshy roots. Short-creeping stems grow laterally for short distances, usually immediately below and parallel to the soil surface. Long-creeping stems may grow laterally for several feet. It is sometimes easy to recognize long-creeping stems from the "trail" of fronds that characterizes their growth habit. Though the descriptions in this book usually include a statement about the appearance and habit of the stem, stem descriptions are usually not used as an identifying feature. Hence, it is not necessary to dig specimens in order to identify them.

Fronds arise from the stem in two primary ways. Most commonly, new fronds are coiled into "croziers" or "fiddleheads," which unroll as the frond matures, a condition called "circinate vernation." In a few instances, as with the several species of *Botrychium*, the developing fronds are folded over from the top before breaking through the soil surface, then unfold rather than unroll as they grow. This latter condition is called "conduplicate vernation."

Unlike flowering plants, ferns reproduce directly from spores, a process which is explained in the following discussion of the life cycle of the ferns. A spore is a tiny reproductive body which can be examined closely only under high magnification. Spores are borne in cases called "sporangia" (sporangium, singular). In some fern species, the sporangia are borne in clusters, or "sori" (sorus, singular), on the lower surface of the pinnae (see photo 54 of *Dryopteris ludoviciana* for an example of typical sori). In some species, the sori are protected by a covering or "indusium" (indusia, plural), in which case they are said to be indusiate. An indusium may arise from a central stalk, umbrella-like (see *Tectaria heracleifolia,* photo 75, be elongated and attached along the side like a miniature hot-dog bun or taco shell (see photo 8 of *Asplenium heterochroum*), kidney shaped (see photo 59 of *Nephrolepis cordifolia*), or cuplike and surrounding the sporangia (see photo 84 of *Trichomanes petersii*). In some instances, for example the members of the genus *Adiantum* (see figure 27, p. 133, the sori are hidden beneath the curled edge of a blade segment. This curled edge is then said to serve as a false indusium.

The position of the sori is helpful in identification. Sori may be borne individually between the margins and midvein of the pinnae or pinnules (see photo 188 of *Thelypteris kunthii*), continuously along the margins or central axis of the pinnae (see photo 155 and 27 of *Pteris cretica* and *Blechnum occidentale,* respectively), in notches at the base of the sinuses between the pinnules (see photo 36 of *Hypolepis repens)*, or naked along fertile fronds or portions of fronds (see photo 110 of *Osmunda cinnamomea).* In the genus *Marsilea* the spores are contained within specialized sporocarps which are borne along the stem (see photo 98 of *Marsilea minuta).* In species of *Botrychium* and *Ophioglossum* the sporocarps are positioned along specialized branches of the frond (see photo 108 and 99 of *Ophioglossum crotalophoroides* and *Botrychium biternatum,* respectively).

Fronds which bear sori are said to be fertile, those which do not are described as sterile. Both fertile and sterile fronds may have the same appearance, in which case the species is said to be monomorphic, meaning "with a single form." In other species the fertile and sterile fronds are slightly to significantly different from each other in appearance, in which case the species is said to be dimorphic. Knowing whether or not a particular species is monomorphic or dimorphic, and being able to recognize the special forms of fertile fronds, can be very helpful to field identification.

The preceding discussion applies more directly to the true ferns than to the so-called fern allies, which are also vascular plants that reproduce by spores. Though the allies are pteridophytes, they are not closely related to the ferns and typically lack a fernlike appearance. The fern allies include only the club-mosses (Lycopodiaceae), spike-mosses (Selaginellaceae), quillworts (Isoetaceae), horsetails (Equisetaceae), and whisk ferns (Psilotaceae).

Fern descriptions often include the overall shape of the blade, or in some cases the entire frond. Most commonly, blades are elliptic, deltate or triangular, ovate, lanceolate, oblong, or linear. Each of these terms is often used in conjunction with adjectival modifiers. For example, a blade described as elliptic is generally about two times longer than it is broad, widest in the middle, and tapering more or less equally toward both ends. However, sometimes blades are described as broadly elliptic, meaning that the blade's length to width ratio is lower, or narrowly elliptic, meaning a higher length to width ratio. Likewise, blades may be described as broadly or narrowly triangular, ovate, or lanceolate. The point at which one shape grades into another is indistinct and subjective and should be used only as a guide in field identification.

The parts of a fern are often covered with hairs, scales, glands, or some combination of these. The term *indumentum* is often used to denote this covering. In some instances, one or more parts of the plant display no indumentum and are then said to be glabrous. Scales are much reduced, hairlike or leaflike structures that often clothe the stem, petiole, rachis, or blade surface. The term is generally applied to structures that are flattened in cross-section and two or more cells wide. The margins, or edges, of scales may be entire (smooth, lacking teeth), toothed, or lined with minute hairs or glands. Hairs, on the other hand, are generally rounded in cross-section and only one cell wide. Both hairs and scales may be segmented, or divided into segments lengthwise, a feature which is usually only clearly visible with good light under magnification of 30x or more. Some hairs are simple, others are branched or fascicled from the base in a star-shaped or brushlike pattern and are called stellate, and some are tipped with tiny glands.

Some surfaces are densely hairy, others moderately so. Such terms as tomentose, hirsute, strigose, and scabrid, all of which appear in the glossary, are useful in describing the hairs on a fern.

Fern Nomenclature

Nomenclature refers to the rules for naming plants established by the International Code of Botanical Nomenclature. These rules attempt to assure that every plant is uniquely named, that the names of plants are appropriately devised and applied, that new or revised names are validly published for the scientific community, and that the earliest name for a species takes precedence over later names.

Complete scientific names are composed of several parts, some of which are required by the rules while others are used only when they apply. The first and most often seen part of the name is made up of a Latinized binomial which includes a genus name followed by a specific epithet. The genus name is analogous to an English surname, and the specific epithet to the given name. Following the epithet, and a required part of the complete botanical name, is an indication of the author or authors who originally named the plant, or reclassified it into a new genus. Some species are further divided into varieties, subspecies, or forms. These further taxonomic divisions are applied to presumably stable differentiations below the species level and are denoted in the complete name by appended Latinized names and their authors.

The scientific name of the resurrection fern *Pleopeltis polypodioides* (Linneaus) E. G. Andrews & Windham var. *michauxiana* (Weatherby) E. G. Andrews & Windham, Florida's most widespread pteridophyte, provides an excellent example for diagramming a complete botanical name. The name *Pleopeltis* is the genus to which the species is currently assigned. The name was formed by combining the Greek words *pleos* ("many") and *pelte* ("shield"), in reference to the stalked scales that cover the immature sori of species assigned to this genus. The specific epithet, *polypodioides* literally means "with the appearance of *Polypodium*," another fern genus to which the current species bears a strong resemblance (the suffix *oides* means "like" or "resembling"). Latinized names, which are most often constructed from Greek, Latin, or Latinized words, are often used to denote a particular salient morphological feature, habit, or ecological niche of the genera (plural for genus) or the species to which they are assigned, though sometimes they are used to commemorate an individual or geographic location.

The authority for our example species includes the name Linnaeus, enclosed within parentheses, followed by two other names joined with an ampersand. This means that the original binomial name for this species was attributed to Carolus Linnaeus, but has since been changed at least once, most recently (in 1993) by Elisabeth G. Andrews and Michael D. Windham. Linnaeus's original name for this fern was *Acrostichum polypodioides* and was first published in his *Species Plantarum* in 1753. Since then at least eight valid names have been applied to the species, all of which are said to be in synonymy with the current name. The most recent synonym is *Polypodium polypodioides* (Linnaeus) Watt. Since the newest binomial combination was applied only in 1993, the latter synonym is still commonly seen listed in both popular and professional manuals, floras, and plant lists. In most cases authority names are shortened to a set of more or less standard abbreviations (such as L. for Linnaeus). In this book I have chosen to use complete names. This has been done in order to provide as much information as possible about the people of botany.

In our example species, the authority name is followed by the abbreviation "var.," and another Latinized name. This designates that resurrection fern has at least two varieties; actually, the species has six. The varietal name *michauxiana* commemorates Andre Michaux (1746-1802), an early French botanist who visited the New World during the late 1700s and described many North American plants. The names of many genera and species honor important botanists or naturalists.

Following the varietal name are the names of the authorities that described and named the variety.

In addition to "var.," the Latin binomial and authority is sometimes followed by the abbreviations "subsp." (short for subspecies) or "f." (forma), or a combination of these three. All three of these levels of classification are referred to as *infraspecific units of classification,* meaning that they recognize differences between individual populations of the same species. The definitions for these three classification levels vary among taxonomists and botanists. In general, a subspecies is a taxon that can be distinguished from the parent species, but that has not yet developed evolutionarily far enough to be considered a separate species. The category of variety is sometimes used interchangeably with subspecies, but has been classically used to recognize stable distinctions within an individual subspecies. *Forma* refers to a relatively minor but recognizable variant of a species.

Most plants are also known by one or more common or vernacular names. Such names often describe a morphological feature, or medicinal or other folk use of the plant. No authority governs the use or acceptability of common names and the same plant may have different names in different regions, countries, or parts of the country. Common names are very useful and often have interesting origins. However, serious fern enthusiasts should make every effort to become familiar with the scientific names of ferns in order to facilitate accurate identification and communication.

Life Cycle of a Fern

Unlike most other vascular plants, ferns produce neither flowers nor seeds. Like all plants, they reproduce through an alternation of generations, which essentially means that an organism passes through two stages during its life cycle, one in which it reproduces asexually, and another in which it reproduces sexually. In the ferns, these two stages typically result in distinct and independent plant bodies which are only briefly connected to one another.

It is the asexual, or sporophytic, generation that draws our attention and is most easily observed in nature. This is the stage which results in the development of the typical fronds with which ferns are associated. During this phase, clusters of sporangia, or spore cases, develop on the fertile fronds. Each typical sporangium (figure 6) is a tiny, stalked, thin-walled case that at first contains a single cell which eventually divides to produce all of the spores in the sporangium. In the typical sporangium the initial, or archesporial, cell first undergoes a succession of several mitotic divisions (mitosis) during which the chromosomes in the nuclei of the initial and succeeding cells first double, then divide, producing daughter cells with a full set of chromosomes and the same genetic makeup as the parent cell. Ordinarily, this series of mitotic divisions results in the production of 16 mother cells, though sometimes only eight are produced. These mother cells then undergo meiosis, or reduction division, which involves a chromosomal duplication followed by two successive nuclear divisions which result in 64 spores, each of which contains only half of the chromosomes of the parent cell. Though 64 is the typical number of spores produced within a single sporangium, some species produce only 16 or 32, while others produce thousands. When cell division is complete, a row of thick-walled cells called the annulus opens to expose the mature spores, then catapults them from the sporangium. Thus begins the fern's sex-cell-producing, or gametophyte generation.

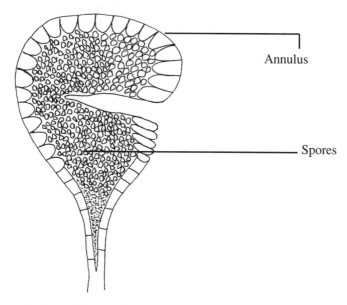

Annulus

Spores

Figure 6. Typical Sporangium Before the Spores Have Been Released

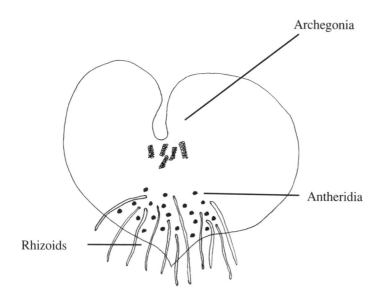

Archegonia

Antheridia

Rhizoids

Figure 7. Heart-Shaped Prothallus

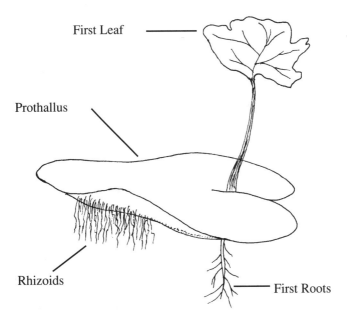

First Leaf

Prothallus

Rhizoids

First Roots

Figure 8. The Prothallus Gives Rise to the First Leaf

A single fern frond produces many thousands of spores, the majority of which never find suitable places in which to germinate. However, those which find a proper substrate develop into a tiny, typically heart-shaped, green, chlorophyll-rich organism called a prothallus (figure 7). The prothallus, which is typically smaller than an average fingernail and remains well-hidden, contains both male (antheridia) and female (archegonia) sex organs which enclose the sperm and eggs, respectively, as well as a collection of hairlike structures (rhizoids) which take in water and minerals. At maturity and with the aid of external moisture (e.g. rain water), the sperm swim to and into the archegonia to fertilize the eggs. Since each sperm and egg contain only half of the required chromosomes, the process of fertilization results in an egg that has a complete set of chromosomes and a full complement of genetic material. The fertilized gametophyte first develops a single leaf (figure 8) before developing into a new sporophyte, or typical fern plant. Many fern enthusiasts enjoy searching for gametophytes, or producing them by germinating spores under controlled conditions.

Hybridization in the Ferns

Hybridization occurs when the sperm of one species crosses with the eggs of another to produce a plant that typically displays morphological features that are intermediate between its parent species. Though somewhat rare in plants in general, hybridization occurs often enough in the ferns to make understanding its process important. This is certainly true for Florida, whose 162 fern taxa include 9 named hybrids, 4 of which are endemic to the state, meaning that they occur nowhere else in the world. Figure 9 on page 34 shows a graphic illustration of the intermediate morphology between two of the state's more important *Asplenium* hybrids and their parent species. The genus *Asplenium,* in particular, is well known for the role hybridization plays in giving rise to new reproductive species.

As might be expected, hybridization occurs only in genetically closely related species, though not always in species that are closely related geographically. In many instances hybrids are nonfertile and produce misshapen spores that abort before maturity and are unable to give rise to prothalli or gametohpytes. In other instances, such as *Asplenium* X *heteroresiliens,* the hybrid gives rise to fertile spores with the ability to reproduce. In still other instances, such as *Botrychium jenmanii,* hybridization may have occurred so far back in time that the hybrid is treated as a species and its hybrid status is only assumed or surmised.

Named hybrids are denoted nomenclaturally by inserting the letter X between the genus and species names. Typically, plants so denoted are considered nonfertile, while the X is sometimes left off for those which are known to reproduce successfully. For example, the X is often dropped for the fertile hybrid *Asplenium heteroresiliens.* Unnamed, or even named, hybrids are sometimes denoted by connecting the specific epithets of the parent species with an X. The unnamed hybrid between *Lycopodiella alopecuroides* and *L. prostrata,* for example, is sometimes seen written as *Lycopodiella alopecuroides* X *prostrata,* while the named hybrid *Lycopodiella* X *copelandii* is also sometimes seen written as *Lycopodiella alopecuroides* X *appressa.* The use of the X is retained in the current volume for most hybrids.

Glossary

Annulus. The ring of thickened cells around the sporangium that ruptures and serves to expel the spores.

Apiculate. Ending with a small, abrupt, flexible tip.

Areole or Areola (plural: Areoles, Areolae). The area(s) enclosed by the veins on net-veined leaf tissue.

Bipinnate. Said of fronds that are divided into pinnae, with the pinnae again divided to the midrib into pinnules that are either stalked or unstalked.

Caudate. With a taillike appendage.

Circinate vernation. Said of a leaf that uncoils from a fiddlehead or crozier as it matures.

Conduplicate vernation. Said of a leaf that unfolds rather than uncoils as it matures.

Coriaceous. Leathery to the touch.

Crozier (syn: crosier). The coiled leaf bud of a new fern frond; fiddlehead.

Dentate. Coarsely toothed along the margin.

Dimorphic. Said of ferns having sterile and fertile fronds that are distinctly different in appearance.

Distal. Towards the apex of a structure.

Entire. Said of a blade, pinna, or other segment with smooth, untoothed margins.

Epithet. The second part of a binomial scientific name.

Epipetric. Growing on rocks.

Epiphytic. Growing on the branches or trunks of trees or shrubs, or on stumps.

Falcate. Curved or sickle shaped.

False indusium. Said of the edge of a leaf blade that curls over and hides the sori.

Farina. A typically whitish or yellowish, waxy exudate that covers plant tissue.

Fertile. Said of a frond or plant that bears sporangia.

Fiddlehead. The coiled leaf bud of a new fern frond; crozier.

Free. Said of veins that run from the midvein to the margin without forming a network.

Frond. The entire leaf of a fern, including the petiole and blade collectively.

Glabrous. Without hairs.

Gland. An epidermal appendage that contains or exudes resinous or waxlike, usually highly-colored substances.

Hair. An elongated epidermal outgrowth consisting of a single cell or column of cells that is typically a single cell in width.

Hirsute. Hairy with erect hairs.

Indumentum or Indument. A covering of hairs on a plant surface.

Indusium (plural: Indusia). A thin membrane that encloses, covers, or subtends a sorus.

Inrolled. Said of leaf edges that are rolled downward and inward.

Monomorphic. Said of ferns having sterile and fertile fronds that are similar in appearance.

Netted (Reticulate). Said of leaf venation that is netlike in appearance.

Pectinate. Said of a frond that is deeply divided into narrow pinnules but not all the way to the rachis; comblike.

Peltate. Said of an appendage that is stalked in the center from below, like an umbrella.

Petiole. The stalk of the frond.

Pinna. The first division or segment in a divided blade.

Pinnate. Divided once.

Pinnatisect. Lobed all the way to the axis.

Pinnule. A division of a pinna.

Protuberance. An outgrowth.

Pubescent. Hairy.

Quadripinnate. Cut to the midrib along four axes; four-pinnate.

Rachis. The central rib of a frond; extension of the petiole.

Reticulate. Said of leaf venation that is netlike in appearance.

Revolute. Rolled downward; inrolled.

Rhizome. The rootstock or stem of a fern that bears the fronds and roots; often belowground and creeping but sometimes erect.

Rootstock. The underground stem that bears the roots; rhizome.

Scabrid. Rough to the touch due to the presence of stiff hairs.

Scale. Reduced, tiny hairlike or leaflike structures that often clothe the stem, petiole, rachis, or blade surface; typically flattened in cross-section and two or more cells wide.

Serrate. Sharply toothed with forward-pointing teeth.

Specific Epithet. See epithet.

Sporangium (plural: Sporangia). The case that contains the spores; spore case.

Sorus (plural: Sori). A collection of sporangia; usually appearing as a dark spot on the lower surfaces of fertile blades.

Sporocarp. A structure containing the sporangia in *Azolla, Marsilea,* and *Salvinia.*

Sporophyll. A blade containing sporangia; fertile blade.

Stellate. Said of tissue clothed with branching, star-shaped hairs.

Stem. See rhizome and rootstock.

Sterile. Said of a blade that lacks sporangia.

Stipe. Petiole.

Stolon. An aboveground, low-arching, or trailing stem or runner.

Strigose. Having stiff, straight, usually appressed hairs.

Strobilus (plural: Strobili). A conelike reproductive structure in the Lycopodiaceae.

Synangium (plural: Synangia). A group of fused sporangia.

Tomentose. Hairy with matted, woolly hairs.

Toothed. Having teeth along the margins.

Tripinnate. Cut to the midrib along three axes.

Ultimate segments/pinnules. Said of the final divisions of a blade.

Vernation. The arrangement of the buds of developing leaves.

Vestiture. Covering.

Key to the Families of Florida Pteridophytes

1. Plants not typically fernlike in appearance; fronds grasslike, scalelike, needlelike, or antlerlike and lacking expanded blades; or cloverlike and four-parted; or undivided and long elliptic or straplike; or pinnately or palmately lobed; or plants freely floating and matlike.

  2. Blades cloverlike and four parted, or simple and undivided, or pinnately or palmately lobed.

    3. Blades cloverlike, four parted, borne on filiform petioles . . . . MARSILEACEAE p. 96

    3. Blades simple or lobed.

      4. Blades simple.

        5. Margins entire.

          6. Blades thin, small, generally rounded to broadly obovate in outline, less than 3 cm long; plants borne in mats on limestone often in association with liverworts; sori borne in tubular cups which are embedded in or protrude from the leaf margins . . . . HYMENOPHYLLACEAE (in part) p. 77

          6. Blades not thin, mature fronds ovate to long-elliptic or strap shaped; plants not growing in mats on limestone; sori not disposed as above.

            7. Blades narrowly elliptic to straplike, exceeding to much exceeding 5 cm long . . . . POLYPODIACEAE (in part) p. 116

            7. Blades ovate, typically held close to the ground; sporangia beadlike and borne in slender spikes at the apex of the fertile stalk . . . OPHIOGLOSSACEAE *(Ophioglossum)* p. 107

        5. Margins serrate . . . . ASPLENIACEAE *(Asplenium serratum)* p. 39

      4. Blades lobed.

        8. Blades pinnately lobed, typically less than 7 cm long; sori borne in tubular cups, which are embedded in or protrude from the leaf margins; plants epiphytic on tree trunks or epipetric.

. . . . HYMENOPHYLLACEAE (in part) p. 77

   8. Blades palmately lobed, sporangia beadlike and borne in spikes situated along the petiole and blade margins; plant epiphytic on sabal palms . . . .

. . . . OPHIOGLOSSACEAE (*Cheiroglossa palmata*) p. 105

2. Fronds grasslike, scalelike, or needlelike and lacking expanded blades; or deeply divided into very narrow segments, if the latter typically aquatic and floating (or some individual plants rooted in mud) and bearing expanded blades near the base of an erect, spongy petiole; or plants matlike, freely floating.

   9. Plants mostly freely floating (individual plants sometimes rooted in mud.

      10. Plants small, fronds minute (< 1 mm long) or rounded to oval and less than 1.5 cm long.

         11. Leaves rounded to oval, mostly 5 - 15 mm long . . . . . . SALVINIACEAE p. 150

         11. Leaves minute, mostly less than 1 mm long, forming dense floating mats on still water

. . . . AZOLLACEAE p. 44

      10. Plants rather large, mostly floating to sometimes rooted in mud; petioles large, erect, spongy; fertile blades deeply divided into narrow segments. . . . .

. . . . PARKERIACEAE p. 114

   9. Plants terrestrial, epiphytic, or if aquatic, rooted in mud and never freely floating.

      12. Leaves grasslike, or multiply divided into narrow branches, each topped with wedge-shaped ultimate segments, or with narrowly linear, stiffly erect leaves divided at the apex into several, very narrow segments; plant aquatic, epiphytic, or terrestrial.

         13. Leaves clustered on 2- to 3-lobed corms, plants occurring in aquatic habits, rooted in muddy bottoms, sori borne in a membranaceous pouch on the corm . . . .

. . . . ISOETACEAE p. 82

         13. Leaves not borne from corms, plants epiphytic or terrestrial.

           14. Leaves pendent, sori borne in marginal grooves; plants epiphytic mostly on sabal palms.

. . . . VITTARIACEAE p. 174

           14. Leaves erect, narrow (or with narrow segments), plants epiphytic or terrestrial.

              15. Fertile fronds branched at the apex into a few narrow, sporangia-bearing segments; plants epiphytic on stumps or in leaf litter, very rare . . . . SCHIZAEACEAE p. 151

              15. Leaves multiply divided into narrow segments, each topped with a wedge-shaped ultimate segment which bears the sporangia . . . .

. . . . DENNSTAEDTIACEAE (*Odontosoria*) p. 51

      12. Leaves scalelike, needlelike, or ovate to lanceolate but less than 5 mm long; plants terrestrial.

         16. Leaves scalelike.

           17. Leaves borne on mostly naked, twiglike stems, spores borne in three-lobed synangia . .

. . . . PSILOTACEAE p. 129

           17. Leaves scalelike, borne in whorls at the nodes of an erect, grooved, mostly hollow stem, which is topped with a conelike structure bearing the sporangia . . . .

. . . . EQUISETACEAE p. 74

         16. Leaves needlelike, elliptic, or lanceolate, less than 5 mm long.

           18. Strobili four-sided or flattened; spores of two sizes . . . .

. . . . SELAGINELLACEAE p. 153

           18. Strobili cylindrical; spores of one size . . . . LYCOPODIACEAE p. 86

1. Leaves with expanded, typically fernlike blades.

   19. Rachis long, twining, sori borne at and constricting the tips of the pinnae lobes; plants high

climbing and vinelike . . . . LYGODIACEAE p. 92

19. Rachis not twining, plants not vinelike and high climbing.

20. Plants conspicuously dimorphic, fertile blades or fertile portions of blades distinctly different from sterile portions and lacking or essentially lacking expanded blade tissue.

21. Sterile blades pinnate-pinnatifid, bipinnate, or more divided.

22. Fertile blades or fertile portions of blades copiously covered throughout with greenish, reddish, cinnamon-colored, or rusty brown sporangia . . . .

. . . . OSMUNDACEAE *(Osmunda)* p. 111

22. Fertile blades not as above.

23. Sporangia capsulelike and borne on branches at the apex of the fertile portion of the blade; stalk of fertile portion somewhat fleshy . . . .

. . . . OPHIOGLOSSACEAE *(Botrychium)* p. 100

23. Sporangia not capsulelike; stalk of fertile portion thin . . . .

. . . . ANEMIACEAE p. 28

21. Sterile blades deeply pinnatifid.

24. Pinnae of sterile blades mostly alternate, pinnae of fertile blades very narrow; sori borne in chainlike rows on the lower blade surface . . . .

. . . . BLECHNACEAE *(Woodwardia areolata)* p. 48

24. Pinnae of sterile blades mostly opposite, sporangia beadlike and borne at the apex of erect fertile blades which lack expanded tissue. . . . .

. . . . DRYOPTERIDACEAE *(Onoclea sensibilis)* p. 67

20. Plants not conspicuously dimorphic, fertile and sterile blades or portions of blades essentially the same in shape, sometimes fertile pinnae smaller or of a different size than sterile pinnae, but not so different as to appear to have a different form.

25. Sori borne in dense rows along the margins or in dense rows adjacent to the midveins on the underside of the pinnae.

26. Sori borne along the margins.

27. Sori borne in dense, continuous, visible bands or rows along the margins on the underside of the pinnae . . . . PTERIDACEAE *(Pteris)* p. 145

27. Sori borne continuously along the margin but partially to completely hidden by the inrolled blade margin . . . . DENNSTAEDTIACEAE *(Pteridium)* p. 52

26. Sori borne in dense rows situated immediately adjacent to the midvein of the pinnae and sometimes the pinnules, extending nearly the entire length of the pinnae, or in some species *(Woodwardia)* contained within areoles and appearing chainlike . . . .

. . . . BLECHNACEAE p. 45

25. Sori otherwise.

28. Sori marginal but borne in cuplike indusia in the lobes of the pinnae, or marginal and borne under the reflexed tips of the ultimate pinnae.

29. Sori borne in cuplike indusia in the lobes of the pinnae . . . .

. . . . DENNSTAEDTIACEAE (in part) p. 49

29. Sori borne under the reflexed tips of the ultimate pinnae . . . .

. . . . PTERIDACEAE *(Adiantum)* p. 133

28. Sori otherwise.

30. Sori completely covering the lower surfaces of fertile pinnae, or sori in lines along the veins and lower surfaces of pinnae coated with a waxy, mealy, whitish to yel-

lowish powder.

    31. Sori completely covering the lower surfaces of the fertile pinnae and obscuring the blade tissue . . . . PTERIDACEAE *(Acrostichum)* p. 131

    31. Sori in lines along the veins, lower surfaces of blades coated with a waxy, mealy, whitish to yellowish powder; blades pinnate, bipinnate or more divided, narrowly lanceolate to nearly linear in overall outline . . . .
. . . . PTERIDACEAE *(Pityrogramma)* p. 143

30. Sori distinctly rounded, kidney shaped, or elongate, usually many per pinna and variously situated on the lower surfaces of the blades but not immediately adjacent to the midvein, not covering the entire lower surface of the pinnae, and not obscured by a whitish to yellowish mealy powder.

    32. Sori rounded or kidney shaped.

      33. Blades pseudodichotomously branched or forked, forks often with hairy dormant buds between the branches, blade segments deeply pinnatifid (pectinate), sori rounded . . . . GLEICHENIACEAE p. 76

      33. Blades otherwise.

        34. Blades deeply pinnatifid or pinnatisect, margins of pinnae entire to sometimes undulate, but not pinnatifid . . . . POLYPODIACEAE (in part) p. 116

        34. Blades otherwise.

          35. Midveins, veins, and tissue between veins at least somewhat hairy below or above with transparent, needle- or star-shaped hairs; blades pinnatifid-pinnatifid, pinnate-pinnatifid, bipinnate-pinnatifid, or more divided . . . .
. . . . THELYPTERIDACEAE p. 158

          35. Midveins, veins, and tissue between veins lacking transparent, needlelike hairs but sometimes with thickened, brownish, hairlike scales or bristles that do not appear needlelike in shape . . . . . . DRYOPTERIDACEAE (in part) p. 53

    32. Sori elongate.

      36. Scales of the belowground stem and sometimes the base of the petiole generally containing transparent to glistening cells surrounded by conspicuously thickened, mostly blackish side walls (as seen with 10x magnification; i.e. scales clathrate), narrowest scales sometimes appearing almost wholly black, sori typically situated along only one side of the vein and commonly oriented at an angle less than perpendicular to the midvein of the pinnae or pinnules, often contained within elongated indusia that have the superficial appearance of tiny hot-dog buns; blades pinnate to bipinnate . . . .
. . . . ASPLENIACEAE p. 29

      36. Scales of belowground stem and petiole base with thin, mostly brownish cell walls, not conspicuously thickened as described above, sori typically situated along both sides of the veins, or curved around the end of the vein . . .
. . . . DRYOPTERIDACEAE (in part) p. 53

Following are the descriptions of the more than 160 fern species that are known to occur or to have occurred in Florida. Each entry includes both common and scientific names of each species, followed by a description of the species' form, fronds, petiole, rachis, blade, pinnae, sori, habitat, and distribution. The remarks section for each species includes tips for field identification and should be studied carefully in order to learn to distinguish between similar species. Scientific synonyms, Latinized names by which a species was previously known, are also included.

Each description also includes references to one or more color photos of the species being described. The photos, which are located in a section between pages112 and 113, emphasize the distinguishing characteristics of the species pictured and are designed to assist with field identification. In a few instances black-and-white photographs or line drawings offer additional assistance with identification. These latter illustrations are referenced by the page number on which they appear.

ANEMIACEAE - FLOWERING FERN FAMILY

In Florida, the Anemiaceae includes only one genus with two species. Two genera and near-ly 120 species are recorded for the family worldwide. Most members of the family are lim-ited to, but widespread in, the tropical and subtropical regions of the world. It is not surpris-ing, then, that both of Florida's species occur in the southern part of the state.

The members of the genus *Anemia* are sometimes referred to as flowering ferns because their fertile fronds (or fertile portions of the fronds in some cases) are held erect above the sterile fronds, and are conspicuously covered with yellow to golden brown sporangia which can be quite showy, though this is not particularly true for the two Florida species. This char-acter, which is reminiscent of both the cinnamon and royal ferns, is the reason that at least one of the species described below was formerly placed in the genus *Osmunda*.

The genus name *Anemia* derives from the Greek word *aneimon,* which means "with-out clothing" and refers to the unprotected sporangia. The several members of this genus, as well as those of the genera *Actinostachys* and *Lygodium,* are often included within the family Schizaeaceae (e.g., Wunderlin, 1998).

A third species *Anemia cicutaria* Kunze ex Sprengel has also been reported for Florida (Correll & Correll), 1996; Mickel, 1979). However, these reports were apparently based on misidentifications of *A. wrightii* (Mickel, 1993).

Pine Fern, Maidenhair Pineland Fern

Anemia adiantifolia (Linneaus) Swartz   **Photo 1**

Form: An erect fern with a creeping rhizome and partially dimorphic fronds; sometimes growing on limestone walls of sinkholes and then somewhat pendent (as in photo1).

Fronds: 17 - 85 cm tall, including fertile portions, 7 - 35 cm wide; sterile portion to about 60 cm tall.

Petiole: 6 - 40 cm long, dark, reddish to chestnut brown below, greenish to straw col-ored above, varying from hairy to essentially without hairs.

Rachis: Greenish, hairy.

Blade: Sterile portion tripinnate, triangular in overall shape, 5 - 25 cm long; fertile por-tion 7 - 18 cm long, borne in one or two pairs arising from the petiole just below the sterile portion of the blade.

Pinnae: Sterile pinnae borne alternate to nearly opposite along the rachis, pinnules minutely toothed and covered with stiff, white hairs when new, hairs disappearing with age; fertile pinnae usually extending beyond the height of the sterile blade.

Sori: Borne in conspicuous, branched clusters on the upper half of the fertile portion of the frond.

Habitat: Open, mostly rocky pinelands, dry hammocks with exposed limestone, rocky woods, limestone rocks, walls of sinkholes.

Distribution: Found mostly in the southernmost counties south of Lake Okeechobee; disjunct pop-ulations are also recorded for Levy, Citrus, Hernando, and Sumter Counties; widespread in the West Indies, Mexico, and central and northern South America.

Remarks: The partially dimorphic fronds with triangular, tripinnate sterile portions are help-ful in identifying this species in Florida. It differs from *A. wrightii* by having a single frond with both sterile and fertile portions; the fronds of the latter species are fully dimorphic with both the sterile and fertile fronds arising separately from the rhizome. *A. adiantifolia* was probably first collected in Florida by J. L. Blodgett from Key West or Big Pine Key in about 1838. The specific epithet means "with leaves like *Adiantum*," in reference to the supposed similarity between the leaves of this species and those of the genus *Adiantum*, a not always evident likeness.

Studies of this species in Jamaica (Walker, 1962) indicate that it is tolerant of wide extremes of moisture and that it can be quite variable from one locality to another in both size and morphology, especially in the degree of leaf dissection and the depth of marginal teeth. Plants in open, sunny situations are generally smaller and coarser than those in shady sites.

Synonyms: *Osmunda adiantifolia* Linneaus

Wright's Pineland Fern
Anemia wrightii Baker   **Photo 2**

Form: An erect fern with dimorphic fronds and creeping, finely hairy stem.

Fronds: Dimorphic; sterile fronds with expanded blades, not exceeding about 6 cm long and 4 cm wide in Florida; fertile fronds with constricted blades, reportedly about 30 cm long in other parts of its range, but generally less than 20 cm long in Florida.

Petiole: Those of sterile blades slender, straw colored to greenish, those of fertile fronds with brown, hairlike scales near the base.

Rachis: Greenish and slender, sometimes with whitish hairs when young.

Blade: Sterile blade pinnate-pinnatifid to bipinnate, generally ovate in outline, 2 - 4 cm wide.

Pinnae: Sterile pinnae borne in two or four alternate to nearly opposite pairs, ascending, margins of pinnules minutely toothed at the apex; surfaces hairy with stiff white hairs when young.

Sori: Borne in branched clusters well above the sterile blade.

Habitat: Rocky glades at the edges of hammocks.

Distribution: Reported and collected in Florida only from Dade County; also distributed in the Bahamas, Cuba, and the West Indies.

Remarks: The fully dimorphic fronds and its much smaller size are helpful in identifying this species and are the distinguishing characters between it and *A. adiantifolia*, with which it grows. Young sterile specimens of *A. adiantifolia* may be mistaken for this species. The specific epithet commemorates the American plant collector Charles Wright (1811-1885). This species is listed as endangered by the Florida Department of Agriculture.

ASPLENIACEAE - SPLEENWORT FAMILY

Six of the 16 taxa of *Asplenium* treated below are listed as endangered in Florida by the Florida Department of Agriculture, and nine are tracked by the Florida Natural Areas Inventory (FNAI). Three of the taxa tracked by FNAI are endemic to Florida. As treated here, all are members of the family Aspleniaceae, which contains but a single genus with about 700 species worldwide. The family's common and scientific names are derived from the root word *splen,* the Greek name for spleen, in deference to the supposition that the Greek god Dioscorides believed the members of this genus to be useful in treating diseases of the spleen.

The family is characterized by monomorphic fronds, latticelike (clathrate) stem scales, and linear or elongated sori covered with flaplike indusia that resemble tiny hot-dog buns or taco shells when viewed with magnification.

At least one additional spleenwort has been reported from Florida but may now be extirpated in the state. The maidenhair spleenwort *(A. trichomanes* Linnaeus), shown in figure 11, is a commonly cultivated species from which several cultivars have been developed. It was collected on Amelia Island, Nassau County in 1857 (Moran, 1981). This species has tiny, rounded pinnae and tufted, erect fronds to about 20 cm tall. It is fairly common in northern Georgia and across much of the eastern United States and is generally found growing on moss-covered limestone rocks in cool, moist woodlands. Its occurrence on Amelia Island is about 270 miles south of its otherwise southernmost station. The voucher for this collection is on deposit at the University of Illinois at Urbana. Whether the species still occurs in Florida is conjectural.

Hybridization among the spleenworts is common. In fact, all three of Florida's endemic taxa are hybrids. Two of these, *A.* X *curtissii a*nd *A.* X *plenum* are found only in the west-central Florida limesink region. See figure 9 for a silhouette of these two hybrids, their parent species, and the closely similar *A. cristatum.* The other hybrid, *A.* X *biscaynianum,* is currently known only from a single population in Dade County. (It should be noted that the specific epithet for the latter species is often seen spelled as *biscayneanum.* However, this latter spelling is incorrect and is not the one used by Eaton in the original description of the species.) These hybrids are treated with one or more of their parent species in the treatments below, but are included individually in the following key to facilitate field identification.

Key to the Species of Asplenium

1. Blades simple and undivided, margins toothed . . . . *A. serratum*
1. Blades divided.
  2. Blades pinnate.
    3. Sori typically more than three per pinna and borne adjacent to and paralleling the lateral veins.
      4. Pairs of pinnae typically more than 4 per blade.
        5. Bases of pinnae with distinctive lobes that often overlap the rachis, plants typically terrestrial (growing in soil, usually not on rocks or trees) . . . . *A. platyneuron*
        5. Bases of pinnae with small to inconspicuous lobes, or lobes absent, lobes not overlapping the rachis, plants typically growing on rocks, trees, or stumps.
          6. Blades mostly more than 4 cm wide.
            7. Pinnae pairs typically numbering more than 10 per blade, pinnae margins sharply toothed, plants growing mostly on trees or stumps . . . . *A. auritum*
            7. Pinnae pairs typically numbering fewer than 10 per blade, pinnae margins bluntly toothed, plants usually growing on limestone . . . . *A. abscissum*
          6. Blades mostly less than 4 cm wide.
            8. Pinnae oblong to oblong-lanceolate, length of middle pinnae typically greater than three times the width.

    9. Pinnae margins mostly entire, sometimes with a few rounded teeth . . . . . .
. . . . *A. resiliens*

    9. Pinnae margins mostly toothed, at least on the upper margin.

        10. Pinnae margins more or less sharply toothed throughout, spores 64 per sporangium . . . . *A. heterochroum*

        10. Pinnae margins more or less bluntly toothed, these mostly confined to the upper margin, lower margin often entire, spores 32 per sporangium . . . . . .
. . . . *A. X heteroresiliens*

    8. Pinnae more or less rounded to egg shaped, length of middle pinnae typically less than two times the width.

        11. Rachis dark only at the base . . . . *A. trichomanes-dentatum*

        11. Rachis dark throughout . . . . *A. trichomanes*

  4. Pairs of pinnae typically less than four per blade, blades triangular to deltoid in outline . . . . *A. pumilum*

3. Sori typically three or less per pinna, these borne parallel to and along the marginal vein on the pinna's lower margin . . . . *A. monanthes*

2. Blades pinnate-pinnatifid, bipinnate, or more divided.

  12. Blades narrowly lanceolate, long elliptic, or linear in outline, longest pinnae not exceeding about 3 cm long, lowermost pinnae shorter than middle pinnae.

    13. Pinnae deeply cut, apical 1/3 of lowermost pinnae cut well over 1/2 way to the midvein.

      14. Plants with blades narrowly lanceolate to long elliptic in outline, lowermost pinnae very much shorter than the middle pinnae, longest pinnae sometimes to about 3 cm long, pinnae closely spaced on the rachis, petioles usually less than 4 cm long . . . .
. . . . *A. verecundum*

      14. Plants with blades linear in outline, lowermost pinnae only slightly shorter than the middle pinnae, pinnae typically not exceeding about 2 cm long, pinnae well-spaced on the rachis, petioles ususally greater than 5 cm long . . . .
. . . . *A. X biscaynianum*

    13. Pinnae not deeply cut, apical 1/3 of lowermost pinnae cut or lobed less than 1/2 way to the midvein . . . . *A. X plenum*

  12. Plants with lowermost pinnae as long as or longer than the middle pinnae.

    15. Apical 1/3 of the lowermost pinnae lobed or cut less than 1/2 way to the midvein.
. . . . *A. X plenum*

    15. Apical 1/3 of the lowermost pinnae cut well over 1/2 way to the midvein.

      16. Pinnae borne mostly at right angles to the rachis, lowermost pinnae mostly descending, at least some pinnae on mature fronds exceeding 5 cm long (ranging 3.8 - 7 cm), width of pinnae at midpoint about equaling that at the base . . . . . . *A. cristatum*

      16. Pinnae borne from the rachis at a slightly ascending angle, lowermost pinnae not descending, pinnae of mature fronds typically less than 5 cm long (ranging 2.0 - 5.1 cm), pinnae widest at the base, gradually tapering toward the apex, wider at base than at middle . . . . *A. X curtissii*

Abscised Spleenwort, Cutleaf Spleenwort

Asplenium abscissum Willdenow   **Photo 3, Page 34**

Asplenium X *curtissii* **Photo 20, 21**

Form: A tufted fern with an erect, unbranched stem and thin, fibrous roots.

Fronds: Upright to somewhat laterally drooping from a limestone substrate, to about 4 dm tall, sterile and fertile similar.

Petiole: 3 - 20 cm tall, green on one side, gray-brown to green on the other, longitudinally furrowed.

Rachis: Green and without hairs.

Blade: Pinnate below to pinnatifid at the apex, somewhat deltate in overall shape, 5 - 20 cm long, 2.5 - 9 cm wide, without hairs.

Pinnae: 3 - 8 cm long, 0.7 - 1.5 cm wide, lanceolate in shape, sometimes with a conspicuous lobe (auricle) on the upward facing edge at the base, borne in 4 - 8 alternate to nearly opposite pairs; margins entire to mostly coarsely toothed.

Sori: Linear, borne in few to several (typically nine or fewer) pairs along the edge of lateral veins, angling acutely away from the midvein toward the margins of the pinna.

Habitat: Hammocks, limestone outcrops, lime sinks, grottoes, often in well-eroded places.

Distribution: Primarily distributed in central Florida in the vicinity of Alachua, Marion, Citrus, Hernando, and Sumter Counties; also collected in Dade County from Everglades hammocks (where it may no longer be extant), and known from a single rocky hammock in Broward County (Keith Bradley, personal communication, 1999).

Remarks: This species is most similar to *A. auritum,* but may be distinguished from it by having mostly eight or less pairs of pinnae which are less sharply toothed and have no or only a small lobe at the base, and by growing mostly on limestone rather than tree trunks or stumps.

   A. abscissum was first collected in Florida in 1878 near Ocala but was first described by Carl Ludwig Willdenow (1765-1812) from the West Indies in 1810. *A. abscissum* hybridizes with the much more dissected *Asplenium verecundum,* a species that is more widely distributed in Florida. The hybrid, *A.* X *curtissii,* is more closely similar to the latter species than the present; the differences between these latter species are detailed in the description of *A. verecundum,* below. See figure 9. The specific epithet for this species denotes the divided base of the lower pinnae, a character that is often not present.

Synonyms: *Asplenium firmum* Kunze, *Asplenium abscissum* var. *firmum* Kunze

Eared Spleenwort

Asplenium auritum Swartz   **Photos 4, 5**

Form: An erect, medium-size, tufted fern with an erect, unbranched stem.

Fronds: Erect, to about 4 dm tall, sterile and fertile similar.

Petiole: 2 - 12 cm long, mostly greenish in color but sometimes purplish black, especially below and toward the base, typically greenish toward the apex, mostly without hairs, often with a few brownish scales toward the base.

Rachis: Typically green above, sometimes purplish to blackish below, sometimes shading to blackish near the base.

Blade: Pinnate (sometimes with a few pinnae so deeply divided as to render the blade bipinnate), 4 - 35 cm tall, 1.8 - 18 cm wide.

Pinnae: Narrowly lanceolate in shape, 1 - 9 cm long (usually about half this length), to about 2.5 cm wide, some with a conspicuous basal lobe on the upward facing margin which may be so deeply divided from the pinna as to be considered a pinnule rather than an auricle (hence the specific epithet); pinnae borne in 10 to 22 pairs; margins irregularly and often sharply toothed.

Sori: To about 10 pairs per pinna, nearly parallel to the pinna midvein.

Habitat: Epiphytic on trunks of mature trees, especially on old live oaks *(Quercus virginiana* Miller) with leaning trunks, or on the base of pop ash *(Fraxinus caroliniana* Miller) and pond apple *(Annona glabra* Linnaeus) trees in the Fakahatchee Strand.

Distribution: A rare species primarily from the central peninsula counties of Citrus, Hernando, Pasco, and Hillsborough; also collected in Volusia, Collier, and Dade Counties, but probably extirpated in Dade.

Remarks: The epiphytic habit in conjunction with mostly pinnate (rarely bipinnate) blades, lanceolate, toothed, short-stalked pinnae, and deeply cut basal pinna lobes help distinguish this species from all other of Florida's ferns. It is most similar to *A. abscissum,* but may be distinguished from the latter by having mostly 10 or more pairs of pinnae which are more sharply toothed and have a conspicuously eared base, and by growing mostly on tree trunks rather than limestone. Its habit of wilting, curling up, and turning brown during dry periods, similar to the fronds of the resurrection fern *(Pleopeltis polypodioides* var. *michauxianum),* also helps set it apart. However, it should be noted that *A. auritum* is quite variable and several forms have been given varietal status. Whether these forms should be given taxonomic rank is unclear, but fern enthusiasts should expect to find wide variations within the species.

A. auritum was first reported in Florida from a hammock in Sumter County and was long suspected of being restricted to this site. Later it was found in Dade and Collier Counties and is still known from the Fakahatchee Strand State Preserve. It was first described to science from Jamaica by Olof Peter Swartz in 1801. *A. auritum* is listed as an endangered species by the Florida Department of Agriculture. It is interesting to note that Lakela and Long (1976) regarded this species as introduced from Jamaica

Synonyms: According to Small (1931), this species was first mistaken for *A. erosum* Linnaeus. Other synonyms include *Asplenium sulcatum* Lamarck var. *auritum, Asplenium auritum* Swartz var. *genuinum* Hieronymus, and *Asplenium auritum* Swartz var. *bipinnatifidum* Kunze.

Hemlock Spleenwort
Asplenium cristatum Lamarck   **Photo 6, Page 34**

Form: A delicate, lacy fern with bright green, clustered fronds and erect, unbranched stems with fibrous roots.

Fronds: 2 - 4 dm tall, sterile and fertile similar.

Petiole: Variable in length, 1 - 17 cm long, greenish to brownish or blackish.

Figure 9.
(left to right) *Asplenium cristatum, A. abcissum, A.* X *plenum, A.* X *curtissii, A. verecundum* (courtesy, *American Journal of Botany* 1967, 54(9), p. 1062)

Rachis: Blackish, grooved, without hairs.

Blade: Bipinnate to tripinnate, 2 - 18 cm long, 2.7 - 10 cm wide, tissue without hairs.

Pinnae: Bipinnate, in 7 to 20 pairs, lower pair descending; pinnules broadly elliptic, to about 1 cm long and 4 mm wide, with strongly toothed margins and evident, unforked to once-forked veins.

Sori: To about six per pinnule, more typically four or less per pinnule, elongated.

Habitat: Hammocks, limestone outcrops, and ledges.

Distribution: Uncommon in several central Florida counties including Alachua, Sumter, Citrus, and Hernando.

Remarks: The bright green leaves help distinguish this species from most other members of the genus. *A. cristatum* is most similar to *A. verecundum.* The former has relatively long petioles and oblong-lanceolate blades with oblong-lanceolate pinnae that are longest nearest the base of the blade, while the latter has very short petioles and narrowly lanceolate blades with ovate to deltate pinnae that decrease in length gradually but conspicuously toward the base of the blade. See figure 9. The specific epithet denotes the crested or crisped pinnae, in reference to their parsleylike margins.

Varicolored Spleenwort

Asplenium heterochroum Kunze   **Photos 7, 8**

Form: A relatively small, dainty fern with erect or at least ascending stem.

Fronds: Evergreen, erect, borne in tufts from the base, 3 - 37 cm long.

Petiole: Dark brown to blackish or purplish black, shiny, 1 - 7 cm long.

Rachis: Black, shiny, without hairs, sometimes shading to brownish toward the apex.

Blade: Pinnate, narrow, 2 - 3 cm wide, to about 30 cm long, widest near the middle and tapering to either end.

Pinnae: Opposite, mostly elliptical in shape with a rounded apex, both margins deeply toothed, bases of some pinnae with a rudimentary lobe at the base on the upward facing margin.

Sori: Longer than wide and somewhat elliptical in overall shape, covered by indusia attached to the pinnule along one side.

Habitat: Limestone outcrops in shady hammocks and sinkholes.

Distribution: Sparsely distributed in northern and north-central Florida.

Remarks: The opposite pinnules with margins toothed along both edges help distinguish this species from other members of the genus. It is similar in appearance to *A. resiliens,* which has nearly entire rather than distinctly and sharply toothed pinna margins, and to *A.* X *heteroresiliens,* a fertile hybrid that is intermediate between *A. resiliens* and *A. heterochroum* (see *A. resiliens,* below, for a description of *A.* X *heteroresiliens).* The margins of the pinnae of *A.* X *heteroresiliens* are only bluntly toothed, while those of *A. heterochroum* are sharply toothed. The specific epithet and the common name both refer to the bicolored rachis.

Synonyms: *Asplenium muticum* Gilbert.

Single-Sorus Spleenwort, Monosoral Spleenwort, San Felasco Spleenwort

Asplenium monanthes Linnaeus   **Photos 9, 10**

Form: A small, rare spleenwort with ascending to erect, scaly stem; scales appressed, lance-olate, blackish near the center, paler toward the edges.

Fronds: To about 3 dm tall, erect, densely clustered, sterile and fertile similar.

Petiole: Typically not exceeding about 10 cm long, purplish to reddish brown, without hairs.

Rachis: Reddish brown to purplish, shiny, without hairs, sometimes narrowly two-winged toward the base.

Blade: Pinnate, 5 - 40 cm tall, to about 3 cm wide, gradually tapering toward the base, light green in color.

Pinnae: Somewhat rectangular to oblong in shape with an asymmetrical base, bluntly toothed toward the apex, longer ones 4 - 15 mm long, to about 5 mm wide.

Sori: Borne mostly one to three per pinna and situated near and parallel to the marginal vein on the lower edge of the pinnae; each sorus protected by a whitish indusium.

Habitat: Limestone outcrops.

Distribution: This species is rare in the United States, somewhat spottily distributed, and thought by some to perhaps be a sterile variant of another, undetermined species. Stations are known from Alabama, Arizona, North Carolina, South Carolina, and Florida. Outside of the continental U.S. the species occurs in Mexico, tropical South America, Africa, and Hawaii. The original Florida record is from a single location in San Felasco Hammock State Preserve, Alachua County, a location that may no longer contain the species. In 1992, Alan Cressler (personal communication) discovered several populations at Florida Caverns State Park, a location at which the species still occurs.

Remarks: *A. monanthes* can be distinguished from other species of *Asplenium* by its pinnate fronds with many pairs of small pinnae (10 to 40), as well as usually having only one to three sori per pinna, situated near and parallel to the pinna's lower margin. The third common name above is a Florida-based appellation and is due to its previous presence in San Felasco Hammock. It is listed as endangered by the Florida Department of Agriculture. The epithet *monanthes* derives from the Greek *mono,* or one, and *anthus,* or flower, in reference to the typically single sorus per pinna.

Synonyms: *Asplenium monanthemum* Linnaeus f. ex Murray.

Ebony Spleenwort, Brown-Stem Spleenwort

Asplenium platyneuron (Linnaeus) Britton, Sterns, & Poggenburg

Photos 11, 12

Form: A relatively common fern with thick stem and both erect and spreading fronds.

Fronds: 15 - 40 dm long, fertile fronds sometimes longer and often more erect than sterile ones, hence the species is often described as more or less dimorphic, or functionally dimorphic.

Petiole: 1 - 10 cm long across its range but usually shorter than 6 cm in Florida, dark brown to nearly black, shiny, scaly, and hairy at or near the base.

Rachis: Dark brown to blackish and shiny.

Blade: Pinnate, 4 - 50 cm long, narrow, usually not exceeding about 5 cm wide.

Pinnae: Up to 45 pairs, borne in an alternate arrangement along the rachis, to about 2.5 cm long, with a conspicuous lobe (auricle) at the base on the upward-facing margin, and often a smaller lobe on the lower-facing margin; margins bluntly toothed.

Sori: Longer than wide, borne on either side of the pinna midvein, developing into protruding, dark brown masses.

Habitat: Rich woods, slopes, open woods, disturbed sites, hammocks; the only species of *Asplenium* in Florida that grows in the ground rather than on rocks or trees.

Distribution: Nearly statewide, but more common in the northern counties, very common north of Florida.

Remarks: This is the common spleenwort across much of northern Florida. It is most easily distinguished from other species of *Aspleniun* by its alternate pinnae, which have a conspicuous lobe on the upward facing margin at the base and often a somewhat smaller lobe on the lower margin; also distinguished by its terrestrial rather than epiphytic or epipetric habit. The specific epithet comes from the Greek "platys" for broad, and "neuron," or nerve, and was awarded based on a early drawing of the species that showed an overly-large and not completely accurate rachis.

Synonyms: *Acrostichum platyneuron* Linnaeus; *Asplenium platyneuron* var. *bacculum-rubrum* (Fernald) Fernald; *A. platyneuron* var. *incisum* (E.C. Howe) Robinson.

Dwarf Spleenwort, Triangle Spleenwort, Hairy Spleenwort, Chervil Spleenwort

Asplenium pumilum Swartz   **Photo 13**

Form: A small, erect fern with clustered fronds, leaves generally deltoid in outline, and erect, unbranched stems with fibrous roots.

Fronds: To about 2 dm tall, bright green in color, sterile and fertile similar.

Petiole: 1.5 - 13 cm long, green on the upper side, brownish on the lower, especially toward the tip, purplish-black to dark brown near the base, often green throughout on young fronds.

Rachis: Dull green, sparsely hairy.

Blade: Pinnate to pinnate-pinnatifid or bipinnate, deltate in overall outline, usually about as wide as long, 1 - 12 cm long, 1 - 8 cm wide; sparsely hairy on both surfaces; margins toothed.

Pinnae: 0.5 - 6 cm long, 0.5 - 3.5 cm wide, deltate to diamond-shaped or lanceolate in overall outline, simple to pinnate or pinnatifid near the apices; margins toothed.

Sori: 2 - 8 mm long and covered with whitish indusia.

Habitat: Rare on limestone outcrops.

Distribution: Known in Florida from the north-central peninsula, especially Alachua, Marion, Volusia, Citrus, and Hernando Counties, but now very rare in the state; widespread in the tropics and first described as a new species from Jamaica in 1766.

Remarks: This is the only *Asplenium* with generally deltoid leaves that are cut into 3 to 7 major segments, which are themselves deltoid to ovate in overall outline. It is interesting to note that though this species is considered a tropical plant, it is not found in the more tropical parts of Florida, instead inhabiting the more north-central region of the state. Small (1938) speculated that if the plant once occurred in southern Florida, it may now be extirpated there. *A. pumilum* is listed as an endangered species by the Florida Department of Agriculture. Its specific epithet means small or dwarf, an allusion to its small size.

Synonyms: *Asplenium pumilum* Swartz var. *anthriscifolium* (Jacquin) Wherry.

Black-Stemmed Spleenwort

Asplenium resiliens Kunze   **Photo 14**

 A. X *heteroreiliens*   **Photo 22**

Form: An erect to spreading fern with tufted leaves and erect, unbanched stems with fibrous roots.

Fronds: 1 - 3.5 dm tall, sterile and fertile similar.

Petiole: Shiny, black throughout, grooved, scaly at the base.

Rachis: Shiny, black throughout, without hairs; grooved.

Blade: Pinnate, broadly linear in overall shape, length of pinnae becoming progressively shorter from the center of the blade toward both the apex and the base, 9 - 30 cm tall, 1 - 2.5 cm wide, without hairs.

Pinnae: Oblong, borne in 20 to 40 opposite to nearly opposite pairs, margins more or less entire, or crenate (with low, rounded or blunt teeth); base of at least the upward-facing margin usually lobed.

Sori: Long elliptic to half-elliptic in shape; small, typically borne less than five per pinna.

Habitat: Limestone outcrops, sinkholes, rocky hammocks.

Distribution: The northern part of the state; uncommon to rare in Florida, fairly frequent north of Florida.

Remarks: Morzenti's spleenwort *(Asplenium* X *heteroresiliens* W. H. Wagner), is a fertile hybrid between the current species and *A. heterochroum.* Its existence was first reported by Wagner and Morzenti at the April 1962 meeting of the Association of Southeastern Biologists (Wagner, 1963) and later by publication (Wagner, 1966). The three taxa are distinguished in the field, though with considerable difficulty, by noting the toothing (or lack thereof) on the pinnae margins. At first glance, all three look quite similar. *A. heterochroum* is distinguished from the other two by having sharply-toothed pinnae margins (see photo 8). *A. resiliens* is distinguished by having mostly entire pinnae. *A.* X *heteroresiliens* (see photo 22), on the other hand, typically has pinnae with blunt or rounded (as opposed to sharp) teeth. Nevertheless, though *A. resiliens* is most often described as having entire pinnae, some pinnae on many specimens have at least a few blunt teeth, especially along the upward-facing margin and near the apex, even though the downward-facing margins of the pinnae are generally entire. Hence, all three of these species can be quite difficult to distinguish in the field and are most clearly separated by microscopic examination of chromosome number. *A.* X *heteroresiliens* has been collected in several counties across northern Florida including Washington, Jackson, Gadsden, Columbia, Levy, Marion, and Citrus, and, according to Wagner (1963 and personal communication, 1998), is much more common and widespread in Florida than *A. resiliens.*

Synonyms: In older fern literature, for example in the writings of both Curtiss (1902) and Noble (1914, 1916), this fern is often referred to as *A. parvulum* M. Martens & Galeotti. However, due to the rules of botanical nomenclature, this name is considered to be illegitimate.

Birdnest Fern, New World Bird's-Nest Fern, American Bird's-Nest Fern, Wild Birdnest Fern

Asplenium serratum Linnaeus   **Photos 15, 16**

Form: A unique, distinctive fern (at least in Florida) usually with several ascending or arching, simple, serrated leaves, and a stout, erect, unbranched stem with fibrous roots.

Fronds: Ascending or arching, 3 - 8 dm tall.

Petiole: Short to apparently lacking, 1 - 8 cm long, sometimes described as vestigial due to the usual presence of a wing that continues down the petiole from the base of the blade to the base of the petiole.

Blade: Simple, 40 - 80 cm long, 6 - 12 cm wide, broadly linear or somewhat rhombic, widest in the middle or slightly above the middle; margins distinctly finely toothed, at least above the middle (hence, the specific eipthet); veins conspicuous, regular, parallel, diverging from the midrib at about a 60- to 70-degree angle.

Sori: Borne in elongated indusia along lateral veins and extending approximately 1/2 to 1/3 way to the leaf margin, hence borne in parallel, ascending rows; generally confined to the upper half of the blade.

Habitat: Bases of trees and on rotten logs and stumps, mostly in hammocks or in swamps, such as Fakahatchee Strand in Collier County.

Distribution: Mostly restricted to the southern tip of the state, especially Lee, Collier, Broward, and Dade Counties; also collected in Volusia County.

Remarks: This species is listed as an endangered species by the Florida Department of Agriculture and was considered rare in the state as early as the turn of the twentieth century (Curtiss, 1902). It is easily distinguished from all other Florida ferns, including the several superficially similar species of *Campyloneurum*, by its simple leaves with finely toothed margins, in conjunction with its parallel, ascending rows of sori that appear as brown lines along the underside of the blade.

Toothed Spleenwort

Asplenium trichomanes-dentatum Linnaeus   **Photo 17**

Form: A small, tufted spleenwort with numerous fronds and erect, nonbranching stems with fibrous roots.

Fronds: Fertile fronds ascending, 9 - 25 cm tall, with widely-spaced pinnae; sterile fronds shorter, 3 - 12 cm long, spreading or prostrate, with more closely set pinnae.

Petiole: Flattish; dull, pale green above the base, brownish at the base, to about 10 cm long, with or without fine scales near the base.

Figure 10.
Asplenium X *biscaynianum*

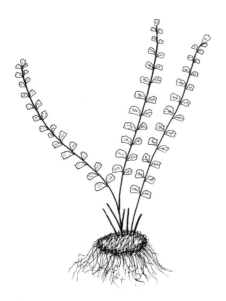

Figure 11.
Asplenium trichomanes

Rachis: Dull green, without hairs.

Blade: Pinnate, linear in overall shape, 3 - 18 cm long, to about 3 cm wide.

Pinnae: Usually not exceeding about 12 pairs and arranged alternately to nearly oppositely along the rachis; oblong, obovate, or narrowly elliptic in overall shape, to about 1.5 cm long, less than 1 cm wide; margins coarsely to bluntly toothed.

Sori: Borne 2 to 5 per pinna in elongated indusia; arranged along the veins.

Habitat: Limestone outcrops, sinks, shaded rocky hammocks.

Distribution: Palm Beach, Broward, and Dade Counties.

Remarks: The pinnae, which are nearly as wide as long (usually less than 1 cm in both width and length) and are toothed along the margins, help separate this species from others in the genus.

Some taxonomists (including Wunderlin, 1998) prefer the name *A. dentatum* Linnaeus for this species, rejecting the name used here because it can be confused with *A. trichomanes,* the name used for a different species. All three names were assigned by Linnaeus: *A. trichomanes-dentatum* and *A. trichomanes* in 1753, and *A. dentatum* in 1759. The latter name was likely the result of Linnaeus's attempt to correct the confusion of his earlier name (Morton and Lellinger, 1966; Lellinger, 1981). Nevertheless, the earlier name has precedence over the latter (Lellinger, 1981) and is the nomenclature used in the treatment of the genus in volume two of the *Flora of North America.* Hence, it is also the name used here.

Small (1918a) reported that in the early part of the twentieth century this species was widespread and reached "its greatest development in the Deering Hammock at Cutler . . . where the plants are so thickly placed that the leaves completely hide the rocks" (p. 43), an observation borne out by Darling (1961) in 1958. Photo 17, which was made at the Deering site, provides evidence that the historical population reported by Small still continues to thrive, though probably less luxuriantly than in Small's and Darling's days. This species is listed as endangered by the Florida Department of Agriculture.

Modest Spleenwort

Asplenium verecundum Chapman ex L. Underwood   **Photos 18, 19, Page 34**

A. X *biscaynianum* **Page 40**

Form: A lacy spleenwort with tufted fronds and an erect, unbranched stem with fibrous roots.

Fronds: Bright green, to about 4 dm long, ascending, arching, curving, or drooping; sterile and fertile similar.

Petiole: Typically short, 0.5 - 5 cm long, brownish, or purplish- or gray-brown.

Rachis: Dull purplish brown to blackish or greenish, grooved, essentially without hairs.

Blade: Bi- to tripinnate, 3 - 30 cm long, to about 5 cm wide, lanceolate in overall shape, tapering toward both the base and apex, but narrower at the apex.

Pinnae: Borne in 8 to 22 alternate and well-spaced pairs, ovate in outline, longer ones to about 3 cm long and 1 cm wide; pinnules divided into up to 5 oblanceolate segments, each segment to about 3 mm long and 2 mm wide.

Sori: Elliptic, borne one per pinnule segment.

Habitat: Limestone outcrops, grottoes, sinkholes.

Distribution: Collected in several scattered locations across Florida from Liberty and Jackson Counties in the panhandle to Dade County in the southern peninsula; the north-central peninsula in the vicinity of Gilchrist, Columbia, Alachua, Marion, Citrus, Hernando, and Sumter Counties constitutes the main part of its distribution in Florida.

Remarks: This plant is listed as an endangered species by the Florida Department of Agriculture. Its narrowly lanceolate, bi- to tripinnate leaves with ovate to ovate-deltate pinnae and short petioles help distinguish it from other members of its genus. Its specific epithet means modest or shy, apparently in reference to the "modest" number of sori per pinnule and meaning that the plant is refraining from reproduction. *A. verecundum* was first collected (though it may have been known earlier in Scott's Spring near Ocala) in Jackson County, Florida about 1840 by A. W. Chapman, an early Florida botanist and physician who lived alternately in Quincy and Apalachicola, but who botanized widely in Florida and the southeast. The three editions of his *Flora of the Southern United States* (1865, 1884, 1897) are important collector's items for avid botanists and a number of southern plants bear his name as the authority, or are named for him. Chapman's collection of *A. verecundum* was reported under the name *A. myriophyllum* (Swartz) Presl in the first and second editions of his flora, with the note that the name was synonymous with *A. anchorita* Chapman. The specimen was not described as a new species until approximately sixty years later (Underwood, 1906). Though Chapman's collection was made in Jackson County, recent populations of the plant have not been found in the region and the species may no longer be present in the central panhandle.

The distinction between *A. verecundum* and *A. myriophyllum* is still unsettled. The latter is a tropical species which occurs in the Antilles and South America. Mickel (1979) noted the use of *A. verecundum* for Florida plants, but reported that he could find no characters by which to reliably separate the two. Lellinger (1981), on the other hand, reported consistent differences in spore size between the two species and purported that *A. verecundum* should be maintained at the species level.

At least two hybrids are reported for this species, both of which are Florida endemics and are listed as endangered in the state. *A.* X *biscaynianum* (D. C. Eaton) A. A. Eaton (see figure 10) is a hybrid with *A. trichomanes-dentatum* (see photo 17), and *A.* X *curtissii* L. Underwood is the hybrid with *A. abscissum* (see photo 3 and 20). The first of these has been collected only in Dade County and may be distinguished from the parent species by combination of its pinnate to bipinnate blades with deeply cut, well-spaced pinnae and long petioles (1 - 12 cm). Small (1918a, 1938) reported that this taxon was first discovered in Florida by Isaac Holden in 1887, and he predicted in 1918 that "it is destined . . . to be exterminated at an early date" (p. 44). He repeated his prediction in 1938, adding that the taxon was then known to occur only sparingly in a few hammocks of the Everglades Keys. Darling (1961) found a few plants in a small hammock near Rickenbacker Causeway, a site that is now probably the location of Alice Wainwright Park. It is not likely that the species still exists at this park. Unfortunately, it appears that Small's prophesy may now be nearly realized.

The second of the hybrids, *A.* X *curtissii,* which was named by Underwood (1906) for A. H. Curtiss, is found in the central peninsular counties of Alachua, Marion, Citrus,

Hernando, and Sumter, and may be distinguished from its parents by its blades being less divided than in *A. verecundum* but more divided than *A. abscissum,* by its long petioles (3 - 15 cm), and by its blade not tapering in width toward the base as in *A. verecundum. A.* X *curtissii* is currently known from only a few stations. See figure 9.

Synonyms: *Asplenium scalifolium* E.P. St. John; *A. suave* E. P. St. John; *A. myriophyllum* (Swartz) C. Presl. misapplied.

Ruffled Spleenwort

Asplenium X *plenum* E. P. St. John ex Small   **Photo 23, Page 34**

    A. X *curtissii*   **Photos 20, 21, Page 34**

Form: A delicate, somewhat lacy fern with short, erect, unbranched stems and fibrous roots.

Fronds: 15 - 25 cm long, drooping, sterile and fertile similar in appearance.

Petiole: 2 - 10 cm tall, without hairs, dull blackish in color.

Rachis: Slender, dull green to grayish, without hairs but sometimes minutely scaly.

Blade: Pinnate to bipinnate, lanceolate in overall shape, 4 - 15 cm long, 1.5 - 5 cm wide, without hairs.

Pinnae: Borne in 5 to 25, ascending pairs, deltate to oblong in shape, 1 - 3.5 cm long, 0.5 - 1.8 cm wide; pinnules oblong to linear, to about 1 cm long, and with notched apices.

Sori: Typically one per pinnule, to about 3 mm long.

Habitat: Limestone outcrops and caverns in dense shade.

Distribution: Collected in Alachua, Sumter, and Citrus Counties. First discovered by E. P. St. John at Lecanto Cave (Citrus County), and later from the so-called Indian Field Ledges (Sumter County) by Thomas Darling (Darling, 1961). Only two stations for this species are known.

Remarks: This species is very similar to *A.* X *curtissii.* The two can be most easily distinguished by differences in their pinnae. Those of the current species are pinnate below grading to pinnatifid toward the apex, the apex is only shallowly notched, and the outermost 1/3 of the lower pinnae are cut less than halfway to the axis. The pinnae of *A.* X *curtissii,* on the other hand, are pinnate throughout, more deeply notched at the apex, and the outermost 1/3 of the lower pinnae are cut more than halfway to the axis. *A.* X *plenum* may be most easily distinguised from the more delicately cut *A. cristatum* and *A. verecundum* by the pinnae being less deeply cut and the pinnules being broadly elliptic rather than nearly linear. Young specimens of *A. abscissum* superficially resemble *A.* X *plenum* until their pinnae lengthen to normal mature proportions.

   A. X *plenum* was discovered in Florida in 1936 and first described in 1938 by Edward Porter St. John in Small's *Ferns of the Southeastern States.* It was previously considered to have arisen as a hybrid between *A. abscissum* and *A. cristatum* (Wagner, 1963). However, later work by Morzenti (1967) rejected Wagner's hypothesis and proposed, instead, that *A.* X *plenum* originated as a backcross between *A. abscissum* and *A.* X *curtissii,* the latter of which is itself a hybrid of *A. verecundum* and *A. abscissum.* This previously unreported, and somewhat remarkable, method of species formation was later confirmed by Gastony (1986) through electrophoretic testing. Figure 9, which was taken from Morzenti's work, provides an excellent comparison of the fronds of these five species. **Synonyms:** *Asplenium subtile* E. P. St. John ex Small.

AZOLLACEAE - AZOLLA FAMILY

The genus *Azolla* was established by French naturalist J. B. Lamarck in 1783. The name means "killed by drought" and refers to the genus's dependence on water. Members of the genus include the world's smallest pteridophytes, and are some of the more difficult ferns to identify due the microscopic nature of a number of their key characters, which include the structure of the megaspores and the number of cells on the hairs of the upper leaf surfaces. Scanning electron microscopy is often used to examine megaspore ornamentation, and at least 40x magnification is needed to examine the hairs.

Azolla is the world's most economically important pteridophyte genus and has been the subject of many scientific papers and symposia (Moran, 1997). Members of the genus are rich in nitrogen, which makes them excellent fertilizers, and at least one species is used extensively in the rice fields of Vietnam and China. The cyanobacteria of the genus *Anabaena* which live within the plant's leaves take nitrogen from the air and combine it with hydrogen to produce ammonium ions which can be absorbed and used by the plant. One of the pigments produced by this group of microscopic organisms accounts for the reddish color often seen in *Azolla* plants. *Azolla* has been cultivated in Vietnam and China since at least the eleventh century. Cultivation is difficult because low winter temperatures kill the plant and high summer temperatures promote insect and fungal attacks. Until the 1950s, only a few families knew the secrets to successfully growing the plant and guarded this asset earnestly. Today, several methods have been developed to mitigate cultivation problems, including warm water irrigation in winter and cold water irrigation in summer.

Eastern Mosquito Fern

Azolla caroliniana Willdenow   **Photos 24, 25**

Form: A small, floating fern with thin, hanging roots; extremely clonal, hence usually forming dense, greenish to reddish mats on the water surface (mats typically reddish only in relatively sunny places). Each plantlet is typically smaller than a centimeter in diameter and may consist of up to 200 leaves.

Fronds: Tiny (less than 1 mm wide and long), banded together, and overlapping in two rows along the stem, scalelike; green when young, often with reddish margins, becoming reddish to dark brown at maturity; largest hairs on the uppermost leaf lobe nearest the stem with two or more cells (requires good light and at least 40x magnification to see clearly).

Sporocarps: Male and female sporangia borne in separate sporocarps at the leaf axils; surface of megaspores typically smooth but vested with tangled filaments (requires high magnification).

Habitat: Typically found floating on still water of ditches, ponds, pools, and stagnant back waters; sometimes stranded on wet mud; in ideal situations forming mats to about 4 cm thick and completely obscuring the water surface.

Distribution: Throughout Florida and the southeastern U. S.; presumably the only member of the genus found in Florida.

Remarks: The current species is one of the few ferns or fern allies that has not been reclassified and whose original name has not been changed since its original description. It is often called mosquito fern due to the belief that its dense covering on the surfaces of ponds retards or prevents the growth of mosquitoes. It is frequently confused with one of the several species of duckweed *(Lemna)* or duckmeat *(Spirodela)*, a collection of green, small-leaved monocots that also float on the water surface. However, these latter species are angiosperms of the family Lemnaceae, not pteridophytes. The several species of *Azolla* are extremely difficult to distinguish and identification is based heavily on reproductive characters, which are seldom present in collected specimens. As far as is known, the present species is the only member of the family that occurs in Florida.

BLECHNACEAE - CHAIN FERN FAMILY

The scientific name for this family derives from the ancient Greek word, *blechnon,* a reference to ferns in general. The family is mostly tropical in distribution and contains approximately 10 genera and 250 species. Six species in two genera are generally reported in North America.

The five species described below do not include the giant vine fern *[Stenochlaena tenuifolia* (Desvaux) T. Moore] (see photo 30), an Old World species first described in 1768 from specimens collected in India. It sometimes escapes cultivation in Florida and was first collected in the state near Tampa in 1932 by Bessie W. Miles (Small, 1938; Lakela & Long 1976), and later by Richard Wunderlin (personal communication, 1998) in Hillsborough County in 1984 and Pinellas County in 1989. More recently (1996), Keith Bradley discovered a small colony of this species at Matheson Hammock Park in Dade County. This colony occurs at the edge of a heavily disturbed rockland hammock near Fairchild Tropical Garden, the likely source of the population. It has apparently not otherwise been recently collected, and has not been considered part of the state's current naturalized flora by Lellinger (1985), Cranfill (1993), or Keller (1994). It is included as a naturalized species by Wunderlin (1998). Its high-climbing habit, in conjunction with its pinnate sterile fronds and bipinnate fertile fronds with linear segments which are continuously covered below with sori distinguish it from other of Florida's ferns.

BLECHNUM - Deer Ferns

The deer ferns include about 220 species worldwide, mostly distributed in the tropics and subtropics. The common name for the family alludes to those species, such as *B. serrulatum,* which are sometimes browsed by deer. Three species occur in North America, two in Florida. The distinctive sori of the genus are borne in dense rows along the midrib of the pinnae and provide an excellent field character. The young fronds of both of Florida's species are often pinkish in color and very attractive (see photo 26). Though a number of species in this genus are used in gardens (Mickel, 1994), neither of our species are among them.

Hammock Fern, New World Midsorus Fern

Blechnum occidentale Linnaeus var. *minor* Hooker   **Photos 26, 27**

Form: A conspicuous, erect fern with erect or ascending stem.

Fronds: 2 - 5 dm tall, usually clustered at the base, erect to somewhat arching.

Petiole: 4 - 34 cm tall, often scaly with narrow, reddish scales at the base, otherwise somewhat hairy near where it joins the blade, straw colored to light brown or bronze.

Rachis: Straw colored, hairy, especially on the lower side, some hairs with glandular tips (requires magnification).

Blade: Pinnate below, pinnatifid at the apex, narrowly to broadly lanceolate to somewhat triangular in overall shape, 10 - 30 cm long, 3 - 12 cm wide, usually longer than the petioles.

Pinnae: Broadly lanceolate to oblong with a bluntly-tapered tip, often curving and slightly sickle-shaped, distinct but without stalks below, pinnae bases joined with the rachis above, margins entire to only minutely toothed, terminal pinna long-tapering to a sharp point.

Sori: Borne in distinct, continuous lines paralleling the mid-veins of the pinnae.

Habitat: Moist woodlands, hammocks, rocky creek banks, woodlands with open shade, over limestone, near seasonally dry streams.

Distribution: Common in the American tropics but only sporadically distributed in central and northern peninsula Florida and in the Fakahatchee Strand; also reported in the United States from small populations in Georgia, Louisiana, and Texas.

Remarks: The specific name for this species, *occidentale,* means western and refers to the presence of this species in the western hemisphere. The varietal name, *minor,* refers to the length of the fronds, which are shorter than those of other varieties of the species. It is easily distinguished from other Florida ferns, except the closely related *B. serrulatum,* by the continuous lines of sori that parallel the mid-vein of fertile pinnae; it differs from the latter species by the pinnae being shorter, and by the margins of the pinnae being entire or only minutely toothed rather than conspicuously toothed. *B. occidentale* var. *occidentale,* which differs from the present variety by lacking gland-tipped hairs on the rachis, has also been reported for Florida but probably does not occur in the state. *B. occidentale* var. *minor* is listed as endangered by the Florida Department of Agriculture.

Synonyms: *Blechnum occidentale* forma *pubirachis* (Rosenstock) Lellinger; *Blechnum occidentale* var. *pubirachis* Rosenstock.

Swamp Fern, Marsh Fern, Dentate Midsorus Fern

Blechnum serrulatum Richard   **Photos 28, 29**

Form: An erect to arching, relatively large fern with creeping to partially erect stem.

Fronds: To about 2 m tall, though often shorter; rigidly erect, stiff, and shorter in stature in the sun, more pliable and taller in the shade, especially in shady swamps.

Petiole: 10 - 55 cm long, grayish to light brown or yellowish, with fine scales near the base, typically without hairs above.

Rachis: Thick, round, grayish green, lacking hairs.

Blade: Pinnate, somewhat oblong to more or less elliptic-lanceolate in overall shape, 25

- 70 cm long, 5 - 28 cm wide.

Pinnae: Alternate, without stalks or with very short stalks, well spaced along the rachis, narrowly lanceolate but sometimes curving (especially the larger pinnae), 3 - 15 cm long, approaching, but less than 2 cm wide; margins sharply toothed.

Sori: Borne in dense lines adjacent to and along either side of the mid-veins of the pinnae.

Habitat: Wet prairies, swamps, marshes, hammocks, moist pinewoods.

Distribution: Throughout the peninsula from about Putnam County southward; also collected in Columbia, Bay, and Escambia Counties; more common in the counties of the southern peninsula, where it is one of the more abundant species. The Bay County population, located at St. Andrews State Recreation Area, is a particularly robust and dense population reminiscent of more tropical locales. It was discovered by Lisa A. O'Kane in January 1995 as part of a science project.

Remarks: Though mostly terrestrial, the stem of this species sometimes, though rarely, climbs onto trees. Its conspicuously-toothed leaves, from which its specific name, *serrulatum,* derives, sets it apart from closely related *B. occidentale.* The distinctive lines of sori adjacent to the midvein distinguish it from other species with superficially similar fronds.

WOODWARDIA - Chain Ferns

The genus *Woodwardia,* named in honor of the English botanist Thomas Jenkinson Woodward (1745-1820), encompasses about 14 species worldwide including three in North America and two in Florida. The Florida species are commonly referred to as chain or netted chain ferns due to the conspicuous, netted, chainlike areoles that parallel both sides of the mid-vein on the lower sides of the pinnae and most pinnules, and impart a distinctive, chainlike appearance to the sori. These "chains" are easily seen without magnification, especially when held up to light, and provide an excellent identifying feature.

A third member of the genus, the European chain fern *[W. radicans* (Linnaeus) J. E. Smith], has also been reported for Florida, first by J. K. Small (1938) and later by Lakela and Long (1976). Lellinger (1985) and Cranfill (1993) both consider this species a nonpersistent escapee in the state, and both discount its inclusion in the state's flora. Wunderlin (1998) lists the species as part of the state's flora since it was collected in Dade County, but notes that is has not been collected since the 1930s. Due to its uncertain status, it is not included in the species descriptions below. It is similar in many respects to *W. virginica,* but may be distinguished by having a scaly bulblet at the tip of the frond.

The genus *Woodwardia* has had a rather unsettled taxonomic history. Both *W. radicans* and *W. virginica* were originally placed in the genus *Blechnum* by Linnaeus in 1771 and only later transferred to the newly established genus *Woodwardia* by J. E. Smith in 1793. In 1851 K. B. Presl established the genus *Anchistea* for *W. virginica* and the genus *Lorinseria* for *W. areolata.* The first of these genera was founded upon the glandular indusia and single row of areoles in *W. virginica.* The latter genus segregated *W. areolata* based on its dimorphic habit and completely areolate venation. Though the generic name *Anchistea* is no longer used by most workers, the name *Lorinseria areolata* is still occasionally encountered.

Members of this genus are host plants to the chain fern borer moth *Papaipema stenocelis,* a tiny, orange-yellow moth whose larvae bore into the rhizomes to obtain food. Like their close relatives of the genus *Blechnum,* their young fronds are often pinkish in color.

Netted Chain Fern

Woodwardia areolata (Linnaeus) T. Moore   **Photo 31**

Form: A dimorphic, bright green fern with distinctive leaves.

Fronds: Dimorphic; sterile fronds 30 - 60 cm tall, fertile ones to about 80 cm tall.

Petiole: Those of sterile fronds 10 - 40 cm long, scaly, straw colored above, darker brown at the base; those of fertile fronds 10 - 60 cm long, shiny, dark reddish brown to purplish black throughout.

Rachis: Straw colored, often greenish toward the tip.

Blade: Sterile blades 13 - 35 cm long, pinnatifid, lanceolate, with expanded pinnae; fertile blades 15 - 35 cm long, pinnate, with very narrow pinnae.

Pinnae: Sterile pinnae long-elliptic to lanceolate with a tapering tip, finely toothed margins, and netted venation, ranging in size from 3 - 11 cm long, 1 - 2.5 cm wide, borne in 7 - 12 alternate pairs; fertile pinnae narrow, linear in outline, 3 - 11 cm long, 0.2 - 0.5 cm wide, borne alternately and widely spaced.

Sori: Oblong to linear, dark brown, arranged in chainlike rows that cover nearly the entire underside of the fertile pinnae.

Habitat: Generally restricted to wet areas, including wet or swampy woods, stream sides, acid bogs and swamps, seeps, floodplains, and limestone sinks.

Distribution: Nearly throughout the state (at least south to Dade County and discovered in 1998 in the Big Cypress Swamp in Monroe County by Keith Bradley and the author); more common in the northern two-thirds of the state.

Remarks: This is an easy fern to identify. It is superficially similar to and may be confused only with *Onoclea sensibilis.* However, the latter species has predominantly opposite rather than alternate pinnae (especially the lower ones) and its pinnae lack the finely toothed margins of the present species. The fertile fronds of the present species are also very distinctive in having linear pinnae rather than beadlike pinnae like those of *O. sensibilis.*

Synonyms: *Acrostichum areolatum* Linnaeus; *Lorinseria areolata* (Linnaeus) C. Presl.

Virginia Chain Fern

Woodwardia virginica (Linnaeus) Smith   **Photos 32, 33**

Form: A large, conspicuous, wetland fern seldom found in sites mostly without standing water but sometimes in ephemeral ponds.

Fronds: Deciduous, 50 - 130 cm tall, stiff, erect.

Petiole: 10 - 60 cm long, shiny, straw colored to greenish above, typically shading to dark, reddish brown, purplish, to nearly black below; bases sometimes with a few, reddish brown scales.

Rachis: Straw colored, sometimes rather darkly so.

Blade: Pinnate-pinnatifid, 25 - 70 cm long, to about 30 cm wide, elliptic to somewhat lanceolate in overall shape, with alternate, well-spaced pinnae.

Pinnae: Narrowly lanceolate, deeply pinnatifid, easily removed from the rachis; larger pinnae to about 16 cm long, 3.5 cm wide; lower surfaces with distinctive, conspicuous, chainlike areoles along the midrib and midvein of the pinnules; margins of pinnules entire.

Sori: Linear, borne in chainlike, parallel rows lining both the midribs of the pinnae and the midveins of the pinnules; indusia with tiny glands.

Habitat: Swampy woods, bogs, marshes, wet flatwoods, acid swamps, roadside ditches, cypress-gum ponds.

Distribution: Statewide.

Remarks: The pinnate-pinnatifid leaves in conjunction with chainlike areoles lining the midveins of the pinnules and midrib of the pinnae distinguish the species. Sometimes confused at a glance with *Osmunda cinnanomea,* with which it is sometimes found, but distinguished at some distance by the dark brown base of the petiole, mostly darker rachis, and by the fronds being well spaced rather than clump forming.

Synonyms: *Blechnum virginicum* Linnaeus; *Anchistea virginica* (Linnaeus) C. Presl.

DENNSTAEDTIACEAE - BRACKEN FERN FAMILY

The bracken or cuplet fern family contains about 20 genera and perhaps 400 species worldwide of which four genera and four species occur in Florida. The family is pantropical with only a few species represented in the temperate regions of the world. Most members of the family are medium to large, thicket forming, and the fronds arise from long-creeping stems (i.e. rhizomes) that can be deeply buried, as in *Pteridium aquilinum.* Most are easily grown but are generally not good garden species due to their sometimes aggressive, weedy tendencies. The type genus of the family is named for August W. Dennstaedt, a German botanist, physician, and director of the Belvedere Garden, who lived from 1776 to 1826.

Hayscented Fern, Bipinnate Cuplet Fern, Cuplet Fern

Dennstaedtia bipinnata (Cavanilles) Maxon   **Photo 34**

Form: A relatively large fern with deeply divided blades, long-creeping stems, and clustered to well-spaced fronds.

Fronds: Large, conspicuous, 0.5 - 2.5 m tall, to about 1 m wide, erect to arching.

Petiole: Shiny, brownish to straw colored above, darker and sparsely hairy at the base.

Rachis: Straw colored.

Blade: Bipinnate-pinnatifid to tripinnate-pinnatifid, shiny bright green, sparsely hairy but less so on the lower surface.

Pinnae: Widely alternate, generally lanceolate in overall outline, lower pinnules opposite to nearly opposite, becoming alternate toward the apex, pinnules rounded toward the apex, sharply narrowed at the base; pinnule margins lobed.

Sori: Rounded to cylindric, borne in dark, cuplike indusia in notches of the pinnule margin.
Habitat: Wet, mucky soil in shaded forests.
Distribution: Rare and local; Duval, Seminole, and Palm Beach Counties; cultivated by fern gardeners in southern Florida.
Remarks: This species is listed as endangered by the Florida Department of Agriculture. It was first found in Florida in 1926 by John Small and C. A. Mosier (Small, 1938) in hammocks along Lake Okeechobee, a site from which it has now apparently disappeared. The cuplike indusia (from which the common name cuplet fern derives) that are borne in notches in the pinnule margins and that open toward the apex of the pinnule are distinctive and help distinguish this species. But see the distinguishing features for *Hypolepis repens,* below. The other common name derives from the haylike aroma of bruised or crushed fronds. The distinctive odor actually emanates from a volatile substance that is released from the glands that adorn the tips of long hairs on the fronds.

   D. bipinnata is one of two species of this genus in eastern North America. The other, *D. punctilobula,* also called hay-scented fern, is common from New England southward to the north Georgia mountains and into Arkansas. It displays a somewhat stronger scent than its Florida counterpart and is often encountered along the Apalachian Mountain's Blue Ridge Parkway.
Synonyms: *Dicksonia bipinnata* Cavanilles

Creeping Bramble Fern, Flaklet Fern
Hypolepis repens (Linnaeus) C. Presl   **Photos 35, 36**

Form: A large, conspicuous, often thicket-forming fern with long-creeping stem.
Fronds: To about 2 m tall.
Petiole: Reddish brown to straw colored, 20 - 60 cm long, often bearing minute but discernible prickles (hence the common name bramble).
Rachis: Hairy to nearly lacking hairs, bearing prickles similar to those of the petiole.
Blade: Repeatedly divided, tripinnate-pinnatifid or sometimes quadripinnate, 25 - 150 cm long, 12 - 60 cm wide, generally deltoid in overall outline; axes of the leaf segments hairy and deeply grooved.
Pinnae: Broadly lanceolate to deltate in overall outline, borne oppositely to alternately along the rachis.
Sori: Borne in notchlike indusia near the base of the lobes at the pinnule margins; indusia formed by thin flaps of blade tissue that curve to partially cover the sori.
Habitat: Swamps, low hammocks, wet woods.
Distribution: Mainly in the central peninsula from about Citrus and Hernando Counties eastward and southward to Highlands and Okeechobee Counties; also collected in Clay, Dade, and Monroe Counties. Easily seen near the head of the ravine at Gold Head Branch State Park.
Remarks: Similar in overall form to *D. bipinnata,* differing from it by the indusium being thin, flaplike, and curving over the sorus rather than being cuplike and holding the sorus. The prickles along the rachis and petiole of most specimens also help distinguish the species.

The genus name comes from the combination of the Greek words *hypo,* or below, and *lepis,* or scale, in apparent reference to the position of the sori below the flaplike tissue at the pinnule margins. The specific epithet, *repens,* means creeping in reference to the thicket-forming, long-creeping stem.

Synonyms: *Lonchitis repens* Linnaeus

Wedgelet Fern

Odontosoria clavata (Linnaeus) J. Smith   **Photos 37, 38**

Form: A delicate fern with sparsely vegetated fronds that arise from a slender, short-creeping stem.

Fronds: Closely spaced, 10 - 50 cm long; lacking or with little expanded tissue, not typically fernlike in appearance.

Petiole: Slender, straw colored to yellowish above, purplish to brownish, and darker at the base, shiny, slightly grooved, without hairs; 5 - 20 cm long.

Rachis: Slender, straw colored, somewhat zig-zag, especially toward the apex.

Blade: Deltoid to narrowly oblong in overall outline, 5 - 25 cm long, 2 - 10 cm overall in width, repeatedly divided into narrow branches, tripinnate or more.

Pinnae: Deltoid to narrowly oblong in outline, ultimate segments wedge-shaped (hence the common name), blunt-tipped; segments borne alternately.

Sori: Borne at the ends of veins at the apex of the leaf segments in an expanded, receptacle-like structure and protected by a cuplike, indusial flap with ragged margins.

Habitat: Limestone outcrops on ledges and sinks, limerock pinelands, rocky glades, margins of solution holes.

Distribution: Rare and local in Dade and Monroe Counties; more widespread across the West Indies.

Remarks: Perhaps confused with whisk-fern *(Psilotum nudum),* but easily distinguished from it by the wedge-shaped leaf segments and distinctive sori as described above, and by habitat. The specific epithet for this species, *clavata,* means "club shaped" and refers to the distinctive, wedge-shaped leaf segments. The genus name derives from the prefix *odonto,* which means toothed, and *soria,* for sorus, an apparent reference to the toothed indusial flaps which protect the sori. *O. clavata* is one of about 22 species in this genus. This species is listed as endangered by the Florida Department of Agriculture.

W. H. Wagner, Jr. (personal communication, 1999) believes that this species is better placed in the genus *Sphenomeris* than *Odontosoria.*

Synonyms: *Adiantum clavatum* Linnaeus; *Sphenomeris clavata* (Linnaeus) Maxon; *Stenoloma clavatum* (Linnaeus) Fee.

Bracken

Pteridium aquilinum (Linnaeus) Kuhn

Pteridium aquilinum var. *cauda-tum* **Photo 39**

Pteridium aquilinium var. *pseudo-caudatum* **Photos 40, 41**

Pteridium aquilinium var. *latiusculum*

Form: A deeply divided, two- to four-pinnate fern of sandy, fire-prone uplands; arising from slender, long-creeping, belowground stems.

Fronds: Ordinarily erect, to about 1 m tall; sometimes somewhat vinelike, climbing trees, and reaching heights above 2 m; coarse to the touch, borne in rows along the stem.

Petiole: 10 - 100 cm long, smooth, becoming somewhat woody, green to brown.

Rachis: Smooth and without hairs.

Blade: Bi- to tripinnate, triangular in outline, 25 - 200 cm long, 15 - 100 cm wide; divided at the top of the petiole into three main divisions.

Pinnae: Narrowly to broadly triangular and with a long, blunt tip; pinnules variously cut, mostly long and narrow.

Sori: Linear in outline and borne along the margins of the pinnules.

Habitat: Dry, sandy, thinly wooded areas where fire is common, often in full sun.

Distribution: Throughout Florida. Bracken occurs nearly worldwide and is one of the earth's most widespread ferns. In his 1941 revision of the genus, Tryon divided the taxon into two subspecies and 12 varieties (four in North America), which partly explains the species' expansive distribution. As might be expected, Tryon's treatment continues to be controversial among taxonomists and there is no clearcut agreement about how the genus should be treated. If Tryon's treatment is accepted, three varieties occur in Florida: *P. aquilinum* (Linnaeus) Kuhn var. *caudatum* (Linnaeus) Sadebeck, *P. aquilinum* (Linnaeus) Kuhn var. *pseudocaudatum* (Clute) A. Heller, and *P. aquilinum* (Linnaeus) Kuhn var. *latiusculum* (Desvaux) L. Underwood ex A. Heller. The second of these varieties is distributed throughout Florida (though it is uncommon in the southernmost peninsula and barely makes it into Dade County), the first from about the middle of the peninsula southward. The last of the three is apparently rare in Florida and has been collected only in Jackson and Escambia counties in the central and western panhandle, but is somewhat more common northward of Florida at least to Canada. The three may be distinguished from each other by the dimensions of their pinnule segments. The fertile ultimate segments of variety *caudatum* are less than 2 mm wide while those of the other two are mostly more than 3 mm wide. Of the latter two, the variety *pseudocaudatum* has terminal pinnule segments that are 6 to 15 times longer than wide, while those of variety *latiusculum* are 2 to 4 times longer than wide.

Whether the interpretation of this taxon remains that of a single species seems improbable. A number of taxonomists believe that at least some of the major varieties should be treated as species. Warren H. Wager (personal communication, 1999), for example, feels especially strong about the status of Florida's plants. He maintains that anyone who studies Florida's plants will readily recognize *P. caudatum* and *P. pseudocaudatum* as distinct species. In summary, Wagner's opinion is "that throwing together into one species the series of perhaps half a dozen or more so-called subspecies or varieties of *Pteridium* is untenable, and it is about time that someone comes along with a set of hard-fast criteria for taxonomically useful specimens and characters, as well as field analyses of populations and produces a sound monograph, whether for one continent or the world."

Remarks: This species is the common bracken of sandy woodlands throughout Florida. Its name comes from the Greek *pteridion* which means "small fern." It generally produces fronds throughout the year and has very deep rhizomes and roots. The latter character makes it well-adapted to fire-prone habitats and it is one of the first species to reappear in the flatwoods following a burn. It is also the only three-parted fern that occurs in dry, sandy uplands.

Through the centuries bracken has been used in many ways including as a tonic, diuretic, astringent, purgative, antiseptic, antiemetic, ointment, and medicinal tea, as well as for tanning and the production of dyes, for making soap and lye, and in glassmaking. Though the fiddleheads have been used as food in a number of cultures, it is now known that they contain carcinogenic and mutagenic compounds and their consumption is not recommended.

Bracken is an aggressive species and can become weedy under ideal conditions. It is extremely clonal and a joke has been made that perhaps the species is comprised of only a single plant with a worldwide distribution. It is probably not a good plant to include in the garden, especially in dry, sandy areas. On the other hand, for restoring longleaf pinelands or flatwoods, it is essential.

Synonyms: The following synonyms include all of those for the several varieties listed above. *Pteris aquilina* Linnaeus var. *pseudocaudata* Clute, *Pteris caudata* Linnaeus; *Pteridium caudatum* (Linnaeus) Maxon, *Pteris latiuscula* Desvaux; *Pteridium latiusculum* (Desvaux) Fries.

DRYOPTERIDACEAE - WOOD FERN FAMILY

This is a large and complex family that has been subject to much taxonomic change. As treated here, the family is represented in Florida by 14 genera, 22 species, and two hybrids. Another member of the family, *Maxonia apiifolia* (Swartz) C. Christensen var. *apiifolia,* a West Indian climbing fern, was reported from Florida in 1921 (see figure 12), but is probably extirpated in the state and is not included below or in the numbers above.

The taxonomic treatment followed here does not enjoy universal acceptance among pteridologists or taxonomists. Wunderlin (1998), for example, divides the following genera into four family groups, including in addition to Dryopteridaceae, the families Lomariopsidaceae (vine fern family), Nephrolepidaceae (sword fern family), and Woodsiaceae (cliff fern family). Lellinger (1985) treats these genera similarly to Wunderlin, but does not recognize the Nephrolepidaceae, preferring instead to place the genus *Nephrolepis* within the family Davalliaceae (Boston fern family). In addition, the Dryopteridaceae also once included many of the species now included within the family Thelypteridaceae, a number of which were placed in the genus *Dryopteris*.

Figure 12.
Maxonia apiifolia

Key to the Genera of Dryopteridaceae

1. Plants vinelike, sterile pinnae 1 - 3 cm long, less than 1.5 cm wide, simple, toothed, fronds strongly dimorphic, but fertile fronds not often seen on Florida populations . . . . . .
. . . . *Lomariopsis*
1. Plants not vinelike.
  2. Blades conspicuously dimorphic, sterile blade expanded, fertile blade lacking expanded tissue and appearing beadlike . . . . *Onoclea*
  2. Blade not dimorphic, or if dimorphic, not conspicuously so, fertile blade differing only slightly from sterile blades, mostly in size.
    3. Pinnae easily and cleanly separating from the rachis, stems creeping, wiry, and running above, along, or just under the soil surface, indusia kidney or U shaped . . . .
. . . . *Nephrolepis*
    3. Pinnae not easily separating from the rachis, creeping, wiry stem not present.

4. Indusia surrounding the sori from below.
  5. Indusia bladderlike or cuplike, typically straddling the lateral veins . . . .
  . . . . *Cystopteris*
  5. Indusia splitting at maturity into scalelike structures that appear starlike in shape
    below the sporangia, scales eventually falling away . . . . *Woodsia*
4. Indusia not surrounding the sori, sori elongate, linear, hooked at one end (J-shaped),
  or circular.
  6. Sori often hooked around one end of a vein, blades bipinnate to tripinnate . . . .
  . . . . *Athyrium*
  6. Indusia elongate, linear, circular, or kidney shaped.
    7. Sori elongate or linear.
      8. Blades pinnate . . . . *Deparia*
      8. Blades bipinnate to tripinnate . . . . *Diplazium*
    7. Sori rounded, circular, or kidney shaped.
      9. Veins of the blade tissue netted (areolate).
        10. Blades simple, lobed, or deeply cut and three parted, or pinnate and typical-
          ly with three or fewer pairs of broad pinnae, the lowermost often conspicu-
          ously and deeply lobed on the lower side, the lobes with the appearance of
          pinnae . . . . *Tectaria* (in part)
        10. Blades pinnate with more than four pairs of pinnae.
          11. Margins of pinnae conspicuously and sharply toothed, predominately less
            than 10 cm long . . . . *Cyrtomium*
          11. Margins of pinnae bluntly toothed, pinnae predominately more than 10 cm
            long . . . . *Tectaria* (in part)
      9. Veins of the blade tissue not netted (free).
        12. Sori round or circular.
          13. Blades pinnate, fronds borne in tufts . . . . *Polystichum*
          13. Blade bipinnately or more divided, stems creeping . . . . *Rumohra*
        12. Sori kidney shaped.
          14. Upper surface of rachis densely hairy, fertile and sterile fronds similar in
            shape and size . . . . *Ctenitis*
          14. Upper surfaces of the rachis not hairy, fertile pinnae borne near the tips of
            fronds and conspicuously different in size from the sterile lower pinnae.
          . . . . *Dryopteris*

Southern Lady Fern, Lowland Lady Fern

Athyrium filix-femina (Linnaeus) Mertens var. *asplenioides*
(Michaux) Farwell   **Photos 42, 43**

Form: A delicate, finely cut fern of wet woodlands with short creeping to erect stems.

Fronds: Borne singly from the ground in close clusters, 30 to 120 cm long.

Petiole: Yellowish green to reddish or straw colored, grooved, 10 to 55 cm long, sometimes with scattered brown to light brown, lanceolate scales, otherwise essentially without hairs.

Rachis: Smooth, similar in color to the petiole, sometimes with a shallow groove.

Blade: Bipinnate-pinnatifid to tripinnate, 20 - 90 cm long, 10 - 30 cm wide, generally ovate-lanceolate to nearly lanceolate in overall shape, broadest from just above the base to about the middle.

Pinnae: Alternate, those in the middle of the blade widely spaced, to about 15 cm long, 3 cm wide, lanceolate to oblong-lanceolate, the lowest pair of pinnae often shorter than those just above; lowermost pinnules very deeply cut, margins of pinnules often toothed.

Sori: Brown to dark brown, longer than wide and partially covered with a curved indusium, borne in two rows on the pinnules, each of which is situated about halfway between the mid-vein and the margin, often so dense on the pinnule as to nearly conceal its lower surface.

Habitat: Swamps, wet woods, along streams and rivers, bluffs.

Distribution: Northernmost peninsula and the panhandle.

Remarks: This species is listed as threatened by the Florida Department of Agriculture. It may be most easily distinguished by its darkish rachis, bipinnate to tripinnate fronds, and the sori being often "hooked" or "J shaped" around one end of the adjacent vein (requires magnification). The specific epithet, *filix-femina,* literally means "lady fern," though the reason for this name is unclear; the varietal name means "like *asplenium*" and refers to the present species' resemblance to members of the genus of the same name, though this resemblance is not always easily seen. This species has given rise to many horticultural forms, including several dwarf forms, as well as numerous forms with crested, cruciate, or finely dissected fronds, and is one of the most dependable and often-used species in fern gardening. The fronds in the numerous cultivars range from over 1 m to less than 8 cm in length. Mickel (1994), in his excellent review of garden ferns, describes more than 25 forms and varieties.

Synonyms: *Nephrodium asplenioides* Michaux; *Athyrium asplenioides* (Michaux) Desvaux; *A. filix-femina* subsp. *asplenioides* (Michaux) Hulten.

Florida Tree Fern, Red-Hair Comb Fern

Ctenitis sloanei (Poeppig ex Sprengel) C.V. Morton   **Photos 44, 45, 46**

Form: A relatively large, conspicuous fern with erect, woody stems that have thick, trunk-like crowns clothed with a dense, soft mass of woolly, golden brown scales; crowns 3 cm thick or more.

Fronds: Clustered, arching, to about 1.6 m tall

Petiole: Pale, reddish brown, 30 - 100 cm tall, grooved, clothed with reddish to orangish scales and covered at the base with a knotted, woolly clump of reddish brown to orange, linear to narrowly linear scales.

Rachis: Brown, densely clothed with fine, hairlike scales, especially on the lower side.

Blade: Bi- to tripinnate-pinnatifid or even more divided, ovate to deltate in general outline, 40 - 100 cm long, 30 - 80 cm wide, medium green in color, surfaces without hairs but sometimes bearing pale yellowish glands.

Pinnae: 15 - 50 cm long, 3 - 23 cm wide, borne in about 12 pairs, the basal pinnae much the longest and widest and somewhat deltate in outline, uppermost and middle pinnae more closely oblong in outline; basal pinnae pinnate-pinnatifid, those nearer the apex of the blade pinnatifid to lobed; midvein with brownish, glandular, hairlike scales.

Sori: Round, small, borne halfway to slightly less than halfway between the central vein and margins of the pinnules.

Habitat: Hammocks, cypress swamps, usually where the subsurface limestone is near ground level.

Distribution: Southernmost peninsula, especially Polk, Manatee, Collier, and Dade Counties.

Remarks: The conspicuous, erect stem with orangish to reddish brown, woolly scales, in conjunction with the large, bi- to tripinnate fronds with long petioles help distinguish this species. The genus name, *Ctenitis,* derives from the Greek word *kteis,* which means comb, in reference to the narrow, comblike pinnae segments of some species in the genus. This species is listed as endangered by the Florida Department of Agriculture.

Synonyms: *Polypodium sloanei* Poeppig ex. Sprengel. The names *C. ampla* (Humboldt & Bonpland ex Willdenow) Ching and its synonym *Dryopteris ampla* (Humboldt & Bonpland ex Willdenow) Kuntze, a rare species from South America, have been incorrectly applied to this species [Morton (1969), Lellinger (1985), Moran (1993)]. Morton, in particular, points out that the two species are distinguished by the apices of the pinnules, which are drawn out in our species and more or less blunt in *C. ampla,* and by the veins beneath on *C. sloanei* bearing minute glandular hairs, a character which is usually lacking in *C. ampla.*

Brown-Hair Comb Fern

Ctenitis submarginalis (Langsdorff & Fischer) Ching   **Photo 47**

Form: A medium-size to large, evergreen fern with short-creeping, erect, woody stems that may be 12 cm tall; clothed with conspicuous reddish brown scales.

Fronds: To about 1 m long or more.

Petiole: Stout, scaly, straw colored, 20 - 45 cm long, conspicuously clothed at and near the base with long, shiny, chestnut or reddish brown scales; scales measuring 1 - 2 cm long; scales not forming a knotted, woolly clump as in *C. sloanei.*

Rachis: Often with scales similar to but smaller and more sparsely distributed than those of the lower petiole and stem crown.

Blade: Pinnate-pinnatifid, bright green, generally ovate to lanceolate or oblong in overall outline, 30 - 60 cm long, 15 - 35 cm wide, surfaces sometimes clothed with pale yellow to brownish, sometimes glandular scales similar to but smaller than those of the lower petiole.

Pinnae: 6 - 18 cm long, to about 3 cm wide, lobed; lobe margins essentially entire.

Sori: Small, rounded, borne at the tips of veins or veinlets near the margin of the pinnae lobes (hence, the specific epithet).

Habitat: Swamps and wet hammocks.

Distribution: Scattered in populations across the southern peninsula from about Seminole County southward. Collected in Seminole, Hardee, Palm Beach, Broward, and Collier Counties.

Remarks: The pinnate-pinnatifid leaves, in conjunction with the long, conspicuous, linear, reddish brown scales at the crown of the stem, on the lower petiole, and on the surfaces of new fiddleheads is diagnostic for this species in Florida.

This fern was first collected in Florida by J. K. Small and C. A. Mosier in an Everglades hammock near the southeastern corner of Lake Okeechobee in 1926 (Small, 1938). In 1933 W. M. Buswell found the first population of this species in the Big Cypress Swamp (Small, 1938), and in April 1934, E. Peterson, a north Miami fern enthusiast and gardener, found it in Royal Palm Hammock and successfully cultivated the plant in her garden (Broun, 1936b). It is now listed as endangered by the Florida Department of Agriculture.

For many years, this species was known in the United States only from Florida. However, on January 31, 1991, Garrie Landry and William Reese discovered a healthy population of this species in a swamp in southern Louisiana (Landry and Reese, 1991). This discovery became the northernmost site known for this fern and was the first report for this species outside of Florida. The discovery also suggests that this species should be searched for along much of the Gulf Coast.

Synonyms: *Polypodium submarginale* Langsdorff & Fischer; *Dryopteris submarginalis* (Langsdorff & Fischer) C. Christensen.

Holly Fern, Japanese Holly Fern, Asian Holly Fern

Cyrtomium falcatum (Linnaeus f.) C. Presl   **Photos 48, 49**

Form: An attractive, robust, evergreen fern with stout, short stem bearing orange brown scales.

Fronds: 28 - 60 cm long or longer, sterile and fertile similar.

Petiole: 10 - 20 cm long, densely covered with long, conspicuous, brown to orange brown scales.

Rachis: Greenish, stout, sometimes hairy, especially near the points of attachment to the pinnae.

Blade: Pinnate, 18 - 35 cm long, 8 - 15 cm wide.

Pinnae: Bright, shiny green on the upper surfaces, duller below, leathery, 4 - 8.5 cm long, typically ovate in overall form but often with an asymmetrical base and a long-tapering and curving tip, borne alternately on short stalks in 4 to 12 pairs along the rachis; margins coarsely and irregularly toothed.

Sori: Round, large, scattered across the lower surfaces of the pinnae.

Habitat: Rocky areas, rock or stone walls, sometimes along the walls of lime sinks.

Distribution: Cultivated widely in the state; collected from Washington and St. Johns Counties but probably escaping into other counties as well; recently (1999) found by the author naturalized in a sinkhole in Leon County. Knappen (1929) reported a population on the walls of the moat at Fort Marion in St. Augustine.

Remarks: No other Florida fern has leaves with the same combination of shape, color, and marginal toothing as *C. falcatum,* making it easy to identify. It is native to east Asia but is often and widely cultivated in Florida and the southern U. S., and has escaped from cultivation in a limited number of places in Florida. The specific epithet *falcatum* means "sickle shaped" in reference to this fern's curving, scythe-shaped pinnae. According to Gledhill (1989), the genus name means "bulged," an apparent reference to the widened bases of the pinnae. Snyder and Bruce (1986), on the other hand, report the genus name to mean "cut in a curve," again in reference to the shape of the pinnae. A second nonnative species, *C. fortunei* J. Smith var. *fortunei,* also occurs as an escape in the southeast, including at least one site in south Georgia not far north of the Florida state line. Its pinnae are similarly shaped but are only minutely toothed with mostly rounded teeth. This latter species is not yet known to have escaped in Florida but is probably to be expected.

Synonyms:*Polypodium falcatum* Linnaeus f.

Southern Bladder Fern, Lowland Brittle Fern
Cystopteris protrusa (Weatherby) Blasdell

Form: Small- to medium-size fern with delicate, lacy fronds and long-creeping stem that is scaly at the apex and densely covered throughout with golden to yellowish hairs; stems often bearing persistent petiole bases.

Fronds: 10 - 50 cm tall, fertile and sterile similar in appearance, clustered just below the apex of the stem, firm in texture, dark green above, lighter green below.

Petiole: Straw colored to greenish above, sparsely scaly and brownish near the base, 4 - 25 cm long.

Rachis: Greenish, without hairs, lower half grooved, upper half flattened.

Blade: Pinnate-pinnatifid to bipinnate-pinnatifid, or sometimes tripinnate; elliptic, ovate, or broadly lanceolate in overall outline, 8 - 25 cm long, 4 - 12 cm wide.

Pinnae: Pinnate to pinnatifid, margins toothed, lowermost pair of pinnae typically well spaced from the next highest pair of pinnae, other pinnae more nearly equally spaced from each other.

Sori: Round, borne near the margins in bladderlike indusia that straddle the lateral veins.

Habitat: Rich woods, moist woodlands, limestone outcrops.

Distribution: Mostly distributed north of Florida from about the Georgia mountains northward, except for one occurrence in Grady County, Georgia, just north of the Florida state line. Known in Florida from a single, 1896 collection from Washington County, near Chipley (Petrik-Ott & Ott, 1982). Dr. Loran Anderson and Angus K. Gholson, Jr., two of north Florida's more avid field botanists, have searched diligently for this species in a number of locations near the original Florida collection site but have failed to find specimens. The plant may now be extirpated in the state.

Remarks: The genus name, *Cystopteris* means "bladder fern" and refers to the bladderlike indusia. The specific epithet, *protrusa,* means "protruding," a reference to the extension of the stem beyond the base of the petioles. Both of these characters help in identifying the species. See the entry for *Woodsia obtusa* for differences between these similar species.

Synonyms: *C. fragilis* (Linnaeus) Bernhardi var. *protrusa* Weatherby.

Japanese False Spleenwort

Deparia petersenii (Kunze) M. Kato   **Photos 50, 51**

Form: A relatively tall, dark green fern with a creeping stem.

Fronds: 30 - 60 cm tall, dark green above, lighter below.

Petiole: 10 - 30 cm long, dark brown to blackish at the base, somewhat lighter near the blade; with pale brown scales; grooved above.

Rachis: Grooved, light brown, with pale to very light brownish, linear scales.

Blade: Pinnate-pinnatifid, 15 - 40 cm long, 6 - 28 cm wide, ovate to somewhat triangular in overall shape, tissue vested with flattened, jointed, sometimes twisted, mostly brownish hairlike scales.

Pinnae: Opposite to nearly opposite, oblong to lanceolate in general shape with long-tapering tips, lowermost pair often smaller and conspicuously reflexed downward; pinnules appearing rectangular with rounded apices; margins of pinnules serrate to entire; veins hairy.

Sori: Elongated and narrow, usually straight but sometimes slightly curved, situated alongside a lateral vein; indusia elongate and attached along one side.

Habitat: Ravines, lowlands, rich woods, moist woods along streams, disturbed sites.

Distribution: Mostly confined in Florida to the counties of the central panhandle from about Leon County westward; also escaped in Georgia and Alabama.

Remarks: According to the treatment in the *Flora of North America* (1993), this species has long been misidentified in Florida as *Diplazium japonicum* (Thundberg) Beddome. Under the latter name, it was first reported as naturalized in the state in a narrow, wooded ravine north of Lake Talquin in Gadsden County (Morton and Godfrey, 1958). It is native to southeastern Asia but is often cultivated in the southeastern United States, where it readily escapes and becomes naturalized. At first glance, this species could be confused with *Thelypteris dentata* due to their similar forms and rachises. The two can be easily separated by their sori, and by the latter species having the first pair of lateral veins of adjacent pinnules joining together and running as a single vein to the base of the sinus. The genus name derives from the Greek "depas," or saucer, in reference to the saucerlike indusia in the type species, a form that does not describe the indusia of the present species. The specific epithet commemorates the Danish collector C. W. Petersen who collected the species' type specimen.

Synonyms: *Asplenium petersenii* Kunze; *Athyrium petersenii* (Kunze) Copeland; *Diplazium petersenii* (Kunze) H. Christ.

Vegetable Fern

Diplazium esculentum (Retzius) Swartz   **Photo 52**

Form: A reportedly edible, garden fern with stout, erect, brown-scaly stems and large, conspicuous fronds.

Fronds: 37 - 150 cm tall (potentially to more than 2 m tall in favorable growing conditions), 15 - 60 cm wide.

Petiole: 30 - 60 cm tall, dark brown to straw colored, hairy, scaly near the base.

Rachis: Grooved, straw colored, finely hairy.

Blade: Bipinnate, bipinnate-pinnatifid, to tripinnate, ovate to triangular in outline, 0.5 - 1 m tall; apex pinnate-pinnatifid.

Pinnae: Pinnate to pinnate-pinnatifid with lanceolate pinnules; pinnules shallowly lobed.

Sori: Elongated, situated along lateral veins of the pinnules; veins bearing sori diverging at an angle slightly less than perpendicular to the pinnule axis.

Habitat: Mostly a garden plant in Florida, sometimes escaped in moist woods and hammocks.

Distribution: Escaped in scattered locations in Florida; collected in Duval, Hillsborough, DeSoto, and Dade Counties.

Remarks: The genus name, *Diplazium,* derives from two Greek words that mean "two" and "oblong," a reference to the pairs of elongated sori that characterize the genus. Hence, members of the genus are often referred to as the "twin sorus ferns." The specific epithet for the current species, *esculentum,* means edible or tasty and refers to its use as a vegetable in eastern and southeastern Asia, where it is native (the species is now suspected of containing carcinogenic properties).

This species was introduced to Florida as a garden plant and was first collected in 1959. It is listed by Lellinger (1985) as only questionably present in the state and is rarely escaped. The large, bipinnate to tripinnate fronds in conjunction with the sori paired back to back along the same lateral vein of the pinnule help distinguish the species.

Another species, referred to as narrow-leaved glade fern, narrow-leaved-spleenwort, or glade fern *[D. pycnocarpon* (Sprengel) M. Broun], has also been reported as present in the Florida panhandle (Mickel, 1979; Lellinger, 1985; Kato, 1993). However, no Florida collections of this species are known and the report of its occurrence in the state appears to be in error (David B. Lellinger, personal communication, 1997). It differs from *D. esculentum* by having pinnate rather than bipinnate leaves.

Synonyms: *Hemionitis esculenta* Retzius.

DRYOPTERIS

The genus *Dryopteris* once encompassed many species now included in other genera and families, especially the genus *Thelypteris* of the family Thelypteridaceae. Worldwide there are about 250 species of *Dryopteris*. The name for the genus is a combination of the Greek words *drys* and *pteris,* which mean tree and fern respectively, and refer to the large size of some members of the genus. Dunbar (1989) reports that the name can also mean "of the oak," an apparent reference to the genus's association with oak trees.

Southern Wood Fern

Dryopteris ludoviciana (Kunze) Small   **Photos 53, 54**

Form: An erect, evergreen fern with a short-creeping stem.

Fronds: 35 - 120 cm tall, 10 - 30 cm wide, upper pinnae of fertile fronds noticeably different (see below) from those below them.

Petiole: 15 - 40 cm long, with scattered, large, pale brown to bronze colored scales, especially near the base.

Rachis: Grooved, with tan to brownish scales.

Blade: Pinnate-pinnatifid, 25 - 120 cm tall, 10 - 30 cm wide, leather, shiny, dark green, elliptic to lanceolate or rhombic in overall shape, fertile blades widest in the middle.

Pinnae: Alternate, deeply cut, long-pointed, fertile pinnae borne on upper 1/2 of the blade and much narrower than sterile pinnae; lateral veins of pinnules forked.

Sori: Round, borne equidistant between the midvein and margins of the pinnules; indusia flattened and pancakelike when new, eventually curling upward and becoming kidney-shaped.

Habitat: Swamps, wet woods, rich hammocks, limestone outcrops; mostly in shade.

Distribution: Throughout northern Florida and the peninsula, southward to Collier County; endemic to the southeastern United States.

Remarks: The widely alternate pinnae in conjunction with constricted fertile pinnae that are confined to the upper half of the blade, and the scaly petiole help distinguish this species in its habitat. The specific epithet *ludoviciana* means "from Louisiana," the state in which the plant was first discovered in the early 1800s by Gustav Kunze (1793-1851). It was first found in Florida in the 1840s.

Synonyms: *Aspidium ludovicianum* Kunze; *Dryopteris floridana* (Hooker) Kunze.

Climbing Holly Fern, Holly Vine Fern, Holly Fern

Lomariopsis kunzeana (C. Presl ex L. Underwood) Holttum   **Photo 55**

Form: A distinctive, dark green fern with unmistakable foliage and a woody, flattened, somewhat twisted stem that climbs or creeps over limerock; stems bearing scattered brown scales.

Fronds: 1 - 6 dm long, pinnae borne in two rows at 0.5 - 2 cm intervals along the stem; sterile and fertile different in appearance.

Petiole: 3 - 12 cm long, straw colored to greenish, sometimes purplish tinged, with scattered scales, especially near the base, winged or grooved throughout.

Rachis: Straw colored, narrowly winged throughout, appearing somewhat zigzagged, terminating with a single pinna.

Blade: Pinnate, 7 - 25 cm long, to about 6 cm wide, widest just below the apex and tapering gradually toward the base.

Pinnae: Sterile pinnae ovate, 1 - 3 cm long, to about 1.5 cm wide, shiny green above, pale green below; margins conspicuously and sometimes sharply toothed with teeth similar to those of several of the hollies *(Ilex* spp.), hence, the common name; fertile pinnae linear in shape and covered below with sporangia; all pinnae borne alternately along the rachis.

Sori: Completely covering the lower side of the narrow, fertile pinnae.

Habitat: Hammocks, limestone sinks.

Distribution: Dade County; A. A. Eaton (1906) reported this species from Castellow, Ross, Timms, and Hattie Bauer hammocks. Today it is known from only a handful of locations in Dade County, none of which contain large populations.

Remarks: The hollylike leaves, winged petiole and rachis, and creeping habit distinguish this species from all others. *L. kunzeana* was first discovered in Florida near Miami by J. K. Small, J. J. Carter, and A. A. Eaton in 1903 (Underwood, 1906; Small, 1938). This is one of only two, simple-leaved ferns in Florida that appear to climb, though in the remaining Florida populations the present species is more appropriately described as scrambling rather than climbing. The other, *Microgramma heterophylla*, is easily distinguishable from the present species. Underwood (1906) noted that "the Florida plants scarcely represent the norm of the species and apparently are straggling plants instead of climbing ones, as in more tropical forests" (p. 197). The genus name refers to its resemblance to the genus *Lomaria,* an old name for *Blechnum.* The specific epithet commenorates German botanist and pteridologist Gustav Kunze (1793-1851). *L. kunzeana* is listed as endangered by the Florida Department of Agriculture.

Synonyms: *Stenochlaena kunzeana* C. Presl ex L. Underwood.

NEPHROLEPIS

Five taxa of the genus *Nephrolepis* occur in Florida, at least three of which are generally referred to by the common name Boston fern. Several members of this genus, particularly *N. exaltata*, which has given rise to at least 100 cultivars, are easily cultivated in potting mix or in moist soil and are common in home landscapes. Most do well in partial to full sun. A sixth species, *N. pectinata* (Willd.) Schott, which is widely distributed in tropical America, has been previously reported for Florida (Wherry, 1964). However, no collections of this species are known or documented. Wherry reported that he had never seen specimens of this species, but included it in his book solely on the basis of a verbal report. Hence, *N. pectinata* has been removed from the state's flora (Darling, 1982).

The genus name *Nephrolepis,* which means "kidneylike scales," derives from the kidney-shaped indusia that characterize many members of the genus. The common name "Boston fern" came into use in the early 1900s because the original variety of *N. exalta* known by this name appeared in nurseries in and near Boston, MA (Benedict, 1916).

Giant Sword Fern, Boston Fern

Nephrolepis biserrata (Swartz) Schott   **Photos 56, 57**

Nephrolepis X *averyi*   **Photo 64**

Form: A relatively large, clump-forming Boston fern with tall fronds and pinnate blades.

Fronds: Ranging 0.35 - 2 m tall, 3 - 35 cm wide.

Petiole: 15 - 55 cm long, sparsely to moderately covered with reddish to light brown, hair-like scales.

Rachis: Pale to dark brown throughout with moderately spaced scales; pinnae attachments to about 3.5 cm apart, hence more widely spaced than on most other members of the genus.

Blade: To about 2.5 m long, scaly, with or without hairs, hairs typically pale brown and often numerous and dense on veins and the lower blade surface.

Pinnae: Oblong to narrowly deltate, not falcate, with a small, often inconspicuous lobe (auricle) on both sides at the base; medial pinnae 2.5 - 23 cm long (most are over 5 cm long), 0.5

- 2 cm wide; margins finely doubly-toothed; apices long-pointed.

Sori: Submarginal; borne under circular to horseshoe-shaped indusia that are approximately 1 mm long and attached either along one side or supported from the center on a small stalk.

Habitat: Typically found in swamps and wet hammocks, but sometimes along roadsides or clearings; usually terrestrial but sometimes epiphytic, especially in cypress and pop ash swamps. In favorable situations, such as in Fakahatchee Strand State Preserve, this species can form dense, nearly impenetrable thickets more than 2 m tall.

Distribution: Southern third of the state from about Manatee and Highlands Counties southward; mostly in the state's more tropical regions.

Remarks: Most easily distinguished from other members of the genus by its relatively large size in conjunction with the densely pubescent undersurfaces of the pinnae. Most similar to and often found in association with *N. exaltata*. The current species has most pinnae longer than 5 cm and submarginal rather than marginal sori. The specific epithet for this species derives from the margins of the pinnae, which are sometimes described as biserrate, meaning doubly toothed. It is listed as endangered by the Florida Department of Agriculture.

In 1979 Nauman described a new hybrid, *N.* X *averyi* Nauman, from Florida (see photo 64). The presumed parent species of this hybrid include the present species and *N. exaltata,* described below. (Some, however, claim that the second parent might be *N. multiflora* rather than *N. exaltata.*) The hybrid was named for George N. Avery, a well-known south Florida botanist and collector. According to Nauman (1979b), the hybrid displays several intermediate characters between its parents. The most easily seen difference is the amount of pubescence on the axes of the pinnae. Whereas the axes in *N. biserrata* are tomentose and those of *N. exaltata* glabrous, those of the hybrid are slightly pubescent. Indusium width also differs between the three taxa: those of *N. biserrata* average 1 mm, those of *N. exaltata* 1.35 mm, and those of *N.* X *averyi* 1.26 mm. Petiole lengths also differ. The length of the petiole in *N. biserrata* averages 2.3 dm, that of *N. exaltata* 1.7 dm, and that of the hybrid 2.7 dm. Nauman takes the increased length of *N.* X *averyi* as evidence of hybrid vigor. *N.* X *averyi* has been collected in a number of counties in central and southern Florida, including Polk, Manatee, Collier, Broward, and Dade.

A single cultivar of this species, the fishtail sword fern *(N. biserrata* cv. 'Furcans'), is sometimes encountered in gardens. The tips of its pinnae are forked and resemble the tail of a fish, and sometimes the forks are themselves forked. This cultivar makes an interesting addition to the fern garden.

Synonyms: *Aspidium biserratum* Swartz

Tuberous Sword Fern, Tuber Sword Fern

Nephrolepis cordifolia (Linnaeus) C. Presl   **Photos 58, 59, 60**

Form: A medium-size, medium-green, pinnately divided Boston fern; often producing belowground, spherical tubers that are densely scaly and reach 1.5 cm in diameter.

Fronds: Ranging 0.25 - 1 m tall, 3 - 7 cm wide.

Petiole: 3 - 20 cm long and densely covered with spreading, pale brown scales.

Rachis: Pale to dark brown and covered with pale, hairlike scales that attach to the rachis at distinctive bases that are much darker than the scales; attachments of the pinnae typically less than 1 cm apart.

Blade: Mostly without hairs and scales.

Pinnae: Mostly oblong to somewhat lanceolate with a distinctive basal lobe on the upper edge and often overlapping the rachis; mostly straight but sometimes slightly curved; 1 - 5 cm long, 0.5 - 1 cm wide; margins entire to crenate or finely toothed; each pinna typically unevenly divided by the central vein, especially toward the base.

Sori: Borne in but protruding from kidney- to crescent-shaped indusia.

Habitat: Limestone ledges, shady, wet places, roadsides; terrestrial or epiphytic.

Distribution: Widely escaped from cultivation throughout much of the state. Wherry (1964) and others regard this species as native to Florida, which is quite doubtful. It has the dubious distinction of being one of only five fern species listed by the Exotic Pest Plant Council as Category I pest plants, which means that it is believed to be invading and disrupting native plant communities.

Remarks: The overlapping bases of the pinnae and two-colored, hairlike scales along the rachis, which are very dark at the base and pale above (seen best with at least 10x magnification), distinguish this species from all other species in the genus (but, see *N. exaltata,* below). This is also the only member of the genus in Florida to produce rounded, belowground tubers (latter character not universally present and requires uprooting the plant to observe).

Synonyms: *Polypodium cordifolium* Linnaeus; *Aspidium cordifolium* (Linnaeus) Swartz.

Sword Fern, Wild Boston Fern

Nephrolepis exaltata (Linnaeus) Schott   **Photos 61, 62**

Form: A medium- to large-size, typical Boston fern often seen under cultivation and in landscape nurseries, or for sale in hanging baskets.

Fronds: 4 - 15 dm tall, arising in spreading clusters.

Petiole: 2 - 40 cm long, with pale to reddish brown scales; scales of a single color or only slightly darkened at the point of attachment, with an expanded base bearing small, marginal hairs which require about 30x magnification to see clearly.

Rachis: Pale to dark brown and moderately clothed with hairlike scales that have expanded bases bearing small, marginal hairs (requires 30x magnification); point of attachment of the scales to the rachis not conspicuously darkened.

Blade: Pinnate, 50 - 100 cm long, to about 11 cm wide, widest at or above the middle.

Pinnae: Deltate to lance shaped, slightly curving to decidedly sickle shaped near the apex, to about 7.4 cm long and 1.8 cm wide, attached to the rachis at intervals of 7 - 21 mm, basally lobed on the upward-facing edge, lobes sometimes overlapping the rachis; pinnae bases usually not overlapping the rachis.

Sori: Marginal; rounded to horseshoe shaped, borne at the tips of forked veins near the margins of the pinnae.

Habitat: Frequent in swamps and wet hammocks, usually terrestrial but also epiphytic on *Sabal palmetto* [(Walt.) Lodd. ex Schultes], several oak species, and on fallen logs.

Distribution: This species has been collected in many counties throughout Florida, from

Leon County eastward and southward. However, it is an often used garden plant and may escape in almost any part of the state. It is sometimes reported as the most common *Nephrolepis* in Florida (Nauman, 1981), an assertion that is most accurate for southern Florida. In other regions of the state, especially the panhandle, it is rivaled in frequency by *N. cordifolia,* a nonnative species with which it is easily confused.

Remarks: The sword fern can be distinguished from other members of the genus by the pinnae being sickle-shaped (at least toward the apex on some pinnae) and lacking or having only a few hairs on the surfaces of their central axes. It is quite similar to and easily confused with *N. cordifolia.* The petiolar scales of the current species are a single color rather than conspicuously bicolored as in the latter species, the pinnae bases of the current species usually do not overlap the rachis, and the stem never produces belowground tubers. It is also similar to and often grows with *N. biserrata.* The current species may be distinguished from the latter by having marginal sori, and by having pinnae usually less than 5 cm long. See *N. biserrata,* above for a discussion of the hybrid *N. X averyi.*

Synonyms: *Polypodium exaltatum* Linnaeus.

Asian Sword Fern

Nephrolepis multiflora (Roxburgh) F.M. Jarrett ex C.V. Morton   **Photo 63**

Form: A medium- to large-size Boston fern with short, woody, underground stems that are covered with two-colored scales that are pale along the edges and have a dark brown central stripe.

Fronds: To about 1.5 m tall, or taller.

Petiole: 4 - 44 cm long, moderately to profusely covered with linear, appressed scales that are similar to the stem scales in being two colored with pale brown margins and a dark brown to nearly black central stripe.

Rachis: Yellowish to grayish brown, clothed with linear, two colored, very hairy scales that impart a hairy appearance to the rachis.

Blade: Pinnate, linear to lance-linear in outline, slightly wider near the middle, 50 - 100 cm long or more, 7 - 20 cm wide.

Pinnae: Linear-oblong, deltate, to narrowly elliptic, 3.5 - 12 cm long or a little longer, scaly and pubescent below with pale brown hairs; margins singly to doubly toothed, apex of marginal teeth sharp to dull.

Sori: Borne near the margins of the pinnae under circular to horseshoe-shaped indusia.

Habitat: Disturbed sites, near canals, roadsides, open waste places, often in full sun.

Distribution: Mostly occurring in the southernmost peninsula, collected as far north as the Tampa area on the west coast and Martin County on the east coast; intolerant of cold and restricted mostly to warmer parts of the state.

Remarks: Three characters help distinguish this species: 1) the dense, short, erect hairs along the central veins on the upper side of the central pinnae, 2) the narrowly lanceolate scales with an expanded hairy base on the lower surfaces of the pinnae, and, perhaps most importantly, 3) the dark brown, appressed petiolar scales that are pale along the margins. *N. multiflora* is native to the Old World tropics but is widely naturalized in the New World. It was first reported in Florida for Dade County in 1975 (Gillis & Proctor), but probably arrived in the state as early as the 1940s. It is listed by the Exotic Pest Plant Council as one of the state's Category II pest plants, which means that it has the potential to invade and disrupt the state's native plant communities.

Synonyms: *Davallia multiflora* Roxburgh.

Sensitive Fern, Bead Fern

Onoclea sensibilis Linnaeus   **Photos 65, 66**

Form: A medium to large, robust fern with wide pinnae and conspicuous fertile fronds.

Fronds: Sterile fronds 35 - 70 cm tall, to about 30 cm wide or a little more, dark green to yellowish green; fertile fronds 25 - 40 cm tall, green when new (in mid-summer), blackish in maturity (late fall and winter).

Petiole: Those of sterile fronds 20 - 40 cm long, grooved, greenish to straw colored, with a darkened base; those of fertile fronds straw colored and with sparsely spaced, brownish scales.

Rachis: Straw colored below, shading to brown at the apex, winged, grooved.

Blade: Sterile blades broadly triangular in overall shape, 15 - 35 cm long, pinnatifid; fertile blades 10 - 15 cm long, narrow and lacking expanded tissue.

Pinnae: Borne nearly opposite along the rachis, typically in 5 - 15 pairs, to about 18 cm long, margins undulate to shallowly lobed but entire.

Sori: Borne in conspicuous, distinctive, beadlike structures at the apex of fertile fronds.

Habitat: Ditches, rich, moist to wet soils, swampy woods, marshes, hammocks, floodplains.

Distribution: Northernmost Florida and the panhandle.

Remarks: Most easily confused with *Woodwardia areolata;* most easily distinguised from it at a glance by the nearly opposite (rather than mostly alternate) pinnae, and by the equally distinctive but quite different fertile fronds of the two species. The common name, sensitive fern, and the specific epithet, *sensibilis,* both derive from this species' sensitivity to cold as well as soil moisture, and its tendency to die back during drought or at the first frost. The genus name derives from the Greek words "onos" (vessel) and "kleiein" (closed), in reference to the sori being enclosed by the tightly inrolled fertile leaf tissue.

Synonyms: *Onoclea sensibilis* forma *hemiphylodes* (Kiss & Kummerle) Gilbert; *O. sensibilis* forma *obtusilobata* (Schkuhr) Gilbert; *O. sensibilis* var. *obtusilobata* (Schkuhr) Torrey.

Christmas Fern

Polystichum acrostichoides (Michaux) Schott   **Photos 67, 68**

Form: A dark green, evergreen fern with a scaly, ascending stem.

Fronds: 30 - 70 cm tall, to about 14 cm wide; sterile and fertile somewhat different in appearance, especially at the apices.

Petiole: 10 - 20 cm long, brown below, somewhat paler above, conspicuously vested with shaggy, light-brown scales.

Rachis: Brownish to pale green, very scaly.

Blade: 20 - 50 cm long, pinnate, lanceolate in overall shape.

Pinnae: Borne oppositely to alternately on short stalks, margins toothed, conspicuously lobed (auricled) at the base on the upward facing margin, lanceolate to oblong in shape, dark green above, pale green below.

Sori: Borne on reduced pinnae at the apices of fertile fronds, at maturity nearly covering the entire lower surface of the fertile pinnae.

Habitat: Rich woods, ravines, shaded slopes, calcareous hammocks.

Distribution: Northern Florida, sparingly southward to about the central peninsula.

Remarks: This is the only fern species of rich mesic woods that displays conspicuously scaly petioles and relatively large, auricled sterile pinnae, and conspicuously reduced fertile pinnae. The genus name of this species means "many rows" and refers to the crowded sori. The specific epithet means "like *Acrostichum*" and refers to the superficial similarity between the sori of this species and those of the leather ferns, which have sori that run together and are described as confluent in botanical parlance. Its common name may derive from its use in Christmas decorations in Colonial America. However, Dunbar (1989) points out the pinnae resemble Christmas stockings when held vertically, and this may also be a reason for the common name. The plant is one of the few evergreen components in the ground cover of mesic slope forests. Hence, it is striking and conspicuous in drab, mid-winter woodlands, which suggests yet another origin of its common name.

Synonyms: *Nephrodium acrostichoides* Michaux.

Korean Rock Fern

Polystichum tsussimense (Hooker) J. Smith   **Photos 69, 70**

Form: A relatively small, compact, glossy blue-green fern of the Asian tropics.

Fronds: To about 60 cm tall.

Petiole: 20 - 30 cm long, slender, about the length of the blade; clothed with dark brown, lanceolate to broadly lanceolate scales that (those at the base, at least) are brown-hairy at the tip.

Rachis: Similar to the petiole but having narrowly lanceolate to more nearly filiform scales that do not exceed about 1 mm in width.

Blade: Bipinnate, rigidly erect to semi-erect, 20 - 30 cm long, 8 - 15 cm wide.

Pinnae: 5 - 10 cm long, to about 3 cm wide, clothed below with small, linear scales; pinnules spine-tipped.

Sori: Compact, protected by rounded indusia, usually produced in a single row on either side of the midvein of the pinnules.

Habitat: Escaped from cultivation in Florida; found in moist, shaded woodlands in its native range.

Distribution: Collected in Florida only in Lake County; native to China, Japan, Taiwan, and Korea; also escaped in Louisiana.

Remarks: This is a hardy fern in its native range and is used in sheltered, moist gardens. It is sold in many Florida nurseries. The specific epithet refers to the Japanese island of Tsussima, for which it is named.

Synonyms: *Aspidium tsus-simense* Hooker, *Polystichum polyblepharum* sensu Nakai, *Polystichum mayebarae* Tagawa, *Polystichum tsussimense* var. *mayebarae* (Tagawa) Kurata.

Leather Fern

Rumohra adiantiformis (G. Forst.) Ching   **Photos 71, 72**

Form: An attractive, medium- to large-size fern with a long-creeping, flattish, stout stem to about 1.5 cm in diameter and clothed with yellowish brown scales that are up to 1.5 cm long and about 4 mm wide.

Fronds: 20 - 150 cm tall, very stiff and firm to the touch.

Petiole: Straw colored and deeply grooved.

Rachis: Multiply grooved, similar to the petiole in color but sometimes darker toward the apex; often scaly.

Blade: Bi- to tripinnate, deltate to somewhat ovate, 15 - 90 cm long, 10 - 75 cm wide near the base, without hairs.

Pinnae: Stalked, lowermost generally deltate in outline, ultimate pinnules more nearly lance-elliptic to ovate-oblong; margins varying from incised to bluntly toothed.

Sori: Large, round, conspicuous, closer to the midveins of the pinnae than to the margins.

Habitat: Disturbed wooded areas in close proximity to human habitations.

Distribution: Leather fern occurs widely in various parts of the tropical and subtropical world from Chile and Argentina to South Africa and New Zealand, a distribution that suggests that the species is quite old (Morton, 1960). Wunderlin (1982) listed it as escaped and rare in Lee County, and Lellinger (1985) reported it as escaped and apparently naturalizing at one Florida locality. It has now been collected in at least five Florida counties (Alachua, Putnum, Volusia, Pinellas, and Lee). Given its availability in landscape nurseries, other naturalizing populations are likely.

Remarks: The genus *Rumohra* was established in 1819 by Guiseppe Raddi in honor of German scholar Karl F. von Rumohr (1785-1843). The genus once included a number of additional species but is now construed to encompass a single, widespread species that ranges throughout the Southern Hemisphere. *R. adiantiformis* is typically epiphytic in its native locations but is used in gardens and landscaping in Florida. The firm texture and durability of its fronds make them an often used component in floral arrangements, and in fashioning corsages. Hence, it is a major component of central Florida's cut foliage trade, but it is also used as a terrestrial garden plant in Florida.

Synonyms: *Rumohra aspidoides* Raddi.

Hairy Halberd Fern

Tectaria coriandrifolia (Swartz) L. Underwood   **Page 70**

Tectaria X amesiana

Form: Relatively small (in Florida) to medium-size, often daintily cut fern with stoutish, decumbent, short-creeping stems.

Fronds: Ascending or arching, 11 - 45 cm long.

Petiole: Dark brown at the base, pale to reddish brown above, pubescent and scaly.

Rachis: Covered with short hairs, at least on the lower side, that are similar to those of the petiole.

Figure 13.
Tectaria coriandrifolia

Blade: Pinnate-pinnatifid, 5 - 28 cm long throughout its range but probably not exceeding about 12 cm long in Florida, 2.5 - 5 cm or more wide, linear-lanceolate to somewhat oblong in outline.

Pinnae: Finely hairy, borne in 1 to 8 pairs, lowermost 1 to 6 pinnae deltate, short stalked, and covered with hairs both above and below (requires magnification), the terminalmost pinna pinnatifid with large lobes below, grading into smaller lobes above.

Sori: Typically few in number, borne in rounded to kidney-shaped indusia.

Habitat: Sinkholes, limerock outcrops.

Distribution: Collected in Hattie Bauer and Gossman's Hammocks, Dade County, where it is apparently no longer extant; otherwise found in the West Indies in both Cuba and Jamaica.

Remarks: This species is most easily distinguished from others in the genus by having blades that are generally less than 15 cm long with 1 to 8 pairs of pinnae. It was first discovered in Florida by A. A. Eaton in 1903 at a site in south Dade County (Underwood, 1906). This species is also known to hybridize with *T. fimbriata* to produce *T.* X *amesiana* A. A. Eaton, which is also restricted to Dade County, and was first described by Eaton (1906) from populations in Hattie Bauer Hammock. However, populations of both *T. coriandrifolia* and the hybrid apparently declined together and neither appear to be extant in Florida's current flora. *T.* X *amesiana* has a dense row of stiff hairs on the upper surface of the petiole, and scattered stiff hairs on the lower surface of the petiole. *T. coriandrifolia* is listed as endangered by the Florida Department of Agriculture.

According to Darling (1961), some attribute the loss of these species in Florida to a combination of the establishment of the Fennell Orchid Jungle at one end of Hattie Bauer Hammock, and to a continued drought during the 1930s. However, Darling further reports that collections made by F. N. Irving in November of 1940 are on deposit in the U. S. National Herbarium, and that Maurice Broun reported thriving colonies from which he collected a number of specimens in February of 1935.

Synonyms: *Aspidium coriandrifolium* Swartz.

Least Halberd Fern
Tectaria fimbriata (Willdenow) Proctor & Lourteig   **Photo 73**

Form: A small fern with horizontal, short-creeping stems.

Fronds: Borne in clusters, less than 35 cm tall

Petiole: Pubescent, 4 - 28 cm long, typically 1 - 3 times the length of the blade, pale brown above, darker toward the base.

Blade: Typically 4 - 11 cm long (or a little longer), 2 - 10 cm wide (or a little wider), bipinnatifid to pinnate-pinnatifid, sometimes without lateral pinnae, sometimes with only 1 to 2 pairs of lower lateral pinnae; apex and sometimes the entire blade deltate and lobed; midvein pubescent on the lower surface; veins netted.

Pinnae: When present, long deltate, 4 - 7 cm long, lower surfaces hairy along the axis.

Sori: Round, borne in single rows adjacent to lateral veins.

Habitat: Sinkholes, solution holes, shaded limestone outcrops.

Distribution: Uncommon and generally reported as occurring in the central and southern peninsula; collected in Citrus, Dade, and Monroe Counties.

Remarks: Most easily distinguished from other members of the genus by having blades typically less than 15 cm long and having, at most, 1 to 2 pairs of lateral pinnae. Underwood (1906) suggested that this species might be confused with young specimens of *T. heracleifolia* because of the similarity of their fronds. However, the presence of sori on the leaves of this species distinguishes it from *T. heracleifolia,* since the latter species only produces sori on its much larger, mature leaves. Wherry (1964) suggested that there may be a hybrid between the present species and *T. heracleifolia.* There is considerable variation among specimens of the present species, but no hybrid has yet been proposed. This species was first described by Underwood (1906) from specimens collected in Dade County. It is now listed as endangered by the Florida Department of Agriculture.

Synonyms: *Aspidium fimbriatum* Willdenow; *A. minimum* (L. Underwood) Clute; *A. trifoliatum* (Linnaeus) Swartz var. *minimum* Clute; *Sagenia lobata* C. Presl; *Tectaria lobata* (C. Presl) C.V. Morton; *T. minima* L. Underwood.

Broad Halberd Fern

Tectaria heracleifolia (Willdenow) L. Underwood   **Photos 74, 75**

Form: A medium-size, halberd fern with a woody, erect or ascending, scaly stem to about 2 cm in diameter.

Fronds: To 60 cm or more tall; dark, shiny green.

Petiole: Grooved, straw colored to pale brown above, dark brown, scaly, and minutely pubescent at the base, 15 - 45 cm long, usually longer than the blade, without hairs above the base.

Rachis: Short or absent, without hairs, becoming the midvein of the terminal pinna.

Blade: Pinnate-pinnatifid, generally deltate-ovate to pentagonal in outline, 12 - 50 cm long, 14 - 45 cm wide; veins netted.

Pinnae: 1 to 3 pairs of lateral pinnae below, lowermost pinnae stalked and often deeply lobed so as to appear as two pinnae, terminal pinna deltate and lobed or toothed, all pinnae terminating in long-tapering apices; axes and lateral veins of lower surfaces of pinnae minutely scaly pubescent; pinnae margins often coarsely toothed.

Sori: Conspicuous, numerous, borne on the lower surfaces of the pinnae in single rows along either side of the veins, to about 3.5 mm wide.

Habitat: Limestone outcrops, rocky hammocks, shaded grottoes, often in association with brittle maidenhair fern *(Adiantum tenerum).*

Distribution: Mostly in the southernmost peninsula; collected in Citrus, Hernando, Martin, Broward, Dade, and Collier Counties.

Remarks: The deeply-lobed lowermost pair of pinnae and blades that are typically over 15 cm long distinguish this species from most other species in the genus. Distinguished from the similar *T. incisa* by the shiny green color, and by lacking hairs on both the lower side of the rachis and the axis of the lower surface of the pinnae.

This species is often found on the walls of lime sinks where the overlapping fronds of separate plants often nearly obscure the substrate. Such situations are quite beautiful and suggestive of a lush, tropical garden. The genus names comes from the Latin "tectum," or roof, in reference to the rooflike indusia that cover the sori. The specific epithet means "with leaves like *Heracleum,*" another fern genus. It is listed as endangered by the Florida Department of Agriculture.

Synonyms: *Aspidium heracleifolium* Willdenow.

Incised Halberd Fern

Tectaria incisa Cavanille   **Photo 76**

Form: A large, coarse fern with an erect, woody stem to about 3 cm in diameter and clothed with dark brown scales that are 3 - 7 mm long.

Fronds: To about 1.5 m tall, clustered on the stem and dull, light green in color.

Petiole: Yellowish to pale brown above, dark brown and scaly at the base, pubescent, grooved, to about 50 cm long, about as long as the blade.

Rachis: Grooved, hairy on the lower surface, especially within the channel of the groove.

Blade: Pinnate, 15 - 75 cm or more long, 20 - 50 cm wide, oblong to somewhat ovate in outline; veins netted.

Pinnae: Terminal pinna deltate and joined at the rachis with the uppermost lateral pinnae, lower five or so pairs of lateral pinnae short stalked, lowermost pair usually so deeply two-lobed that both lobes appear to be pinnae; lateral pinnae mostly linear-oblong; margins mostly entire but wavy.

Sori: Round, in single rows on either side of lateral veins.

Habitat: Rare in rocky hammocks.

Distribution: Broward, Dade, and Palm Beach Counties.

Remarks: The deeply-lobed lowermost pair of pinnae in conjunction with blades that are typically over 15 cm long distinguish this species from most other species in the genus. Distinguished from the superficially similar *T. heracleifolia* by the multiple pairs of dull green pinnae, and by having pubescence on the lower side of the rachis. The specific epithet comes from the deeply cut fronds.

Blunt-Lobed Cliff Fern, Blunt-Lobed Woodsia

Woodsia obtusa (Sprengel) Torrey subsp. *obtusa*   **Photos 77, 78**

Form: A small, delicate, somewhat lacy-appearing fern with few to many petiole bases of unequal lengths.

Fronds: 2 - 5 dm tall, lanceolate in overall shape, sterile and fertile similar in appearance.

Petiole: 5 - 20 cm long, green with a dark base and pale, reddish brown to light brown scales.

Rachis: Yellowish to greenish or straw colored, scaly and finely pubescent.

Blade: Pinnate-pinnatifid to bipinnate-pinnatifid, 10 - 30 cm long, to about 12 cm wide.

Pinnae: 5 to 15 pairs, borne well spaced along the rachis (especially so toward the base), nearly opposite, decreasing in length toward the base; pinnules toothed to deeply lobed; with glandular hairs.

Sori: Round, borne in cuplike indusia that split into narrow, ribbonlike segments at maturity. As the indusia split, their segments form a starlike arrangement under the sporangia, making each sporangium/indusium combination take on the appearance of a tiny flower. These flowerlike clusters are very small and require at least 15x magnification to see clearly.

Habitat: Uppermost, shaded ledges above major rivers, moist open woods, rocky outcrops, banks within and adjacent to floodplains.

Distribution: Very limited in Florida and known from only three stations. This species was previously reported from two stations along the Apalachicola River, one in 1936 (apparently the first record for the state) by Edward P. St. John, in conjunction with Herman Kurz, John K. Small, and others (specimen on deposit at the University of Florida Herbarium, FLAS P1449), and another in Jackson County by Angus K. Gholson, Jr. (specimens on deposit at FSU and at AKG Herbarium in Chattahoochee, Florida). Recent searches indicate that neither of these populations is still extant. A third population, reported in 1968 from Lafayette County (FLAS P8110) also seems to be extirpated. The sporadic appearance and disappearance of this species in Florida may be due to its being brought to the state via large rivers that originate outside of Florida. Small populations that become established in this manner are very susceptible to the vagaries of river fluctuation and bank erosion. I have seen this species just across the Florida state line in Georgia on bluffs along the east side of the Chattahoochee River in a similar situation.

Remarks: The widely-spaced pinnae that become increasingly shorter toward the base of the frond and the star-shaped sori help to distinguish this species. *W. obtusa* is similar in general aspects to *Cystopteris protrusa,* another of Florida's very rare ferns. The two may be distinguished by their indusia. The rachis and petiole of the present species are generally paler in color and somewhat more scaly than those of *Cystopteris.* The petiolar scales of the present species are also more conspicuous and extend farther up the petiotle and onto the rachis.

The genus name of this species commemorates British botanist Joseph Woods (1776-1864). The specific epithet refers to the bluntly-tipped, or obtuse, lobes of the pinnae.

Synonyms: *Polypodium obtusum* Sprengel, *Woodsia perriniana* (Sprengel) Hooker & Greville.

EQUISETACEAE - HORSETAIL FAMILY

The Equisetaceae includes 15 species worldwide, 11 in North America, and two in Florida. Members of the family, all of which are included within the single genus, *Equisetum,* have erect, grooved, jointed, hollow stems and small, whorled leaves that are fused with sheath-like structures and are borne at regular intervals along the stem. The sporangia are borne in conelike structures (strobili) at the top of the more or less erect stems. The family is of ancient lineage and the single surviving genus has remained relatively unchanged over the past 200 million years. Many of the species of *Equisetum* are quite similar and very difficult to distinguish in the field. Scanning electron microscopy and close examination are often required for accurate determination.

The common name, horsetail, derives from the appearance of the stems. The appellation scouring rush, another common name for members of the family, derives from the rough surfaces of the stem which rendered them useful for scouring. The scientific name for the genus comes from the Latin *equis,* or horse, and *seta,* or bristle, and refers to the stiff, black roots of the non-Florida species river horsetail *(E. fluviatile* Linnaeus), which occurs across much of the northern North America.

Scouring Rush

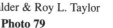

Equisetum hyemale Linnaeus subsp. *affine* (Engelmann) Calder & Roy L. Taylor

Photo 79

Form: An erect, unbranched fern ally with a characteristic hollow, rounded stem, 18 - 100 cm tall (or taller); stem minutely longitudinally ridged and grooved with 18 to 40 ridges; fertile and sterile stems similar in appearance.

Leaves: Borne in whorls and fused into sheathlike structures; sheaths, at maturity, narrow with brown to blackish bands above and below, and with 12 to 30 dark brown, narrow teeth with white margins.

Cones: Pointed, borne at the tips of the stems, somewhat reminiscent of a tiny pineapple in appearance.

Habitat: Riverbanks, flood plains, moist woodlands, sandy shores, and other moist situations, including agriculture fields in southern Florida.

Distribution: Throughout the state, but sparingly so in southern Florida; perhaps more common along larger rivers of northern Florida.

Remarks: This is the only species likely to be seen in Florida, except in the far western panhandle. It is most easily distinguished from *E. ramosissimum,* the other Florida species, by the sheaths being about as wide as long, and by the stem being mostly unbranched (except in cases where the stem has been injured) rather than branched (but see remarks in the entry for the latter species). The common name of this species results from its stems being used for sanding wood and scouring pots. The specific epithet *hymale,* means "of winter," in reference to the plant's evergreen habit.

Synonyms: *Equisetum robustum* A. Braun var. *affine* Engelmann; *E. hyemale* var. *affine* (Engelmann) A. A. Eaton; *E. hyemale* var. *californicum* J. Milde; *E. hyemale* var. *pseudohyemale* (Farwell) C.V. Morton; *E. hyemale* var. *robustum* (A. Braun) A. A. Eaton; *E. prealtum* Rafinesque

Branched Scouring Rush

Equisetum ramosissimum Desfontaines subsp. *ramosissimum*

Form: Stems regularly branched, especially from near the base, 32 - 250 cm tall, with 10 to 16 longitudinal grooves and ridges.

Leaves: Borne in whorls at nodes along the stem and fused into leaf sheaths that are conspicuously longer than wide; upper sheaths greenish, lower darker, shading to brownish; teeth numbering 5 - 16.

Cones: Pointed at the apex and borne at the tips of the stems, somewhat resembling a tiny, narrow pineapple.

Habitat: Railroad embankments, moist, sandy, or clay areas.

Distribution: Reported in Florida only from Escambia County.

Remarks: This is an Old World species which ". . . is widely distributed in the Eastern Hemisphere, ranging through southern, eastern, and Mediterranean Africa, the Canary and Azores islands, Europe, north to southern Germany and Lithuania and east through the Balkans and Asia Minor to Mongolia, Korea, and Japan" (Hauke, 1979). It has been introduced to the United States, probably through discarded ballast many years ago, and is currently known in the United States only from Louisiana, North Carolina, and Florida (Hauke, 1979, 1984, 1992). As might be expected, it is uncommon and local in Florida, and is likely to be seen only in Escambia County in the far western panhandle where it was first collected by Ward and Burkhalter in 1975. However, it should probably be looked for throughout the southeast, especially near old ports.

E. ramosissimum can be mistaken for *E. hymale,* the more common Florida species. It may be distinguished by the combination of long internodes, flattened sheath segments that are generally longer than wide, regularly branched stems (at least near the base), and persistent and shriveling sheath teeth that do not exceed about 15 in number. The specific epithet means "many branched."

GLEICHENIACEAE - FORKING FERN FAMILY

The common name for this family derives from the unique branching pattern of the fronds. The apex of the petiole divides into three buds, one of which aborts, two of which develop into repeatedly forking blades. The name for the single genus of the family that occurs in Florida, *Dicranopteris*, derives from the Greek word *dikranos*, or twice-forked, and *pteris*, or fern. The family name commemorates the German botanist, F. W. Gleichen.

Forked Fern, Net Fern

Dicranopteris flexuosa (Schrader) L. Underwood   **Photos 80, 81**

Form: A distinctive fern with wiry, firm, several-forked fronds and coarse stems that are clothed when young with reddish brown hairs.

Fronds: Leathery, stiff, firm to the touch, to about 1 m tall.

Petiole: Green at first, straw colored to brown with age, without hairs except near the base, stiff and wiry.

Rachis: Straw colored and without hairs, stiff.

Blade: Branched and repeatedly forking, the ultimate branches lanceolate in outline, 9 - 30 cm long, 2 - 6 cm wide, deeply pinnatifid with alternate pinnules, light yellowish green above, typically with a whitish bloom below; blade tissue typically without hairs; lateral veins 2- to 4-forked; margins strongly inrolled.

Sori: Borne nearer the midrib than the margin and consisting of clusters of 4 - 12 round, yellowish sporangia.

Habitat: Open pinelands, embankments along roadside and drainage ditches.

Distribution: Native to and widespread in tropical America; collected in Osceola, Hillsborough, Bay, Palm Beach, and Franklin Counties.

Remarks: This is the sole species of the family Gleicheniaceae in North America. It was originally described from Brazil in 1824 and was first discovered in the United States on a Gulf coast island near Mobile, Alabama in 1913, presumably where it arrived by natural means (Small, 1938). It was subsequently collected in Florida in both Osceola County in 1947 (Singletary, 1950) and Hillsborough County in 1955 (Wherry, 1964; Darling, 1961). Recent accounts (Lellinger, 1985 and Lakela & Long, 1979) reported that the species had not been collected in recent years and was only questionably present in our flora. Lellinger even elected to leave it out of the main part of his manual due to its uncertain status. However, recent discoveries in Bay (Burkhalter, 1985), Palm Beach (Moyroud and Nauman, 1989), and Franklin (Nelson, 1998) Counties indicate that the species is still present in Florida. Nauman (1993c) considers this species a natural part of our flora. Others describe it as a tropical waif, meaning that it arrives in the state periodically but typically dies out before becoming naturalized. Its somewhat wide-spaced distributional pattern in the state suggests that it may appear, albeit in small numbers, in other regions of Florida, especially those areas impacted by hurricanes or strong tropical depressions. It is interesting to note that nodding club-moss (*Palhinhaea cernua*) is an important associate of the current species in all of the extant Florida populations as well as at least one of its lost populations (Darling, 1961). Hence, this latter species may be a useful indicator of suitable habitat. The forked fern's distinctive form makes it unlikely to be confused with any other of the state's pteridophytes.

Synonyms: *Mertensia flexuosa* Schrader; *Gleichenia flexuosa* (Schrader) Mettenius.

HYMENOPHYLLACEAE - FILMY FERN FAMILY

The common name for this family derives from the thin, filmy leaves of the genus *Hymenophyllum,* two species of which occur in the southeastern United States outside of Florida, and one in Alaska. There are six genera and approximately 650 species in the family; only five species of the single genus, *Trichomanes,* have been found in Florida.

Two other species have been reported for Florida, one questionable, the other in error. *T. boschianum* Sturn, was reported by Small (1931) as questionably present in western Florida. However, in his 1938 *Ferns of the Southeastern United States,* he remarks that "The Florida station for it appears to be lost to science" (p. 57). Since there are no known herbarium specimens or documented records of this species for the state, whether it ever occurred here is conjectural. Mickel's (1979) report of *T. membranaceum* Linnaeus for Florida was apparently an error, since it also has not been documented in the state.

Members of the genus *Trichomanes* are commonly referred to as bristle ferns, a name that alludes to the bristlelike structure that protrudes from the mature sporangia. The scientific name for the genus comes from the Greek word *thrix,* which translates as "hair," and *manes,* or "cup," a reference to the hairy, cuplike receptacle in which the sporangia are held. These small, flaring, cuplike structures, which are typically borne at the tips of lateral veins, are often referred to as soral involucres. In normal botanical parlance, the term involucre is used to describe a series of (often nestlike) bracts that closely subtend a flower or flower cluster. In this instance, however, it refers to a cone- or funnel-shaped indusium, a character which distinguishes the Hymenophyllaceae.

Most members of the genus *Trichomanes* are small to minute plants. Nearly all of the 320 or so species in the genus occur naturally primarily in the tropics; only a few, such as the Appalachian filmy fern *(T. boschianum* Sturm), occur naturally in temperate regions.

Entire-Winged Bristle Fern

Trichomanes holopterum Kunze   **Photo 82**

Form: A small, epiphytic fern with erect, sparingly-branched stems.

Fronds: Small, clustered along the stem, 2.5 - 10 cm long throughout its range, typically shorter in Florida, and not exceeding about 7 cm long to about 2 cm wide.

Petiole: Short, 1 - 3.5 cm long, winged.

Blade: Pinnatifid, oblong, 1.5 - 6 cm long, pinnules lobed near the apex; margins of blades lacking hair.

Sori: Borne along the margins of the blade segments at the tips of veins in flaring, funnel-shaped, cuplike structures (involucres), which are easily visible to the naked eye.

Habitat: Epiphytic on stumps, fallen logs, the bases of cypress trees in cypress swamps.

Distribution: Rare in Collier and Monroe Counties.

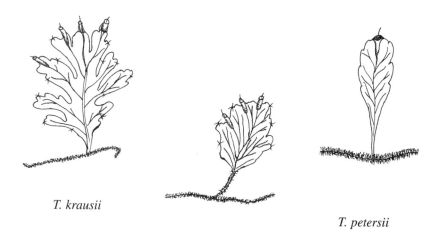

T. krausii

T. petersii

T. punctatum subsp. *flori-danum*

Figure 14. Fronds in *Trichomanes*

Remarks: This is the largest of Florida's filmy ferns. The small, flaring, cuplike structures (soral involucres) near the leaf margins that bear the sporangia distinguish the genus. The present species is distinguished from others in the genus by having pinnatifid leaves that are generally longer than 4 cm. The specific epithet and common names allude to the entirely winged petiole. This species is listed as endangered by the Florida Department of Agriculture.

Kraus's Bristle Fern

Trichomanes krausii Hooker & Greville   **Photo 83, Page 78**

Form: A small fern with small leaves and long-creeping, intertwining, hairy, rootless stems.
Petiole: Shorter than the blade, hairy to bristly hairy.
Frond: Borne well-spaced along the long-creeping stem, 1 - 6 cm long.
Blade: Deeply pinnatifid to bipinnatifid, to about 4 cm long and 1.5 cm wide, oblanceolate to diamond shaped in overall outline, with branched (stellate), dark to black hairs (requires magnification) scattered along the lobe margins.
Sori: Borne along the margins of the blade segments at the tips of veins in flaring, funnel-shaped, cuplike structures (involucres).

Habitat: On limestone in rocky hammocks and in sinkholes; also epiphytic on stumps and fallen trees.

Distribution: Known from a few stations in Dade County.

Remarks: The small, flaring, cuplike structures (soral involucres) near the leaf margins that bear the sporangia distinguish the genus. The present species is most similar to *T. holopterum* because of its typically pinnate-pinnatifid fronds. However, the mature fronds of the current species are generally shorter than 4 cm, have narrow pinnules, and display branched hairs along their margins, while those of the former are typically longer than 4 cm, have wider pinnules, and lack marginal hairs.

In his 1918 treatise on the ferns of tropical Florida, J. K. Small describes this species as occurring on trees and shrubs in at least six hammocks in southern Florida, "sometimes completely covering trunks and limbs with masses that can be stripped off as mats of several square feet" (p. 6). It is much less common and conspicuous today and is listed as endangered by the Florida Department of Agriculture. Its specific epithet commemorates Christian Ferdinand Fredrich von Krause (1812-1890), a German zoologist who collected plants in South Africa.

Synonyms: *Didymoglossum krausii* (Hooker & Greville) C. Presl

Lined Bristle Fern

Trichomanes lineolatum (Bosch) Hooker   **Page 80**

Form: A small fern with small leaves and rootless, threadlike stems that are clothed with blackish hairs (requires magnification).

Fronds: Numerous and often borne in overlapping tufts along the stem, dull green in color, to about 3 cm long.

Petiole: Shorter than to about as long as the blade.

Blade: Simple or, more commonly, irregularly lobed, 1 - 2 cm long, typically less than 1 cm wide (at least in Florida collections); orbicular, obovate, to somewhat spatulate in overall outline; lobes to about 5 mm long and 3 mm wide; margins with dark, branched (stellate) hairs (requires magnification) that sometimes slough off with age.

Sori: Borne along and extending slightly beyond the margins of the blade segments at the tips of veins in narrowly funnel-shaped to cylindrical, cuplike structures (involucres) that are about 2 mm long and only slightly or not at all flaring at the mouth.

Habitat: On limestone in rocky hammocks and in sinkholes; very occasionally on stumps and fallen trees.

Distribution: Dade County; originally known from Castellow, Ross, and Hattie Bauer Hammocks, but now apparently no longer extant in Florida (Lellinger, 1985; Wunderlin, 1998).

Remarks: The small, cuplike structures (soral involucres) near the leaf margins that bear the sporangia distinguish the genus. The present species is distinguished from others in the genus by having irregularly-lobed to simple leaves that are generally 1 - 3 cm long and that bear cylindric (as opposed to distinctly funnel-shaped), essentially non-flaring soral involucres. This latter characteristic in conjunction with its overall slightly longer leaves distinguishes it from the closely similar *T. petersii* and *T. punctatum* subsp. *floridanum*. The specific epithet

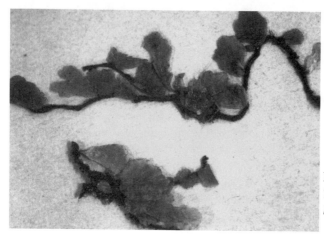

Figure15.
*Trichomanes
lineolatum*

refers to the species' relatively wide veins in comparison to other members of the genus.

T. lineolatum is fairly common in the West Indies and South America, and was original-ly collected in Jamaica in 1863 (Proctor, 1985). It was first collected in Florida in Ross Hammock by J. K. Small and J. J. Carter in 1906 (Small, 1938), but has not been seen in the state in recent years. It may no longer be present in Florida's fern flora but is still listed as endangered by the Florida Department of Agriculture.

Synonyms: *Didymoglossum lineolatum* Bosch

Dwarf Bristle Fern, Peters' Bristle Fern

Trichomanes petersii A. Gray　　　　　　**Photo 84, Pag 78**

Form: A minute, epiphytic fern with a rootless, long-creeping stem and a generally mat-ted appearance.

Fronds: Borne in congested clusters at intervals along the stem.

Petiole: To about 7 mm long and about as long as the blade.

Blade: Less than 2 cm long (often not exceeding 1 cm), to about 5 mm wide, simple, elliptic to obovate, adorned along the margins with branched, black hairs (requires magnification).

Sori: Borne at the leaf apex in a single, funnel-shaped cup (soral involucre); involucre entire-ly within the leaf tissue and not edged in black.

Habitat: In Florida, mostly on limestone boulders and along the edges of lime sinks. Also epiphytic on tree trunks in areas of high humidity in other parts of its range, especially on American beech *(Fagus grandifolia* Ehrhart) and southern magnolia *(Magnolia grandiflora* Linnaeus) and in association with mosses, liverworts, resurrection fern *(Pleopeltis polypodi-oides* var. *michauxianum)*, and green fly orchid *(Epidendrum conopseum* R. Brown).

Distribution: Collected in Florida in Sumter, Citrus, and Hernando Counties but potentially present in other locations

Remarks: The small, cuplike structures (soral involucres) near the leaf margins that bear the sporangia distinguish the genus. The current species is most likely to be confused only with the equally minute *T. punctatum* subsp. *floridanum*. However, each leaf of *T. petersii* has only a single soral involucre, the lips of which are not dark-edged and do not extend beyond the margin of the blade. But also see *T. lineolatum.*

This plant was first discovered in 1853 in Winston County, Alabama, by Judge Thomas Minott Peters, for whom Asa Gray named the plant. Peters was a New Englander who studied law at the University of Alabama. He was a state legislator, a state senator, and later served a six-year term as a judge on the Alabama Supreme Court. He was also an avid amateur botanist who corresponded with many of the leading botanists of the day and was well respected for his knowledge of the lichens, the fungi, and sedges of the genus *Carex*. The divergent southeastern distribution of the fern that bears his name, coupled with its minute size, suggests that it is likely overlooked in Florida as well as other southern states.

Synonyms: *Didymoglossum petersii* (A. Gray) Copeland

Florida Bristle Fern

Trichomanes punctatum Poiret subsp. *floridanum* Wessels Boer

Photo 85, Page 78

Form: A minute, epiphytic fern with rootless, long-creeping, threadlike, intertwining stems.

Fronds: Scattered in matted clusters along the stems.

Petiole: To about 8 mm long, mostly shorter than the blade.

Blade: To about 1.5 cm or a little longer, 2 - 9 mm wide, simple, oblong, elliptic, diamond shaped, to nearly circular in outline; margins vested with black, star-shaped hairs (requires magnification).

Sori: Borne in funnel-shaped cups (soral involucres) at the margins of the blade; lips of the soral involucres brown to blackish edged; involucres several per blade, and typically extending beyond the blade margin.

Habitat: Hammocks, epiphytic on tree trunks, edges of lime sinks, and on the vertical faces of limestone boulders, sometimes in association with mosses and liverworts.

Distribution: Endemic to Florida; collected in Dade, Sumter, and Citrus Counties.

Remarks: The small, cuplike structures (soral involucres) near the leaf margins that bear the sporangia distinguish the genus. The current species is most likely to be confused only with the equally minute *T. petersii*. However, each leaf of *T. petersii* has only a single soral involucre, the lips of which are not dark-edged and do not normally exceed the margin of the blade. (But also see *T. lineolatum.*) Like several other species of *Trichomanes*, this taxon is small, indistinct, and may be easily overlooked. It was first collected in Florida by J. K. Small in October of 1901. Today it is known primarily from small populations in Dade and Sumter Counties and is listed as endangered by the Florida Department of Agriculture.

ISOETACEAE - QUILLWORT FAMILY

The quillworts constitute a genus of fern allies. Like other fern allies, they are pteridophytes but not true ferns. The common name for many of the species derives from the resemblance of their leaves to the quill of a feather. The scientific name for the genus *Isoetes* derives from the Greek words *isos,* which means "equal," and *etos* or "year," and apparently refers to the evergreen habit of several of the species, though all of the species that occur in Florida appear to be evergreen.

The stems of the various quillwort species are cormlike and buried just underground, below the leaves. The leaves, which are curled in cross-section rather than flat, are arranged in spirals around the corms and, in the Florida species, number from about 10 to 100 per plant.

Quillworts are heterosporous, which means they have spores of two sizes rather than of only a single size as in the majority of pteridophytes. The larger spores are called megaspores and are often helpful in identifying the species; the smaller spores are called microspores. The spores are borne in sporangia on the upper side of the leaves at the swollen leaf bases and are covered by a thin membrane called a velum (see figure 19).

Many of the quillworts are extremely similar and their correct identification can present a significant challenge to even accomplished field botanists as well as casual plant enthusiasts. Learning to identify them often requires specialized knowledge, 30x to 50x magnification, and close attention to detail. Minute characters of the megaspores and velum, as well as distribution are all helpful in recognizing the species of *Isoetes* in Florida.

Three species of quillwort are confirmed as occurring in Florida: *I. appalachiana, I. flaccida,* and *I. hyemalis.* However, another species, thought by Dan Brunton (personal communication, 1999) to be *I. boomii* N. Luebke, has been collected in Clay County and may be Florida's fourth species. Considerable research is ongoing on the *Isoetes* of the southeastern United States (Daniel Brunton, personal communication, 1998), which may result in several additional species being reported from Florida, some of which may be newly described species. Much of the descriptive data presented below for both *I. applachiana* and *I. hyemalis* was adapted from the work of Brunton and Britton (1997), and Brunton, Britton, and Taylor (1994).

For many years, both *I. engelmannii* and *I. riparia* were reported as occurring in Florida. Recent interpretation has concluded that the Florida collections of *I. engelmannii,* a diploid species, are actually representative of the newly described *I. appalachiana,* a tetraploid (Brunton & Britton, 1997). Morphological differences between taxa of the *I. engelmannii* complex, and between *I. engelmannii* and *I. applachiana,* are very difficult to discern in the field and normally require detailed comparisons of megaspore size and ornamentation. According to Brunton (personal communication, 1998), the Duval County collection of what was formerly determined to be *I. riparia* (site now destroyed) has reticulate megaspores, effectively ruling out the possibility that the specimen has been correctly identified.

Appalachian Quillwort

Isoetes appalachiana Brunton & Britton   **Photo 86**

Form: An evergreen (or mostly evergreen), "grasslike" plant of wet areas; often found in standing water.

Leaves: 25 - 30 cm long, 1 - 2 mm wide at mid-leaf, dull olive green but whitish green to pale brownish green toward the base, erect to loosely reflexed; arising from two-lobed, rounded corms subtended by fibrous roots; corms 1.5 - 2.5 cm wide; well-developed by late April in Florida.

Sporangia: Sporangia oblong to oval, brown streaked, to about 10 mm long; velum covering 20 to 25 percent of the sporangium, rarely 45 percent.

Spores: Megaspores 450 - 600 microns in diameter, averaging about 534 microns, maturing early to midsummer, white to cream colored, surfaces with ragged-crested ridges.

Habitat: Clay soils at the edges of swamp forests in Florida; in other parts of its range occurring in shallow waters of lakes, ponds, creeks, and gravely streams.

Distribution: Sporadically distributed in the eastern United States (mostly along the Appalachian Mountains, hence the specific epithet) from Pennsylvania southward to northern Florida; apparently absent from northern and western Virginia, Maryland, and West Virginia, or at least not reported; found in Florida mostly in the counties of the Big Bend and in northeast Florida.

Remarks: This is a newly described species (Brunton & Britton, 1997). It differs from *I. flaccida,* the most common Florida species, by the velum covering only 20 to 25 percent of the sporangium rather than more than 80 percent. It differs from *I. hyemalis* by the surfaces of the megaspores forming an interlocking network (reticulate) rather than being covered with mostly unconnected protuberances or tubercles (tuberculate).

Florida Quillwort

Isoetes flaccida Shuttleworth ex A. Braun

Form: An evergreen (or mostly evergreen) aquatic or emergent "grasslike" plant with rolled, somewhat limp (hence the specific epithet) leaves; often in standing water.

Leaves: 10 - 60 cm long, bright green, in-rolled, spirally arranged and arising from two- to three-lobed, rounded corms subtended by fibrous roots; quite flaccid and often prostrate when not in standing water, numbering 10 to 35 per plant.

Sporangium: Elliptical, to about 6 mm long; velum covering the entire sporangium.

Spores: Megaspores 250 - 540 microns in diameter, maturing in summer and early autumn, white to cream colored, surfaces with tiny tubercules or dull-pointed protrusions which require at least 40x magnification to see clearly.

Habitat: Wet pinelands, marshes, and in shallow water of lakes, ponds, streams, and ditches.

Distribution: Throughout much of the northern two thirds of Florida, especially nearer the coast.

Remarks: This is the common *Isoetes* of the Florida Gulf coast and is the quillwort most likely to be found in the state. It is most easily distinguished from Florida's other species by the velum covering more than 80 percent of the sporangium. Two varieties of this species are recognized as occurring in Florida. *I. flaccida* var. *chapmanii* (Engelmann) Small, known only from Jackson County, and *I. flaccida* var. *alata* Pheiffer. The two are distinguished by microscopic characters of their megaspores (Pfeiffer, 1922; Boom, 1983).

Synonyms: *Isoetes chapmanii* (Engelmann) Small

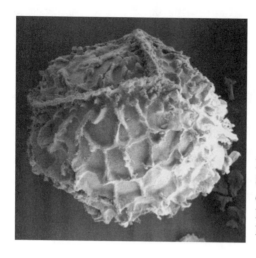

Figure 16.
Scanning Electron Micrograph
of a *Isoetes appalachiana*
Megaspore - courtesy, D. F.
Brunton & D. M. Britton

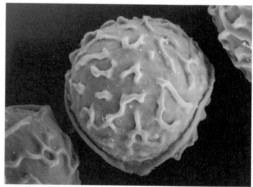

Figure 17. Scanning Electron
Micrographs of Two Views of a
Megaspore of *Isoetes flaccida* -
courtesy, D. F. Brunton & D. M.
Britton

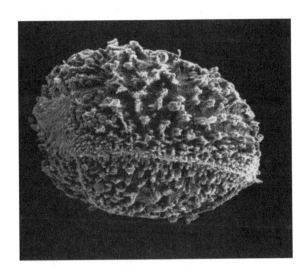

Figure 18.
Scanning Electron
Micrograph of
Megaspore of *Isoetes
hyemalis* - courtesy, D. F.
Brunton & D. M. Britton

Figure 19.
Isoetes sporangium and velum

Wintergreen Quillwort

Isoetes hyemalis Brunton

Form: An evergreen (or mostly evergreen), typically submergent to emergent, aquatic species similar in overall features to Florida's other two species of *Isoetes*.

Leaves: 30 to 105 in number, 23 - 27 cm long, less than 1 mm wide at mid-leaf, bright green when new, darkening to dark green or brownish green with age, but paler toward the base; arising from two-lobed, rounded corms.

Sporangia: Oval, 5.3 mm tall, 2.2 mm wide, densely dark brown streaked or spotted; velum clear, covering 10 to 20 percent of the sporangium.

Spores: Megaspores measuring 400 - 580 microns in diameter, averaging 522 microns, grayish white, round, with irregular crests and tubercles (sometimes appearing somewhat networked [reticulate] on the lower sides), maturing in early to midsummer.

Habitat: Shallow running water of creeks, sloughs, rivers; also in swamps.

Distribution: Recorded in Florida only from Holmes County; otherwise distributed in the Piedmont of Virginia and North Carolina, and on the Coastal Plain of Virginia, both North and South Carolina, and Georgia.

Remarks: This is a newly described species from North Carolina (Brunton, Britton, and Taylor, 1994). It was discovered in Florida by Jim Allison in the spring of 1997. It differs from *I. appalachiana,* the other Florida species with a similar velum, by the velum covering less than 20 percent of the sporangium. The specific epithet, *hyemalis,* means "of winter" and was given based on the plant's evergreen habit.

LYCOPODIACEAE - CLUB-MOSS FAMILY

The club-moss family (some species are also referred to as ground-pines or ground-cedars) encompasses a large and diverse group of primitive plants with ancient lineage. As currently interpreted, the family includes up to 15 genera and as many as 400 species worldwide in both temperate and tropical regions. As treated here, four genera represent the family in Florida. All of Florida's six species, as with all members of this family, have at one time or another been included within the genus *Lycopodium.*

The family is characterized by a combination of erect, arching, or pendulous stems with multiple rows of small, narrow, pointed, often crowded and overlapping, spirally-arranged leaves, and the conelike structures, or strobili, that bear the sporangia. The cylindrical strobili (strobilus, singular) are typically situated at the top of erect or lateral branches and are composed of spore-bearing leaves (sporophylls). The sporangia are borne near the base of these fertile leaves and may be easily seen with 10x magnification.

The club-moss family has undergone considerable taxonomic revision in the past few years and the interpretation adopted here still does not enjoy universal acceptance. Wunderlin (1998), for example, includes only two genera in the family: *Huperzia,* treated here as *Phlegmariurus,* and *Lycopodiella,* segregated here into the genera *Lycopodiella, Palhinhaea,* and *Pseudolycopodiella.* A treatment similar to Wunderlin's is followed by Tryon and Moran (1997) for the ferns of New England (with the addition of the genus *Lycopodium,* which under current interpretation has no representatives in Florida). Earlier volumes (Clewell, 1985; Lakela & Long, 1976; and Wunderlin, 1982), on the other hand, include all of Florida's *Lyocopsids* within the genus *Lycopodium,* the traditional view of the family. Part of the reason for the historical "lumping" of species into a single genus probably stems from the facts that earlier workers could not find enough characters with which to differentiate species, that some taxonomists may have been more familiar with flowering plants than pteridophytes, and because many of the species tend to be superficially similar in appearance. (This is especially apropos for Florida since several species often occur together in the same habitat.) More recent developments have allowed diligent study of these plants's gametophytes (sexual phase), and new technology has made possible closer examination of their spores, chromosome numbers, and sporangial structure (Wagner & Beitel, 1992). Regardless of the taxonomic refinement that has occurred in recent years, the number of species treated in Florida has remained at six since the late 1800s, and the validity of these taxa at the species level has long been accepted.

Whitehead (1941) reports that the spores of several species of *Lycopodium,* especially the more northern *L. clavatum,* were once used medicinally in the production of dusting powder for coating surgeon's gloves as well suppositories. However, he notes that such use is dangerous and not recommended. Whitehead also adds that species of the genus tend to burn quickly when thrown into a fire and were also once used in the development of fireworks and powders for colored signal fires.

LYCOPODIELLA - Club-Mosses

The genus name *Lycopodiella* was established by Holub in 1964 and derives from a combination of the genus name *Lycopodium* and the diminutive *ella.* The name refers to the similarity of species in the two genera. In addition to the common name club-moss, some species of the genus have occasionally been referred to as ground pines due to their resemblance to young branches of some gymnosperms, though this latter appellation more appropriately fits several species in the genus *Lycopodium* that occur to the north of Florida. The Florida species are recognized by their typically prostrate to arching horizontal stems and erect fertile stems topped with expanded strobili.

Foxtail Bog Club-Moss

Lycopodiella alopecuroides (Linnaeus) Cranfill   **Photo 87**

          Lycopodiella X *copelandii*

Form: Relatively low-growing, evergreen (though sometimes yellowing in cold winters) species with arching, long-creeping horizontal stems and many-leaved, erect stems tipped by bushy strobili.

Stems: Horizontal stems long-creeping, arching, densely leaved, rooting at intervals, 5 - 40 cm long, about 1 cm wide, with 5 to 8 erect stems; erect stems typically 15 - 25 cm tall with an expanded, bushy fertile tip, 2.5 - 6 cm long and about 1.5 cm wide.

Leaves: Sterile leaves spreading, densely crowded along the stem, linear with sharp-pointed tips, margins conspicuously toothed (seen best with magnification), 5 - 7 mm long, less than 1 mm wide.

Strobili: To about 6 cm long, averaging 1.5 cm wide; bushy in appearance with spreading to slightly ascending (less than 45 degrees from the stobilus) sporophylls.

Habitat: Wet meadows, moist pine flatwoods, swamp edges, sphagnum bogs, ditches.

Distribution: Northern half of the state, southward to at least Highlands and Okeechobee Counties.

Remarks: This species is most commonly listed and described under its synonym, *Lycopodium alopecuroides* Linnaeus. Its common name as well as its specific epithet *(alopecuroides* literally means "like a fox's tail") derives from its brushlike strobili, which somewhat resembles the tip of a fox's tail. It is one of Florida's more common members of the genus and is most easily recognized by the combination of its relatively robust erect stems and strongly arching horizontal stems. See *L. prostrata* below for discussion of similarities between these two species.

The present species is known to hybridize with *L. appressa* to form the hybrid *L.* X *copelandii* (Eiger) Cranfill. The hybrid has arching stems like the present species, but its strobili are more narrow, ranging 0.4 - 1.2 cm wide, intermediate between the parent species. The hybrid is difficult to identify and is not discussed in the *Flora of North America,* though it and all of the known *Lycopodiella* hybrids and their relationships are illustrated in the diagram on page 35 of the latter volume.

Synonyms: *Lycopodium alopecuroides* Linnaeus

Appressed Bog Club-Moss, Southern Club-Moss

Lycopodiella appressa (Chapman) Cranfill   **Photo 88**

    Lycopdiella X *brucei*

Form: A slender clubmoss with closely appressed leaves.

Stems: Horizontal stems creeping, prostrate, 15 - 45 cm long, rooting throughout, with many spiral rows of leaves; erect stems 1 to 15 in number, upright, 15 - 40 cm tall, with conspicuously appressed leaves that typically do not completely obscure the surface of the stem beneath; erect stems tipped with long, slender but somewhat expanded strobili ranging 2.5 - 6 cm long and 3 - 4 mm wide.

Leaves: Sterile leaves 5 - 7 mm long, tightly appressed to the erect stem, with 0 to 3 marginal teeth; those of the horizontal stem similar in appearance and often with a few teeth.

Strobili: Long, slender, 2.5 - 5 cm long, less than 6 mm wide; sporophylls tightly appressed, incurved, without marginal teeth.

Habitat: Bogs, lake shores, meadows, wet sand barrens, ditches, marshes, moist flatwoods.

Distribution: Statewide, except, perhaps, for the southernmost tip.

Remarks: Similar to both *Pseudolycopodiella caroliniana* and *Lycopodiella prostrata,* distinguished from the former by having more densely leafy stems, and from the latter by leaves of erect stems lacking or having only a few marginal teeth and not completely hiding the surface of the stem, and by the strobili being generally less than 8 mm thick. The specific epithet refers to the appressed leaves of the strobili and erect stems.

In an 1878 article in the Botanical Gazette, A. W. Chapman (1809-1899), one of north Florida's most important early botanists, awarded the varietal name *Lycopodium inundatum* Linnaeus var. *appressum* to this species and later so included it in the second edition of his *Flora of the Southern United States* (1884). The variety was raised to species level in 1900 by Lloyd and Underwood and reassigned to the genus *Lycopodiella* by Cranfill in 1981.

The present species is known to hybridize with *L. prostrata* to form the hybrid *L. X brucei* Cranfill. Its strobili range 0.5 - 1.2 cm in width, intermediate between the parent species, and is somewhat bushy like *L. prostrata*. The sporophylls are typically somewhat ascending rather than wide-spreading from the axis of the strobilus, again intermediate between the parent species. The hybrid is difficult to identify and is not recognized in the *Flora of North America*.

Synonyms: *Lycopodium inundatum* Linnaeus var. *appressum* Chapman; *L. appressum* (Chapman) F. E. Lloyd & L. Underwood; *L. inundatum* var. *bigelovii* Tuckerman

Prostrate Bog Club-Moss, Harper's Club-Moss

Lycopodiella prostrata (R.M. Harper) Cranfill   **Photo 89**

Form: A relatively low-growing club-moss with prostrate horizontal stems and upright erect stems.

Stems: Horizontal stems borne flat on the ground, 10 - 45 cm long, with spreading leaves, rooting throughout; erect stems 1 to 3 per plant, 15 - 35 cm tall.

Leaves: Those on horizontal stems spreading but often appearing mostly lateral from above, leaves on the upper side of horizontal stems ascending; leaves of erect stems ascending or appressed to the stem and overlapping so as to hide the surface of the stem; leaves predominantly less than 1 cm long, with 1 to 10 marginal teeth (which may require magnification to see clearly).

Strobili: Bushy in appearance, 4 - 8 cm long, 1 - 2 cm wide; sporophylls strongly toothed and spreading.

Habitat: Sandy, acidic soil, roadsides, ditches, wet pine flatwoods, meadows, bogs.

Distribution: Northern Florida, southward to about Manatee and Highlands Counties.

Remarks: At first glance this species might be confused with *L. alopecuroides* (a species with which it is sometimes thought to be conspecific (see for example, Clewell, 1985) because of its bushy strobili. However, the ground-hugging horizontal stems of the present species easily set the two apart. This conspicuous latter character gives this species its specific epithet as well as one of its common names. The present species is also similar to *L. appressa,* but is distinguished from it by the strobili generally being greater than 10 mm wide, and by the margins of the erect stem leaves having numerous spinulose teeth and overlapping so as to hide the surface of the erect stem. The specific epithet refers to the plant's prostrate habit.

Synonyms: *Lycopodium prostratum* R.M. Harper; *L. inundatum* Linnaeus var. *pinnatum* Chapman

Nodding Club-Moss

Palhinhaea cernua (Linnaeus) Vasconcellos & Franco   **Photo 90**

Form: An erect, delicate, many branched club-moss that gives the appearance of a tiny tree.
Stems: Horizontal stems reclining, often inconspicuous and appearing rootlike, with sparse, needlelike leaves; erect stems 20 - 80 cm tall with spreading leaves and many, spreading branches; branches drooping at their extremities and tipped by short (to about 1 cm long), compact strobili.
Leaves: Sterile leaves linear to needlelike, to about 5 mm long, those at the bases of both the erect stem and the lateral branches curved downward, those toward the tips curved upward.
Strobili: Borne at the drooping tips of lateral branches, fertile leaves of the strobili shorter and requiring magnification to see clearly.
Habitat: Moist, sandy banks, margins of stream and spring runs, moist meadows, ditches, bog edges, dried lake bottoms.
Distribution: Distributed nearly statewide; also occurs outside of Florida on the Coastal Plain in Alabama, Georgia, Louisiana, Mississippi, and South Carolina.
Remarks: The slender, erect stems, many drooping branches, and tiny treelike habit distinguish this species from all other members of the genus in Florida. The specific epithet means drooping, nodding, or curving forward and refers to the orientation of the branch tips. The genus name is in honor of Portugese botanist R. T. Palhinha (1871-1950). This plant is listed as commercially exploited by the Florida Department of Agriculture (under the name *Lycopodium cernuum*). It should not be removed from the wild.

This species is a common associate with the forked fern *(Dicranopteris flexuosa)* in its Florida locations and may be treated as an indicator of appropriate habitat for the latter species. See additional comments under the entry for forked fern.
Synonyms: *Lycopodium cernuum* Linnaeus

Hanging Fir-Moss

Phlegmariurus dichotomus (Jacquin) W.H. Wagner & Beitel   **Photo 91**

Form: A long-lived, epiphytic club-moss found on trunks and branches of hammock trees in tropical America and the West Indies.
Stems: Pendent from tree trunks and branches, to about 30 cm long, averaging 1.5 cm wide including the leaves, dividing into 1 to 3 pairs of dichotomous forks (hence the specific epithet).
Leaves: 1.5 - 2 cm long, averaging about 1 mm wide, spreading to ascending, gradually narrowing to a long-pointed tip; margins entire.
Sporangia: Borne at the base of fertile leaves near the ends of the branches; 2 to 3 times as wide as the subtending leaf.
Habitat: Stems and branches of pop-ash (*Fraxinus caroliniana* Miller) and pond apple *(Annona glabra* Linnaeus) trees in mixed swamp forest.
Distribution: Extremely rare; known in North America only from three Florida locations, each of which contains but a single plant and all of which are located in the Fakahatchee

Strand Preserve of the Big Cypress Swamp in Collier County.

Remarks: This is a member of a large, primarily tropical, and poorly known genus with at least 300 species, many of which are epiphytes. The present species is the only member of the genus in Florida and is listed as endangered by the Florida Department of Agriculture (under the name *Huperzia dichotoma*). It is often seen on Florida plant lists and publications as *Lycopodium dichotomum,* and is easily distinguished as the only epiphyte among Florida's Lycopodiaceae.

Hanging fir-moss was first discovered in Florida April 15, 1934, by C. A. Mosier, E. Peterson, and J. B. McFarlin (Broun, 1936b; Small, 1938). Peterson, a fern gardener, successfully potted and cultivated the species in her slat-house in North Miami (Broun, 1936b) following its discovery. Today, however, the species is extremely rare.

Synonyms: *Lycopodium dichotomum* Jacquin; *Huperzia dichotoma* (Jacquin) Trevisan

Slender Bog Club-Moss
Pseudolycopodiella caroliniana (Linnaeus) Holub   **Photo 92**

Form: A diminutive, creeping plant with slender, upright stems; rhizome tips sometimes forming underground tubers (probably less than 10 percent of cases); roots emerging on the lower side of rhizome, typically between about every other pair of leaves; roots extending to depths sometimes exceeding 5 cm, holding the plant fast to the ground.

Stems: Horizontal stems evergreen, more or less flat to the ground, irregularly branched, rooting throughout their extent, with laterally spreading leaves that appear two ranked; erect stems slender, relatively sparsely leaved in comparison with the horizontal stems and with the erect stems of members of the genus *Lycopodiella;* strobili 1 - 9 cm long, less than 5 mm wide.

Leaves: Narrow, scattered, not typically overlapping, and often strongly ascending along the erect stem; leaves of horizontal stems awl shaped, spreading, and larger than those of the erect stem.

Strobili: 3 - 8 cm long, less than 4 mm side, yellowish in color; sporophylls borne in six ranks in alternating whorls of three, wider at the base and narrowed to a long-pointed apex, often tightly appressed when new, sometimes spreading and more or less perpendicular to the strobili, or even slightly downcurved, at the tip at maturity.

Habitat: Moist, sandy soils, bogs, meadows, wet pinewoods, ditches, wet pineland depressions, flatwoods.

Distribution: Throughout most of the state, except perhaps for the southernmost tip; generally distributed along the Gulf and Atlantic coasts from Long Island, NY, to Texas.

Remarks: The genus name for this species literally means "false little *Lycopodium,*" and suggests its similarity to the genera *Lycopodium* and *Lycopodiella.* The specific epithet means "of Carolina" because the type specimen for the plant came from the "Carolinas," a geographic entity that once included much of the territory now encompassed by the southeastern United States. The species' slender, sparsely-leaved erect stem in combination with its tightly rooted horizontal stem is diagnostic for field identification in Florida.

Synonyms: *Lycopodium carolinianum* Linnaeus

LYGODIACEAE - CLIMBING FERN FAMILY

Three species in a single genus represent this family in North America, only two of which definitely occur in Florida. The climbing habit, which is accomplished by an elongated twining and climbing rachis, makes the members of the family unusual among the ferns. Most members of the family are tropical and occur naturally in mesic habitats of Asia, Africa, New Zealand, and the Pacific Islands. The two species described below, one of which is native to Japan, the other to Southeast Asia, are noxious alien weeds that are extremely difficult to eradicate or control. Both were introduced for horticultural purposes and both are listed by the Florida Exotic Pest Plant Council as Category I pest plants, which means that they are currently known to be invading and disrupting native plant communities. Anyone who has seen the dense, climbing masses of *L. microphyllum* in Jonathan Dickinson and other state parks and roadsides of south-central Florida will understand the threat these plants pose to native flora (see photo 95).

The American climbing fern *[Lygodium palmatum* (Bernhardi) Swartz (synonym: *Gisopteris palmata* Bernhardi)] is the only temperate member of the family in North America and is restricted essentially to the eastern United States from New Hampshire to Georgia, but is nowhere common. In the earlier parts of the 20th century the American climbing fern, or Hartford fern as it is sometimes called, was so sought after and heavily collected for its horticultural utility that the Connecticut legislature passed a law making it illegal to remove it from private land. Hence, this dainty, vinelike fern became the first of America's plants to receive protected status.

Lygodium palmatum is included in the Florida flora primarily on the strength of an herbarium specimen on deposit in New York. The specimen was apparently collected by W. W. Calkins in the late 1800s and the location of the collection is recorded merely as "Florida" (Wunderlin, personal communication, 1997). A second specimen, which is on deposit at the Florida State Museum at the University of Florida and labeled "Brooklyn Institute of Arts and Sciences," is dated February 17, 1895, and was collected in Lemon City, Dade County. Wherry's (1964) report of the species from Dade County was probably based upon this collection, which was likely from a cultivated plant. A. W. Chapman reported *L. palmatum* for Florida in all three editions of his *Flora of the Southern States* (1865, 1884 [1883], 1897), and Small (1931, 1938) reported *L. palmatum* as rare in Florida but did not specify a location. In his checklist of Florida Ferns, Correll (1938) notes the specimen from Dade County as "very unusual." According to Judith Garrison (personal communication, 1998), who revised the genus in 1998, it is unlikely that this species actually occurs in the state today.

L. palmatum is distinguished from the two exotic species by having all pinnules palmately lobed and by the fertile lobes nearly lacking sterile tissue. Though not described below, it is pictured in figure 20, and should be searched for in northern Florida, especially along larger rivers and streams that have their sources outside of the state.

It is interesting to note that this now questionably present species is the only member of the genus Small (1931) includes in his treatment of Florida's ferns. The other two species now present in the state, both of which are aggressive and ubiquitous in their respective regions, were introduced into Florida sometime between the late 1930s and early 1960s. Correll (1938) includes *Lygodium japonicum* in his Florida checklist for Liberty County and notes, unfortunately somewhat prophetically: "The recent discovery of the Japanese climb-

Figure 20.

Lygodium palmatum

ing fern in northern Florida adds another state to the range of this rapidly spreading species. The writer has collected this Old World species in Georgia and South Carolina where it has become well-established. It has also been found in Alabama, and may be expected in other southern states" (p. 46).

Japanese Climbing Fern

Lygodium japonicum (Thunberg ex Murray) Swartz   **Photo 93**

Form: A high-climbing, trailing and twining, viney fern with wiry stems and medium- to dark-green leaves; top killed in winter, then forming dense, brownish, rather unattractive mats covering the supporting vegetation.

Fronds: Trailing and twining, to at least 6 m long (sometimes much longer).

Petiole: Twining, 2 - 35 cm long, straw colored to pale greenish, wiry.

Rachis: Twining, to about 3 m long, straw colored to greenish, with or without hairs.

Blade: With numerous, alternate pinnae that are, themselves, divided once or twice more into pinnaelike segments.

Pinnae: Dimorphic; borne oppositely on the rachis; axis of pinnae straw colored to pale green, darker toward the tip; sterile pinnae lanceolate to triangular in overall shape, 8 - 15 cm long, to about 13 cm wide at the base, borne on 1.5 - 3.5 cm long stalks, each pinna pinnately or bipinnately divided, ultimate segments lanceolate and typically lobed at the base; fertile pinnae similar in shape to the sterile ones but appearing smaller and lacy due to the presence of marginal sporangia.

Sori: Sporangia borne in narrowed, fingerlike lobes at the ends of fertile pinnules, giving fertile plants a distinctly lacy appearance.

Habitat: Disturbed sites, yards, secondary woods, pinelands, floodplains, woodland margins, roadsides, banks of ditches and streams, marshes, other moist sites.

Distribution: Primarily found in the northern two-thirds of Florida, but reported as far south as Dade county; native to Japan, introduced to the U.S. as a landscape plant and now escaped and established in large parts of the southeastern United States, especially in the Coastal Plain.

Remarks: This plant is easily distinguished from all other Florida ferns, except *L. microphyllum,* by its twining and climbing habit. See the remarks for this latter species for characters that distinguish the two.

L. japonicum was reported as escaped from cultivation in Thomasville, GA, just north of the Florida state line, in the early 1900s (Underwood, 1906). According to Small (1938), it was first collected in Florida only in 1932 at the old Aspalaga Landing area on the eastern banks of the Apalachicola River by Drs. Herman Kurz and E. T. Wherry. Hence, it was not included in Small's 1931 *Ferns of Florida.*

In 1941, Mary Diddell, a Jacksonville-based fern enthusiast and gardener reported finding this species "growing plentifully in a swamp within the city limits of Jacksonville." She continued, "A few years ago I noticed this fern growing as an escape, in great profusion, over the grounds of the Glen St. Mary Nursery," then mused that "it would be interesting to know if it has spread outside the nursery" (p. 49). In a later article, she reported having found what was presumably the first of these populations in 1934 or 1935, which she described as "three or four small plants . . . growing in the edge of a swamp about a mile from my place" (Diddell, 1956, p. 27). She acknowledges that these plants likely got their start from airborne spores produced in her own garden. Diddell would no doubt be flabbergasted at the range of this plant today and at the deleterious effects it has on native flora. Since the time of her observations, Japanese climbing fern has become widely naturalized across much of the northern part of Florida and is often seen in dense, climbing mats in a number of the state's natural areas, as well as in urban and suburban landscapes. It is considered to be a troublesome exotic weed and is listed as a Category I pest plant by Florida's Exotic Pest Plant Council. It is extremely difficult to control or eradicate once established and should never be planted or used in landscaping. Freezing temperatures will top kill the plant, but with the return of warm weather, growth will again commence and typical populations may return to their previous levels within a single growing season.

Synonyms: *Ophioglossum japonicum* Thunberg ex Murray

Small-Leaved Climbing Fern, Old World Climbing Fern

Lygodium microphyllum (Canvanilles) R. Brown   **Photos 94, 95**

Form: A thicket-forming, climbing, and extremely invasive fern with a thin, creeping, blackish stem that is covered with stiff, brownish black hairs.

Fronds: Trailing and twining, to about 10 m long.

Petiole: 7 - 25 cm long, very thin, borne 2 - 5 mm apart on the stem, straw colored to brownish, darker toward the base.

Rachis: Trailing and twining, wiry.

Blade: To about 10 m long, bearing alternate, short-stalked, pinnate pinnae.

Pinnae: 3 - 14 cm long and 2.5 - 6 cm wide, each sterile pinna with several pairs of more or less triangular segments with pointed to rounded tips; fertile pinnae somewhat longer than sterile pinnae and bearing constricted, fertile lobes along the margins; lower surfaces lacking hairs.

Sori: Borne on constricted marginal lobes on fertile pinnae.

Habitat: Swamps, cypress swamps, river banks, wet disturbed sites, pinelands, cabbage palm hammocks.

Distribution: Well established and spreading in the central to southern peninsula from about Polk County southward.

Remarks: This is a pernicious exotic weed, especially in southern Florida. It is closely related and somewhat similar in appearance to *L. japonicum*. The two species may be distinguished in their region of overlap by their pinnae. Those of *L. japonicum* are at least bipinnate to sometimes tripinnate, with the lowermost pinnae segments often being deeply cut, while those of *L. microphyllum* are pinnate with simple segments. In addition, the lower surfaces for the blade tissue of *L. japonicum* are sparsely to moderately hairy, while those of *L. microphyllum* lack hairs (requires at least 10x magnification to see clearly).

Biologists and managers at various south Florida parks and refuges report spending much of their time and resources attempting to control this species and to keep it from overtaking natural habitats. Though it was first reported as adventive only in the late 1960s (Beckner, 1968; Nauman and Austin, 1978), it is now listed as a Category I pest plant by Florida's Exotic Pest Plant Council and should never be planted or used in landscaping. It is interesting to note that Lakela and Long (1976) reported this species as rare in Florida just 30 years ago!

Two excellent recent papers in the *American Fern Journal* (Pemberton and Ferriter, 1998 and Pemberton, 1998) outline the history and threat of this species as well as the potential of biological control to manage it. These authors point out that in 1978 the plant was confined to a few acres in the eastern third of Martin and Palm Beach Counties, but that by 1997 had covered more than 39,000 acres. More importantly, they point out that most of the natural areas of the southern third of the state are likely vulnerable to invasion. They further suggest that, like *L. japonicum,* the plant is only top killed by freezing termperatures and recovers from frost rapidly. Hence, its potential northern limit is currently undetermined.

Synonyms: *Ugena microphylla* Canvanilles

MARSILEACEAE - WATER CLOVER FAMILY

The water clover family includes three genera and about 50 species worldwide. A single genus occurs in Florida. The family and type genus names commemorate Count Luigi Marsigli, an Italian mycologist who lived from 1656-1730.

The family is represented in Florida by the genus *Marsilea*. Five species are typically listed for the state; none are widespread or common and at least one may no longer be extant in the state; photo 96, 97, and 98 illustrate two of Florida's species. Though often difficult to distinguish from each other, members of the genus are easily distinguished from other ferns and fern allies by their typical "four-leaf clover" appearance, hence one of the common names of the genus.

All members of the Marsileaceae produce sporocarps, capsule- or beanlike structures that contain the sporangia. These sporocarps resemble a peppercorn in both shape and size and members of the genus are sometimes referred to as pepperworts. Members of the family are also heterosporous, meaning that they produce two kinds of spores: megaspores and microspores. Both types are borne within the same sporocarp. The sporocarps are very useful in identification; most species of *Marsilea* cannot be accurately determined when sporocarps are absent. Some claim that the order Marsileales, with which the water-clover family is alligned, are surviving members of the order of seed ferns, an extinct order of gymnosperms that contained the earliest seed plants and flourished some 270 to 350 million years ago (Meeuse, 1961).

The most recently reported species of *Marsilea* in Florida was collected in a roadside ditch in Pensacola in 1992 (Burkhalter, 1995). *M. minuta* is a common and widespread weed in India and Africa but is known in the western hemisphere only as an introduced species in eastern Brazil and the Caribbean islands of Trinidad and Tobago. Burkhalter suggests that the origin of the Pensacola population is relatively recent and may possibly be attributed to migratory waterfowl. It is known that waterfowl feed on members of the genus and Malone and Proctor (1965) have shown that *Marsilea* sporocarps will pass unaffected though the digestive system of several waterfowl species. Since Pensacola is within one of the eastern United States's migratory flyways, and the area where the *M. minuta* population was found is in close proximity to waterfowl wintering sites, Burkhalter concludes that the birds may have transported the sporocarps here from South America. No matter how it originated, the population seems well established, stable, and unaffected by cold winter weather.

Due to their similarity of appearance and infrequent occurrence in Florida, only a single species of the genus is described below. However, the accompanying table summarizes the genus in Florida and should prove helpful in learning to distinguish the species that occur in the state.

Water Clover

Marsilea vestita Hooker & Greville

Form: An aquatic, sometimes floating fern with slender stems, clustered fronds, and roots arising at the leaf nodes.

Petiole: Slender, 2 - 35 cm long, sparsely hairy with appressed hairs.

Blade: Divided into four, spreading, sparsely to densely hairy, radially symmetrical segments giving the overall appearance of a four-leaf clover, circular in overall outline, 0.4 - 2.7 cm in diameter.

Pinnae: 4 - 19 mm long, 4 - 16 mm wide, broadly obovate or wedge-shaped, with a rounded apex.

Sori: Borne in a hairy sporocarp on a stalk that is no longer than the sporocarp, sporocarp with an acutely pointed apical tooth ranging 0.4 - 1.2 mm long.

Habitat: Moist soils of roadsides and roadside ditches, moist to dry soil of lawns and flower beds.

Distribution: Ranging mostly west of the Mississippi River; introduced in Florida and collected in scattered locations across the state, including Franklin, Lake, and Hillsborough counties.

Remarks: *M. vestita* is not a common plant in the state and not easy to find. It is easily distinguished as *Marsilea* by the four-leaf clover appearance. It may be distinguished from other members of its genus in Florida by the apical tooth of the sporocarp being generally longer than 0.4 mm and acutely pointed.

Small (1931) erroneously reported that this species was first discovered in Florida in 1891, a reference to Underwood's (1891 [1892]) published report of his 1891 travels through Florida. Underwood found the plant near a rail station in Lake County and considered his find the first record of this species east of the Mississippi River. In 1895, Nash rediscovered and confirmed Underwood's report. In the early 1960s, Dan Ward also attempted to rediscover the plant at the Lake County location. He and students from the University of Florida found the site of the old train depot and what they believed to be the ditch from which the Underwood and Nash collections had been made. Unfortunately, the ditch "was largely filled with dry cinders, and no *Marsilea* could be located" (Ward & Hall, 1976).

The actual first report for Florida appears to have been made by D. C. Eaton in 1872 based upon an 1860 collection made in Apalachicola by Dr. A. W. Chapman. However, since Chapman did not list Florida within the range of this taxon in the third edition of his *Flora of the Southern United States,* Ward and Hall (1976) suggested that the label on Chapman's collection may have been made in error and that the plant, if it had ever occurred in Apalachicola, likely occurred there no longer. In more recent years Loran Anderson rediscovered the plant in two locations in Apalachicola (Anderson, 1986), thereby supporting the theory that Apalachicola was the first reported site for the species in Florida. Both of these latter populations are still extant.

Two other records of *M. vestita* have been reported for Florida. The first, in Dade County in 1891, was considered by Ward and Hall (1976) to be spurious and to actually represent the Lake County collection. The second collection, made by David Hall in 1975, was from a population in Hillsborough County ". . . from a very extensive stand on the moist to dry soil of lawns and flower beds in a residential area ninety miles southwest . . ." of Underwood's 1891 collection (Ward & Hall, 1976). Ward and Hall speculated that the source of this population was likely from garden plantings brought from New Orleans.

Synonyms: *Marsilea fournieri* C. Christensen, *M. mucronata* A. Braun, *M. tenuifolia* Englemann ex A. Braun, *M. vestita* subsp. *tenuifolia* (Engleman ex A. Braun) D. M. Johnson.

Figure 21. Florida Species of *Marsilea*

Species	Identification	Counties	Remarks
M. ancyclopoda A. Braun	Petiole 1 - 18 cm long and sparsely hairy; sporocarp 2.5 - 6 mm long, 2 - 5 mm wide, 2.1 - 3.2 mm thick, without an apical tooth, borne belowground on prostrate to recurved stalks; roots mostly at the leaf nodes.	Lake	known in N. America only from Florida; last collected at the turn of the century and perhaps no longer extant
M. hirsuta R. Brown	Petiole erect, 1.5 - 15 cm long, without hairs; sporocarps 2.4 - 6 mm long, 3 - 4 mm wide, 2 - 3 mm thick, with a blunt apical tooth, borne on unbranched stalk above the rootstock, 3 - 11 mm long; roots at leaf nodes and internodes.	Pinellas	native to Australia; known in Florida from a vacant residential lot at one intersection in St. Petersburg
M. macropoda Englemann ex A. Braun in Kunze	Petiole 5 - 39 cm long, hairy; sporocarps 6 - 9 mm long, 4.5 - 5 mm wide, ~2 mm thick, without an apical tooth, strongly ascending on branched stalk, 3 - 11 mm long; roots mostly at the leaf nodes.	Sarasota Hillsborough	native to southern Texas but introduced elsewhere, including Alabama, Louisiana, and Florida
M. minuta Linnaeus	Petiole 5 - 30 cm long; sporocarps 4.5 - 5 mm long, 3.5 - 4 mm wide, 1.3 - 2 mm thick, with an apical tooth 0.3 - 0.6 mm long; margins of some leaves bluntly toothed; roots at both nodes and internodes.	Escambia	first discovered in Florida in 1992, and known in the state only from a roadside ditch in Pensacola
M. vestita Hooker and Greville	Petiole 2 - 35 cm long; sporocarp 3.6 - 7.6 mm long, 2 - 6.5 mm wide, 1.5 - 2 mm thick, with an acutely pointed apical tooth 0.4 - 1.2 mm long; roots mostly at the leaf nodes.	Dade, Franklin, Hillsborough, Lake	native to the western United States; populations in Franklin and Hillsborough counties are still extant

OPHIOGLOSSACEAE - ADDER'S-TONGUE FAMILY

The adder's-tongue family consists of 5 genera and about 80 species worldwide. Four genera and 11 specie occur in Florida, many of which are small and difficult to find without diligent searching. The family is quite divergent from all other ferns. Both the common and scientific names for the family derive from the superficial resemblance of the tip of fertile segments in the genera *Ophioglossum* and *Cheiroglossa* to the tongue of a snake. *Ophis* is Greek for snake, *glossa* for tongue.

All but two of Florida's species are terrestrial. Terrestrial members of the family have fleshy rather than fibrous roots, and reproduce sexually by subterranean gametophytes. Mature sporophytes appear above ground for only a brief period, often for only a few weeks, after having developed below ground for a year or more. Both the fleshy roots and below ground sexual phase—adaptations that are uncommon among the modern ferns—probably arose to insure competitive advantage with terrestrial species. Both also probably contributed significantly to the family's overall evolution. The subterranean habit allows the developing gametophyte to take advantage of a unique niche that is relatively unused by other spore-bearing plants, while the fleshy roots act as food reservoirs to nourish the plants during the long periods they remain hidden from the sun. According to E. P. St. John (1949), this phenomenon may be the single most important factor insuring the survival of this family of plants to the present.

St. John also argues that the subterranean habit is responsible for the relatively unchanged morphology of this family throughout its evolution:

> The connection between the life history of the plants and this course of evolution is clear. When crowding of the more favorable habitats by other plants brought about the transition from terrestrial growth of the gametophyte to the subterranean habit the opportunity for cross-fertilization through close association of the gametophytes was greatly reduced; and the ease with which self-fertilization was accomplished in the changing but not yet fully adapted gametohpyte was also lessened. Hence any variation that would facilitate self-fertilization would have high selective value. The tendency toward self-fertilization enabled the gametophyte to descend to lower levels where the supply of moisture was better, and this action again increased the selective value of self-fertilization. . . . The evolutionary effect of this condition is very great. The almost complete absence of inter-breeding between varying forms eliminates the most effective means of bringing about recombination of genes, and the range of variation can little exceed the limits of mutation and recombination in the individual plant. (E. P. St. John, 1949, p. 211)

As many as nine species of *Ophioglossum* were once attributed to Florida (E. P. St. John, 1941). However, five of these taxa are no longer recognized as valid species (Clausen, 1938b; Wagner, et al., 1981). Hence, only four species are described below. A fifth species, *O. vulgatum* Linnaeus [=*O. pycnostichum* (Fernald) A. Love & D. Love, and *O. vulgatum* var. *pycnostichum* Fernald], known as southern adder's-tongue, is also often reported for Florida (Small 1931, 1938; Lakela & Long, 1976; Lellinger 1985; Wagner & Wagner 1993). All of these reports seem to be founded on the original reports by Small (1931, 1938), which are based upon an early 1800s collection by John LeConte, an early southeastern naturalist. According to Wunderlin (personal communication, 1997), this record is a misidentification of *O. petiolatum*. Hence, the former species is not currently known in Florida's flora. However, it is present in the northern half of Georgia (Snyder & Bruce, 1986), and is distributed in Louisiana (Thieret, 1980), Alabama (Clausen, 1942), and other southeastern states (Wagner & Wagner, 1993; Cranfill, 1980). Hence, it would not be surprising for it to be discovered in the northern panhandle. It is distinguished from Florida's other species by its relatively large (10 x 3.5 cm), dark, shiny green leaves, which have netted veins, the larger areoles of which include only free veins rather than smaller areoles.

Of the more than 60 species of Ophioglossaceae, only two are epiphytes: *Cheiroglossa palmata* and *Ophioderma pendula*. The first of these is listed as endangered in Florida and is a rare component of cabbage palm hammocks in the southern peninsula. The other is distributed primarily in the Old World Tropics but has recently been collected in Dade County, where it probably escaped cultivation. Both require moist habitats and high humidity to remain vital.

Members of the genus *Botrychium*, the other genus found in Florida, are often referred to as grape ferns. The genus name comes from the Latin botry, or bunch, and oides, or like, in reference to the sporangia, which are borne in minute grapelike clusters. Members of the genus typically produce only a single leaf per year, but do not produce "fiddleheads" as most ferns do. Instead, their leaves form underground, where they may stay dormant for a period of several years, then unfold rather than unroll as they grow upwards.

Though interesting in nature, none of the following species, except perhaps *O. petiolatum*, are particularly conducive to gardening and all are also extremely difficult to transplant. Hence, none of the members of this family should ever be taken from the wild.

Southern Grapefern, Sparse-Lobed Grapefern

Botrychium biternatum (Savigny) L. Underwood   **Photo 99**

Form: A low-growing, dimorphic fern typically with a single frond per season, this usually in late spring and summer.

Fronds: Often green in winter but brownish and fading as spring approaches; new fronds appear in late spring to early summer, with fertile portion of fronds maturing in spring and summer.

Petiole: Relatively dark brown to greenish, those of sterile fronds 5 - 15 cm long, those of the fertile portion of the frond often much longer, to about 45 cm, but typically not exceeding about 35 cm; sterile and fertile frond segments arising together but diverging within about 6 cm above ground, hence measurements of the petiole sometimes recorded as not exceeding about 6 cm.

Rachis: Greenish, fleshy.

Blade: Sterile blade portion bipinnate to tripinnate, triangular in overall outline, 5 - 22 cm long, to about 25 cm wide at the base; fertile blade segment pinnate-bipinnate with filiform segments, each of which is covered with conspicuous clusters of sporangia, arising well below the base of the sterile blade; fertile frond segments produced mostly in late spring and summer, then withering away in late fall or early winter; sterile segments of fronds often remaining green throughout the winter.

Pinnae: Two to three pairs, each pinna with two to five pairs of pinnules and an extended, oblong to lanceolate, irregularly- to finely-toothed, blunt-tipped terminal segment.

Habitat: Most often in moist, rich woodlands, along stream banks, or in mesic hammocks, but sometimes also in drier woods.

Distribution: Generally ranging across northern Florida and sparingly southward to about DeSoto County.

Remarks: This fern is not uncommon in mesic woodlands and hammocks but is easily overlooked in the ground cover. Its single, typically triangular-shaped, sterile blade and taller, more delicately cut fertile blade segment, which arises well below the base of the sterile blade, distinguish it from all other Florida ferns in similar habitat except the extremely similar and difficult-to-distinguish *B. dissectum* (see remarks under the latter species for a discussion of distinguishing characters, as well as the possible conspecific status of these species).

Synonyms: *Osmunda biternata* Savigny; *Botrychium dissectum* Springel var. *tenuifolium* (L. Underwood) Farwell; *B. tenuifolium* L. Underwood.

Dissected Grapefern, Lace-Frond Grapefern

Botrychium dissectum Sprengel   **Photo 100**

Form: A low-growing, dimorphic fern typically with a single fertile and sterile blade segment per season; with an erect stem.

Fronds: To about 45 cm tall, appearing in late summer and fall to at least November, fertile segments of fronds maturing in fall.

Petiole: 2 - 6 cm long, yellowish to yellow green to straw colored or brownish, round, grooved.

Rachis: Similar to the petiole.

Blade: Sterile blades very variable, bipinnate to tripinnate or more divided, shiny green when new, turning bronze in winter (a feature often used as a distinguishing character of the plant), to about 40 cm long and 30 cm wide or more at the base, margins profusely toothed or lacerated and appearing lacy, borne on a stalk 3 - 15 cm long; fertile blade segments far exceeding the sterile in height, arising well below the base of the sterile blade, produced mostly in fall.

Pinnae: Sterile pinnae up to about 10 pairs, 1 - 4 cm long, margins lacerated and lacy.

Sporangia: Borne in branched clusters near the apex of tall, fertile blade segments.

Habitat: Seepages, moist woods, stream banks, open grassy areas.

Distribution: Collected or reported from many counties in north and central Florida; from about Calhoun and Gulf Counties eastward and southward to at least Hendry County. This species was reported by Long and Lakela (1976) only from a single location near

Jacksonville. More recent accounts (e.g., Wunderlin, 1998) show it as distributed across much of Florida. The form found in Florida is difficult to distinguish from *B. biternatum* (if the two are distinct, see remarks below), which has led to the two often being confused in the state.

Remarks: This plant may be distinguished from *B. virginianum* by the fertile blade segment arising well-below the base of the sterile blade segment. Some forms are very similar to *B. biternatum* and the two taxa may, in fact, not be distinct. It is generally reported to differ from the latter by having bipinnate to 4-pinnate (mostly tripinnate) leaves rather than the mostly bipinnate leaves (occasionally tripinnate) of *B. biternatum,* by the lateral lobes of the pinnae or pinnules being mostly rhomboidal and angular rather than oblong and subround, by the terminal segments being more lacerated, incised, or toothed than in the latter, by producing spores mostly in fall rather than summer, and by its leaves often turning brown or bronze colored in winter rather than remaining green. Wagner (Wagner, 1963; Wagner & Wagner, 1993) holds that these two taxa are closely allied but distinct species. However, not all taxonomists and pteridologists agree with this separation. Alice and Rolla Tryon (pesonal communication, 1998), for example, "treat both *B. biternatum* and *B. dissectum* Spreng var. *obliquum* Clute as synonyms under *B. dissectum* Sprengel. . . . We regard *B. dissectum* as a highly variable species." However, Wunderlin, in the upcoming comprehensive flora of Florida, treats the complex as *B. biternatum,* since a form of the species' specific epithet was first applied by Savigny *(Osmunda biternata)* in 1797, hence predating the first use of the epithet dissectum in 1804. This author is highly inclined toward Wunderlin's treatment as the most defensible taxonomic rendering of the taxa, especially for Florida's plants, but has chosen here to maintain consistency with the *Flora of North America.*

The fronds of *B. dissectum* are quite variable (see for example Graham & Wagner, 1991 and R. M. Tryon, 1936) and there are at least two (some say as many as four) distinct forms of this species, only one of which occurs regularly in Florida. Populations north of Florida more commonly have deeply dissected sterile leaves with narrow pinnules (sometimes referred to as forma *dissectum)* and are easier to recognize in the field. The sterile leaves of most Florida populations, on the other hand, are much less dissected (forma *obliquum)* and quite similar in appearance to *B. biternatum.* Both *B. biternatum* and *B. dissectum* may be found in the same habitat.

Synonyms: *Botrychium obliquum* Muhlenberg in Willdenow

Alabama Grapefern

Botrychium jenmanii L. Underwood **Photo 101**

Form: A relatively low, somewhat fleshy fern with a short, erect stem and fleshy roots; usually not exceeding about 20 cm tall.

Fronds: Sterile portion of fronds typically produced one (sometimes more) per season and appearing in mid to late summer, fertile portion of fronds maturing mostly October to November and dying back by spring; sterile portion of frond grayish green in color, spreading and more nearly parallel to the ground, fertile portion erect, narrow, taller, and without expanded blade tissue.

Petiole: Yellowish brown, round, fleshy, dividing about 3.5 cm above the ground into sterile and fertile portions, complete petiole to about 15 cm long.

Rachis: Similar in color and shape to the petiole.

Blade: Sterile portion bipinnate-pinnatifid to tripinnate, generally triangular in overall outline, to about 18 cm long and 26 cm wide; fertile portion bipinnate, to about 30 cm long.

Pinnae: Sterile pinnae bipinnate, well spaced along the rachis, divided into small, typically ovate to fan-shaped pinnules with finely toothed margins; pinnules borne alternately and well spaced along the pinna axis.

Sporangia: Borne in clusters near the apex of the fertile portion of the blade.

Habitat: Relatively dry, well-drained sites, including pine woods, and open lawns; cemeteries.

Distribution: Rare; collected in Florida only in Gadsden and Duval Counties.

Remarks: This species is similar in some respects to *B. lunarioides,* but is larger and its sterile blades are erect whereas those of *B. lunarioides* are typically inconspicuous and prostrate. *B. jenmanii* was first and long known as *B. alabamense,* a name given it by William Maxon who discovered it in Alabama in 1906, hence its common name. It appears in both Small (1938) and Lakela and Long (1976) under this combination. In 1983 Wagner determined that the taxon was actually conspecific with *B. jenmanii,* which was first described by L. M. Underwood in 1900. *B. jenmanii* is generally thought to be a fertile hybrid between *B. lunarioides* and *B. biternatum,* and is often found growing in association with these latter species. Hence, it is sometimes reported as *B. X jenmanii,* and sometimes superficially resembles either *B. biternatum* or *B. dissectum.*

Synonyms: *Botrychium alabamense* Maxon

Winter Grapefern, Prostrate Grapefern

Botrychium lunarioides (Michaux) Swartz   **Photo 102**

Form: A diminutive, dimorphic, difficult-to-find fern of open grassy areas; plants appearing February to April, dying back by summer.

Fronds: Sterile portion of the frond small, to about 10 cm long, but often not exceeding about 6 cm, often held close to the ground, concealed by, and not easily distinguished from the associated grassy ground cover; fertile portion 7 - 15 cm long, often to the shorter of this range, held erect, but sometimes barely conspicuous above closely cropped grass.

Petiole: Greenish to straw colored, grooved, 1 - 3 cm long on sterile fronds, 1 - 6 cm on fertile frond segments.

Rachis: Light brown to straw colored.

Blade: Sterile blade bipinnate to tripinnate, to about 6 cm long, broad and triangular in overall shape, typically lying prostrate; sterile segments rounded with entire to irregularly toothed margins; fertile blade portion with narrow segments that are covered with brownish sporangia.

Habitat: Mostly found in closely cut grassy areas, especially cemeteries.

Distribution: Known in Florida primarily in Gadsden, Jackson, Liberty, and Jefferson Counties, but likely overlooked in other north Florida locations.

Remarks: This fern and the several species of *Ophioglossum* are sometimes referred to collectively as "little people" due their diminutive stature. The most effective way to find this fern is to search for it in closely cut lawns, especially cemeteries, by crawling on hands and knees or by laying one's face close to the ground, then looking laterally across the top of the grass for fertile frond segments.

Wagner (1992) has placed this species into its own monotypic section (sect. *Hiemobotrychium*) within the genus *Botrychium*. According to Wagner, *B. lunarioides* differs from other members of the genus in several ways. It is ". . . wholly underground and dormant for 8 to 9 months of the year, including most of spring, summer, and fall, rather than being essentially evergreen and visible at all seasons... [and it has] numerous, yellow brown narrow roots rather than few, blackish thick roots . . ." (p. 267). It typically has two, short-stalked, mostly prostrate portions of the sterile frond segments, rather than one, long-stalked, upright sterile portion. The venation of the pinnules is fan-shaped and forking, whereas the venation in other members of the genus is generally pinnate, and the stalk of the fertile portion of the frond is usually conspicuously flattened and fleshy, rather than round (to only slightly flattened) and only moderately fleshy. *B. lunarioides* is most similar to *B. jenmanii,* which is more erect in stature with a long-stalked sterile blade segment and round-stalked fertile blade segment, and which produces sporangia in fall rather than early spring.

Synonyms: *Botrypus lunarioides* Michaux

Rattlesnake Fern, Common Grapefern

Botrychium virginianum (Linnaeus) Swartz   **Photos 103, 104**

Form: An erect, relatively low fern producing a single frond per season from an erect stem with fleshy roots.

Fronds: To about 60 cm tall; appearing early spring to summer, dying back in the fall; sterile portions spreading and nearly parallel to the ground, fertile portions erect, narrow, taller, without expanded blade tissue.

Petiole: 10 - 35 cm tall, fleshy, round, pale green to straw colored, grooved.

Rachis: Similar to the petiole, pale brown to straw colored and grooved.

Blade: Sterile portion bi- to tripinnate-pinnatifid (or more), triangular in overall outline, appearing to be divided at the base into three major divisions, 10 - 35 cm long, 15 - 40 cm wide, pale green in color; fertile portion bipinnate, erect, arising at the base of the blade, narrow, 11 - 40 cm long and extending well above the sterile portion.

Pinnae: Pinnate-pinnatifid to bipinnate, segments deeply incised, toothed, and pointed at the apices

Sporangia: Borne in clusters near the apex of the fertile portion of the blade.

Habitat: Rich, deciduous, well-drained but moist forests.

Distribution: Sporadically distributed in Florida, but sometimes fairly abundant from the central panhandle eastward to about Alachua County and southward to Hernando County; much more common north of Florida.

Remarks: At first glance this species may be confused with *B. biternatum* or *B. dissectum*. It is most easily distinguished from these and all other similar members of the genus by the fertile portion of the blade arising at the base of, rather than well below the base of, the sterile portion of the blade, in conjunction with the deeply cut sterile blades. The name rattlesnake fern derives from the supposed similarity of the spore clusters to the rattles of the rattlesnake. It has also been reported that a salve made by boiling the roots of the plant was used by the Cherokee Indians in the treatment of snake bites.

Synonyms: *Osmunda virginiana* Linnaeus

Hand Fern, Hand Adder's Tongue Fern, Dwarf Staghorn

Cheiroglossa palmata (Linnaeus) C. Presl   **Photos 105, 106**

Form: An epiphytic fern with conspicuous, pendent leaves, tan, finely brown-hairy stems, and succulent roots that are generally hidden from view under the humus at the bases of sabal palm leaves. The roots are often branching and may extend for considerable distances. Mature plants may bear as many as six mostly fertile leaves.

Petiole: 3.5 - 17 cm long, with conspicuous tufts of whitish hairs at the base.

Blade: Bright green, to about 45 cm long and 35 cm wide, broadest at the base and divided near the middle into several long (typically 8 - 15 cm), fingerlike or tongue-shaped lobes that taper to a more or less bluntly pointed apex; young fronds unfold rather than uncurl as in many ferns, and are pinkish green, soft, fleshy, and are much smaller than and out of proportion to the much more robust petioles (Luis Diego Gomez, 1976).

Sori: Borne from the petiole and blade margins in two yellowish, marginal rows on stalked spikes; spikes numbering to about 15 (occasionally more) per leaf, 1 - 7 cm long with stalks 1 - 2 cm long; the sporangia typically mature between December and May.

Habitat: Subtropical hammocks; in Florida epiphytic mostly in humus at the leaf bases of sabal palms *(Sabal palmetto* [Walt.] Lodd. ex Schultes). In other parts of its range, the hand fern has been reported on trees other than palms, as well as on rocks, and from the root masses of bromeliads (Mesler, 1974), and Small (1938) implies that this species might have once occurred on more than one tree species in peninsula Florida. Whether or not this was widely true during Small's sojourns in the state, more recent evidence suggests the species is today confined essentially to *S. palmetto*. However, it should also be noted that this species has more recently been reported, but only once, to occur in Florida on the trunks of saw palmetto *[Serenoa repens* (Bartram) Small] (Nauman and Moyroud, 1986), and that a single specimen on an oak tree has been reported from Palm Beach County.

Distribution: Currently known only from southernmost peninsula Florida, the West Indies, Mexico, Central and South America, South Vietnam, Madagascar, the Seychelles, and Reunion; previously collected in Florida as far north as St. Johns County on the east coast and Pasco County on the west coast. Small (1938), Lakela and Long (1976), and Chrysler (1941) suggest that this species might have been more frequent in Florida only a few decades ago. Today, it has disappeared from much of the Everglades, where it was once more common, and its continued existence seems to be in jeopardy. It is listed as endangered by the Florida Department of Agriculture.

The history of its demise is well documented. In 1906 Eaton noted that inhabitants of the Everglades regularly "set fire to whatever will burn, and the time seems not far distant when this [species] will be exterminated" (p. 459). Mesler (1974) suggests that its decline in the state may be attributed in minor part to over collecting, and, perhaps more importantly, to the extensive drainage and water diversion activities that have altered the Everglades. *C. palmata* requires nearly continuous high humidity and moist conditions to reproduce and grow. The draining of the Everglades has decreased moisture and increased the frequency of fire, hence destroying or altering the hand fern's only available habitat. Once reported by Small as being so common along the edges of the Everglades that one could "collect it by the wagon load" (Chrysler, 1941), its population today is restricted to a few hammocks that have escaped fire, and its future in Florida is uncertain. However, though fire has been advanced as a major reason for the decline of this species, this assumption has not been adequately proven. More research is needed to clarify answers to this question.

Remarks: This species was discovered in Florida by Dr. A. W. Chapman in 1875 on the banks of the Caloosahatchee River, and later included in the second edition of his *Flora of the Southern United States.* Smith (1911) also reported it from the banks of the Caloosahatchee in March, 1878, the very month in which Chapman published his find three years earlier. Its conspicuous hand-shaped leaves (from which the specific epithet, *palmata,* is derived), epiphytic habit, and preference for sabal palms make it unmistakable among Florida's fern flora. It is superficially similar to species of *Platycerium,* the nonnative staghorn fern, and has erroneously been collected for cultivation as such, hence the common name dwarf staghorn.

While the other epiphytic member of the family, *Ophioderma pendula,* is often grown in cultivation, plants of *C. palmata* are impossible to transplant or cultivate and begin withering immediately upon removal from the tree. Hence, the species has no horticultural value and should never be collected from the wild.

Synonyms: *Ophioglossum palmatum* Linnaeus.

Ribbon Fern

Ophioderma pendula (Linnaeus) Presl   **Photo 107**

Form: An evergreen, epiphytic, straplike or ribbonlike fern with pendent fronds.

Fronds: Tufted, green, rather fleshy, to about 90 cm long and to about 3 cm wide at midfrond in Florida (but reported to reach lengths of 4 m and widths of 9 cm [Mesler, 1974] in other parts of its range), slightly narrowed toward the straw-colored base, rounded to often divided and mittenlike at the apex; margins entire.

Sporangia: Enclosed in leaf tissue and borne along the margins of the sterile blade in conspicuous, stalked, linear, straight, slightly flattened clusters, to about 10 cm long and 6 mm wide, with a blunt, blackish, tiny toothlike projection at the apex; stalk stout, sometimes branched, to about 4 cm long.

Habitat: Florida's only naturalized record of this species was collected from a population growing on a date palm *(Phoenix* sp.); epiphytic on palms, a variety of trees, and rocks in other parts of its range, sometimes in humus on tree trunks, more often in palms with persistent leaf bases (Mesler, 1974).

Distribution: Reported in Florida only in Dade County; also distributed in the Old World

Tropics including Formosa, Phillipines, Malaysia to India, and Australia, but also in Polynesia (including Hawaii).

Remarks: This species was discovered growing spontaneously in the Miami area in March, 1998 by Adrian Tejedor, a student at Miami-Dade Community College. Bruce McAlpin (personal communication, 1999) suggests that this plant has been introduced to the state through cultivation. According to McAlpin, this species has been grown in southern Florida for at least 25 years and regularly shows up at plant raffles of the local fern society.

Valier (1995) reports that a cough remedy is brewed from the endemic subspecies *falcatum* in Hawaii, and that one of the Hawaiian names for this subspecies is Puapuamoa, because its arching fronds are reminiscent of a cock's tail feathers. It is recommended for cultivation in hanging baskets in the tropical and subtropical portions of Australia and New Zealand, with the caution that it is too cold sensitive to be used in temperate regions (Goudey, 1988).

Synonyms: *Ophioglossum pendulum* Linnaeus

Bulbous Adder's-Tongue, Dwarf Adder's-Tongue Fern

Ophioglossum crotalophoroides Walter   **Photo 108**

Form: A diminutive, inconspicuous fern with a bulbous stem.

Fronds: Sterile frond with one or two blades; fertile frond filiform, to about 10 cm tall.

Petiole: 1 - 3 cm long on sterile fronds.

Blade: Sterile blades heart shaped with netted veins, held close to the ground, somewhat resembling the blades of pony-foot *(Dichondra carolinensis* Michaux), a common, low-growing yard weed often found in association with the present species; fertile fronds erect and bearing beadlike sporangia in two rows near the tip; sporangial spike to about 1 cm long.

Habitat: Lawns and cemeteries, roadsides; often in association with *Botrychium lunarioides.*

Distribution: Frequent but often overlooked, sporadically reported in the western peninsula from about Manatee County northward and westward to at least the west-central panhandle; also collected in Duval County.

Remarks: This is an easily overlooked species due to its small size and the fact that it is only visible during a few months of the year. Its common names come from its bulbous stem and the supposed resemblance of its fertile spike to a snake's tongue; its specific epithet derives from the superficial resemblance of its fertile spike to the rattles of a rattlesnake. It is easiest to find in early spring before the flush of new growth in closely cut lawns when the sporangial spikes are most visible. The bulbous, rounded, field-pea-size stem distinguishes this species from the other members of the genus. Wherry (1964) recognized var. *nanum* for this species, which he called a dwarf variety. However, this taxon is not recognized, even in synonymy, in the *Flora of North America* or in Wunderlin (1998).

Many species of *Ophioglossum* reproduce primarily asexually by the formation of clones through the process of root budding. According to Mesler (1974), due to its bulbous stem, *O. crotalophoroides* seemingly lacks the ability to develop root buds, reproducing, instead, primarily or solely by sexual means. Mesler further points out that whereas colonies of other species of *Ophioglossum* often conform to a pattern of crowding or ordering which tends to accompany root proliferation, populations of *O. crotalophoroides* are more randomly spaced.

The tendency toward sexual reproduction has made *O. crotalophoroides* very useful in the study of the subterranean, and hence difficult-to-find, gametophytes that are common in the Ophioglossaceae family. Given that most individuals in most populations of *Ophioglossum* result from root budding, locating examples of their belowground phase is extremely difficult and may require disturbing nearly every plant in a population. On the other hand, since all individuals in a population of *O. crotalophoriodes* likely result from sexual development, such populations offer prime sites for discovering and studying their underground gametophytes. However, finding these tiny, somewhat globular plants requires excavating an individual specimen at first leaf appearance, then examining it carefully under sufficient magnification, preferably with a binocular, dissecting microscope.

Limestone Adder's-Tongue, Engelmann's Adder's-Tongue

Ophioglossum engelmannii Prantl   **Page 109**

Form: A relatively low-growing fern with simple leaves and fleshy stem with tan to brownish roots.

Fronds: 5 - 20 cm long (including fertile spike), appearing in early spring, borne two per stem.

Petiole: Those of sterile fronds to about 9 cm long, those of fertile fronds 4 - 14 cm long.

Blade: Simple, to about 10 cm long and 4.5 cm wide, pale green, typically more or less folded upward from the central axis, ovate in outline, veins netted with smaller areoles inside larger ones, margins entire.

Sporangia: Borne in slender, beadlike spikes on the apical 1 - 3 cm of the fertile stalk.

Habitat: Rocky glades, limesinks, showing a distinct preference for calcium-rich habitats.

Distribution: Sparsely distributed in Florida with collections reported only from Jackson, Citrus, Hernando, Hillsborough, and Manatee Counties; otherwise widespread across the south from west-central Georgia and the western Carolinas westward to Arizona and northward to Missouri, Illinois, and Ohio.

Remarks: The combination of its overall size, netted leaf venation, and relatively large, folded leaves, and distinctly apiculate (or flexible and pointed) tip distinguish *O. engelmannii* from all other members of the genus in Florida. German botanist Karl Prantl (1849-1893) named this species in 1883 for St. Louis botanist George Engelmann (1809-1884), who first recognized the plant as distinct.

Figure 22.

Ophioglossum engelmannii

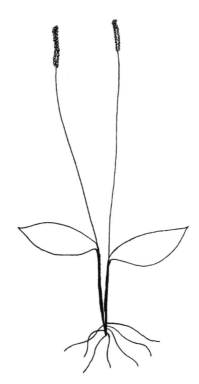

Figure 23 .
Ophioglossum nudicaule

Slender Adder's-Tongue
Ophioglossum nudicaule Linnaeus　　　　　　　　**Page 109**

Form: A low-growing, simple-leaved fern with a fleshy stem and yellowish to pale brown roots.
Fronds: 3.5 - 12 cm tall (including fertile spikes), appearing in late winter to very early spring, borne two to three per stem.
Petiole: Those of sterile portion of blades less than 1 cm long, those of fertile portions to about 11 cm long.
Blade: Sterile portion to about 2 cm long, typically less than 1 cm wide, dull green, mostly elliptic in outline, not folded upward from the central axis, venation netted, margins entire.
Sporangia: Borne in slender, beadlike spikes in the apical 1 - 1.5 cm of the fertile portion of the frond.
Habitat: Open woods, disturbed lawns, cemeteries, sometimes with *O. crotalophoroides*.
Distribution: More widespread than *O. crotalophoroides* but perhaps less common; from about the central panhandle eastward and southward to at least Lee County on the west coast, Broward on the east coast, and Highlands County in the central peninsula.
Remarks: The combination of small size (leaves generally less than about 1.5 cm long), flat leaves with netted venation, leaves arising at the base of the plant, and non-bulbous stem distinguishes this species from others in the genus. Like other "little people," this species can be very difficult to find and is easily overlooked without diligent searching.

E. P. St. John (1941) recognized at least three additional species in the *O. nudicaule* complex: *O. pumilio, O. dendroneuron,* and *O. mononeuron*. However, more recent researches have determined all three of these to be ecological variants of *O. nudicaule* (Wagner, et. al., 1981). Much of the evidence for the variation found in this species was determined from the study of a large population of *O. nudicaule* discovered by Steve Leonard in 1976 in Leon County, on the outskirts of Tallahassee.
Synonyms: *Opgioglossum dendroneuron* E. P. St. John; *O. ellipticum* Hooker & Greville; *O. mononeuron* E. P. St. John.; *O. pumilio* E. P. St. John.

Stalked Adder's-Tongue
Ophioglossum petiolatum Hooker　　　　　　　　**Photo 109**

Form: A low-growing, two- to three-leaved adder's-tongue with a slightly erect stem and pale brown roots; propogating by root budding, hence forming small colonies.
Fronds: With two distinctive parts, one sterile and one fertile, the latter to about 20 cm tall and tipped with a cylindrical fertile spike that resembles the "rattles" of a rattlesnake.
Petiole: Fertile stalk 2 - 13 cm tall, sterile stalk 1 - 7 cm long but usually longer than 3 cm.
Blade: Expanded portion of sterile blade gray green, erect to spreading, essentially flat, broadly lanceolate with an acute apex, 1 - 6 cm long, to about 2 cm wide, thick and fleshy, the veins forming areoles that do not contain smaller areoles; fertile portion of the blade to about 2 cm long.
Sporangia: Borne in distinctive, crowded rows at the apex of the fertile stalk.
Habitat: Lawns, moist roadsides and grassy areas, open woods, disturbed sites.
Distribution: Nearly throughout the state, sporadically collected from Escambia County eastward

and southward to Collier and Palm Beach Counties; also distributed in, but not limited to, the West Indies, Mexico, northern South America, tropical Africa, India, Ceylon, China, Japan, Philippines, Borneo, New Zealand, and Samoa. *O. petiolatum* is most likely a nonnative species, introduced to the state through nurseries and horticulture (Wagner and Wagner, 1993; W. H. Wagner, personal communication, 1999).

Remarks: This species is distinguished from *O. crotalophoroides* by having consistently longer petioles and by lacking the bulbous stem; from *O. nudicaule* by having larger leaves; and from *O. engelmannii* by being smaller and by the vein areoles lacking smaller areoles. The scientific epithet refers to the petiole, which is somewhat elongated below the sterile leaf blade, thus raising the blade slightly above the ground. This species is particularly known for developing root buds and a single plant can fill a pot quickly through root proliferation. Incorrect identification has caused this species to have a much larger collection of scientific synonyms than the single synonym listed below. According to Clausen (1938a):

> The history of *Ophioglossum petiolatum* is one of taxonomic blundering and misinterpretation. Although the species was already known somewhat before the publication of the first edition of the *Species Plantarum*, yet there seems to have been no end of misunderstanding concerning its proper status, its distribution, and its range of variation. It has been almost periodically described as new, each time with a different name and usually without any mention of the previous descriptions or an examination of the literature which should always be consulted before a new name is placed on record, to avoid renaming long-known species. (p. 6)

It was first described as *O. simplex* by Rumphius in 1750, a name that cannot be used since it was given prior to 1753, the official year in which current nomenclature conventions were first established, and it has been described many times since.

One of these descriptions was by Edward P. St. John from material collected in central Florida. St. John named the plant *O. floridanum* (E. P. St. John, 1936b), based partly on the length of the petiole of sterile blades. However, Clausen (1938a) discounts the use of this character as one of slight taxonomic importance and certainly not worthy for separating a new species. He maintains that St. Johns's plants are in every way the same as *Ophioglossum petiolatum*, a conclusion that is universally accepted today.

Synonyms: *Ophioglossum floridanum* E. P. St. John.

OSMUNDACEAE - ROYAL FERN FAMILY

Two species of the royal fern family occur in Florida and are two of the state's best known and most often recognized ferns. Both are conspicuous and have easily identified fertile fronds. The family is distributed nearly worldwide in temperate and tropical regions and includes three genera and up to 36 species. Florida's two species are well-known as garden plants and are listed as commercially exploited on Florida's Regulated Plant Index. Neither should be removed from the wild.

Only the genus *Osmunda* occurs naturally in the United States. Members of the genus are well-known native ferns and are excellent for use in the garden. Neither of the Florida species is invasive or weedy, and both are dimorphic, with unique and attractive fertile fronds, and tall, broad, conspicuous sterile fronds that provide an excellent background to smaller fern species. At least the cinnamon fern is a host plant of the osmunda borer moth *(Papaipema speciosissima)*, which deposits its larvae on the plant's petioles and stem and is closely related to the borer moth that attacks members of the genus *Woodwardia.*

The genus name was given by Linnaeus and is most commonly said to be in honor of the Saxon god Osmunder, another name for Thor, the god of war. Other interpretations (Dunbar, 1989) suggest that the name means "flowering fern," in reference to the showy fertile fronds, and "to cleanse," in reference to the supposed medicinal properties of the genus. In addition to their attractive fertile fronds, the fronds of members of this genus often turn rusty orange in the fall, much like the fall colors associated with eastern deciduous forests.

Cinnamon Fern

Osmunda cinnamomea Linnaeus   **Photo 110**

Form: A large, conspicuous, pale green, wholly dimorphic fern, the sterile and fertile fronds of which arise from a thick, sometimes stout stem in tall, dense tufts.

Fronds: 60 to 150 cm tall; sterile fronds pale green and relatively large; fertile fronds lacking leafy pinnae, green at first, becoming mostly cinnamon colored or brownish, as tall as or exceeding the height of the sterile fronds, appearing mostly in spring and early summer; fiddleheads are typically covered with silvery hairs that turn cinnamon colored as they unfold.

Petiole: Typically straw colored to sometimes greenish; grooved; with reddish brown, woolly hairs when new; 10 - 45 cm long.

Rachis: Greenish, with woolly, reddish brown hairs when young, becoming smooth and nearly hairless with age.

Blade: Sterile blades pinnate-pinnatifid, 30 - 120 cm long, to about 30 cm wide, elliptic in overall outline with 15 to 25 pairs of pinnae; lower side of the base of each pinna vested with a conspicuous tuft of reddish brown hairs; fertile blades to about 45 cm long, with strongly ascending pinnae that contain copious masses of brownish sporangia.

Pinnae: Sterile pinnae lobed, lanceolate in overall shape, arranged alternately on the rachis.

Habitat: Wet woods, floodplains, acid swamps, wet flatwoods, sphagnum bogs.

Distribution: Throughout Florida, except the southernmost peninsula and Keys.

Remarks: When fertile fronds are present, this species is unmistakable; when absent, the conspicuous patch of pubescence on the lower side at the base of each pinna is diagnostic. It is superficially similar to *Woodwardia virginica* but is easily distinguished at some distance by the latter's overall darker rachis. As might be expected of such a common and conspicuous fern, several parts of the cinnamon fern have been widely used both medicinally and as food by American Indians. This species is listed as commercially exploited by the Florida Department of Agriculture.

A distinctive form of this species, *O. cinnamonea* forma *frondosa* (Torrey & Gray) Britton, has been reported by a number of authors (House, 1933; Kittredge, 1941; Werth et. al., 1985), including a report of its occurrence in Florida (Carter and Faircloth, 1986). Florida specimens of this form are also held in several of the state's major herbaria, indicating that it

1.   Pine Fern   Page 28
Anemia adiantifolia

2.   Wright's Pineland Fern   Page 29
Anemia wrightii

3.   Abscised Spleenwort   Page 32
Asplenium abscissum

5.   Eared Spleenwort   Page 32
Asplenium auritum

4.   Eared Spleenwort   Page 32
Asplenium auritum

8.   Varicolored Spleenwort   Page 35
        Asplenium heterochroum

6.   Hemlock Spleenwort   Page 33
        Asplenium cristatum

7.   Varicolored Spleenwort   Page 35
        Asplenium heterochroum

10.   Single-Sorus Spleenwort   Page 36
        Asplenium monanthes

9.   Single-Sorus Spleenwort   Page 36
        Asplenium monanthes

11. **Ebony Spleenwort**   Page 36
Asplenium platyneuron

13. **Dwarf Spleenwort**   Page 37
Asplenium pumilum

12. **Ebony Spleenwort**   Page 36
Asplenium platyneuron

14. **Black-Stemmed Spleenwort** Page 38
Asplenium resiliens

15. **Birdnest Fern**   Page 39
Asplenium serratum

16. Birdnest Fern Page 39
     Asplenium serratum

17. Toothed Spleenwort Page 39
     Asplenium trichomanes-dentatum

18. Modest Spleenwort Page 41
     Asplenium verecundum

19. Modest Spleenwort Page 41
     Asplenium verecundum

20. Curtiss' Spleenwort Page 43
     Asplenium X curtissii

21. Curtiss' Spleenwort Page 43
     Asplenium X curtissii

23.   Ruffled Spleenwort   Page 43
Asplenium X *plenum*

24.   Eastern Mosquito Fern   Page 44
Azolla caroliniana

22.   Morzenti's spleenwort   Page 38
Asplenium X *heteroresiliens*

25.   Eastern Mosquito Fern   Page 44
Azolla caroliniana

26.   Hammock Fern   Page 44
Blechnum occidentale

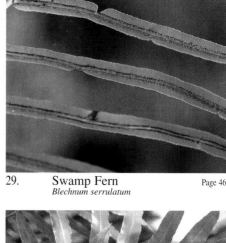

29.   Swamp Fern   Page 46
Blechnum serrulatum

27.   Hammock Fern   Page 46
Blechnum occidentale

30.   Giant Vine Fern   Page 45
Stenochlaena tenuifolia

28.   Swamp Fern   Page 46
Blechnum serrulatum

32.   Virginia Chain Fern   Page 48
Woodwardia virginica

33.   **Virginia Chain Fern**   Page 48
Woodwardia virginica

34.   **Hayscented Fern**   Page 49
Dennstaedtia bipinnata

35.   **Creeping Bramble Fern**   Page 50
Hypolepis repens

31.   **Netted Chain Fern**   Page 48
Woodwardia areolata

36.   **Creeping Bramble Fern**   Page 50
Hypolepis repens

38.   Wedgelet Fern   Page 51
       Odontosoria clavata

37.   Wedgelet Fern   Page 51
       Odontosoria clavata

39.   Bracken   Page 52
       Pteridium aqulinum var. *caudatum*

41.   Bracken   Page 52
       Pteridium aqulinum var. *pseudocaudatum*

40.   Bracken   Page 52
       Pteridium aqulinum var. *pseudocaudatum*

43. **Southern Lady Fern** Page 56
Athyrium filix-femina subsp. *asplenioides*

42. **Southern Lady Fern** Page 56
Athyrium filix-femina subsp. *asplenioides*

44. **Florida Tree Fern** Page 56
Ctenitis sloanei

45. **Florida Tree Fern** Page 56
Ctenitis sloanei

46. **Florida Tree Fern** Page 56
Ctenitis sloanei

47.　　Brown-Hair Comb Fern　Page 57
Ctenitis submarginalis

48.　　Holly Fern　Page 58
Cyrtomium falcatum

50.　　Japanese False Spleenwort　Page 60
Deparia petersenii

49.　　Holly Fern　Page 58
Cyrtomium falcatum

52. Vegetable Fern   Page 60
Diplazium esculentum

54. Southern Wood Fern   Page 61
Dryopteris ludoviciana

55. Climbing Holly Fern   Page 62
Lomariopsis kunzeana

51. Japanese False Spleenwort   Page 60
Deparia petersenii

53. Southern Wood Fern   Page 61
Dryopteris ludoviciana

56.   **Giant Sword Fern**   Page 63
Nephrolepis biserrata

57.   **Giant Sword Fern**   Page 63
Nephrolepis biserrata

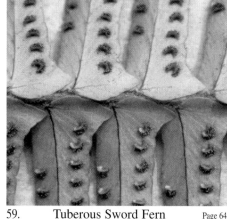

58.   **Tuberous Sword Fern**   Page 64
Nephrolepis cordifolia

59.   **Tuberous Sword Fern**   Page 64
Nephrolepis cordifolia

60.   **Tuberous Sword Fern**   Page 64
Nephrolepis cordifolia

61.   **Sword Fern**   Page 65
Nephrolepis exaltata

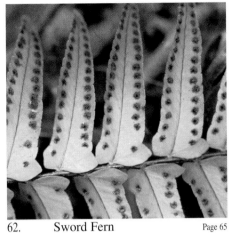

62.   Sword Fern   Page 65
Nephrolepis exaltata

64.   Avery's Sword Fern   Page 63
Nephrolepis X averyi

63.   Asian Sword Fern   Page 66
Nephrolepis multiflora

66.   Sensitive Fern   Page 67
Onoclea sensibilis

65.   Sensitive Fern   Page 67
Onoclea sensibilis

67.   Christmas Fern   Page 67
Polystichum acrostichoides

68.   Christmas Fern   Page 67
Polystichum acrostichoides

69.   Korean Rock Fern   Page 68
Polystichum tsussimense

71.   Leather Fern   Page 69
Rumohra adiantiformis

70.   Korean Rock Fern   Page 68
Polystichum tsussimense

72.   Leather Fern   Page 69
Rumohra adiantiformis

73.   Least Halberd Fern   Page 71
Tectaria fimbriata

75.   Broad Halberd Fern   Page 72
Tectaria heracleifolia

74.   Broad Halberd Fern   Page 72
Tectaria heracleifolia

76.   Incised Halberd Fern   Page 72
Tectaria incisa

78.   **Blunt-Lobed Cliff Fern**   Page 73
Woodsia obtusa

77.   **Blunt-Lobed Cliff Fern**   Page 73
Woodsia obtusa

80.   **Forked Fern**   Page 76
Dicranopteris flexuosa

79.   **Scouring Rush**   Page 74
Equisetum hyemale var. *affine*

81.   **Forked Fern**   Page 76
Dicranopteris flexuosa

83. Kraus's Bristle Fern   Page 78
Trichomanes krausii

82. Entire-Winged Bristle Fern   Page 77
Trichomanes holopterum

84. Dwarf Bristle Fern   Page 80
Trichomanes petersii

86. Appalachian Quillwort   Page 82
Isoetes appalachiana

85. Florida Bristle Fern   Page 81
Trichomanes punctatum subsp. *floridanum*

87.   Foxtail Bog Club-Moss   Page 87
        Lycopodiella alopecuroides

88.   Appressed Bog Club-Moss   Page 88
        Lycopodiella appressa

90.   Nodding Club-Moss   Page 90
        Palhinhaea cernua

89.   Prostrate Bog Club-Moss   Page 89
        Lycopodiella prostrata

91.   Hanging Fir-Moss   Page 90
        Phlegmariurus dichotomus

93.   Japanese Climbing Fern   Page 93
Lygodium japonicum

92.   Slender Bog Club-Moss   Page 91
Pseudolycopodiella caroliniana

94.   Small-Leaved Climbing Fern   Page 95
Lygodium microphyllum

96.   Bristly Water-Clover   Page 98
Marsilea hirsuta

95.   Small-Leaved Climbing Fern   Page 95
Lygodium microphyllum

98.   Small Water-Clover   Page 98
Marsilea minuta

97.   Small Water-Clover   Page 98
Marsilea minuta

100.   Dissected Grapefern   Page 101
Botrychium dissectum

99.   Southern Grapefern   Page 100
Botrychium biternatum

101.   Alabama Grapefern   Page 102
Botrychium jenmanii

102.   Winter Grapefern   Page 103
Botrychium lunarioides

104.   Rattlesnake Fern   Page 104
Botrychium virginianum

103.   Rattlesnake Fern   Page 104
Botrychium virginianum

106.   Hand Fern   Page 105
Cheiroglossa palmata

105.   Hand Fern   Page 105
Cheiroglossa palmata

108. **Bulbous Adder's-Tongue** Page 107
Ophioglossum crotalophoroides

107. **Ribbon Fern** Page 106
Ophioderma pendula

109. **Stalked Adder's-Tongue** Page 110
Ophioglossum petiolatum

110. **Cinnamon Fern** Page 112
Osmunda cinnamomea

111. **Royal Fern** Page 113
Osmunda regalis var. *spectabilis*

113. Water Sprite   Page 115
Ceratopteris thalictroides

112. Floating Water Fern   Page 114
Ceratopteris pteridoides

115. Narrow Strap Fern   Page 118
Campyloneurum angustifolium

114. Narrow Strap Fern   Page 118
Campyloneurum angustifolium

116. Tailed Strap Fern   Page 119
Campyloneurum costatum

117.   *Campyloneurum latum*   Page 118

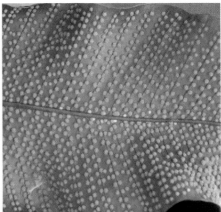

118.   *Campyloneurum latum*   Page 118

119.   Long Strap Fern   Page 119
        Campyloneurum phyllitidis

121.   Climbing Vine Fern   Page 120
        Microgramma heterophylla

120.   Long Strap Fern   Page 119
        Campyloneurum phyllitidis

122.   Climbing Vine Fern   Page 120
Microgramma heterophylla

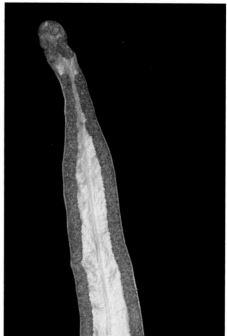

123.   Ribbon Fern   Page 122
Neurodium lanceolatum

124.   Widespread Polypody   Page 123
Pecluma dispersa

125.   Plume Polypody   Page 123
Pecluma plumula

126.   Plume Polypody   Page 123
Pecluma plumula

127.   Comb Polypody   Page 124
Pecluma ptilodon var. *caespitosa*

128.   Comb Polypody   Page 124
Pecluma ptilodon var. *caespitosa*

129.   Comb Polypody   Page 124
Pecluma ptilodon var. *caespitosa*

131.   Goldfoot Fern   Page 124
Phlebodium aureum

130.   Goldfoot Fern   Page 124
Phlebodium aureum

132.   Serpent Fern   Page 125
Phymatosorus scolopendria

133.   Serpent Fern   Page 125
Phymatosorus scolopendria

134.   Resurrection Fern   Page 127
Pleopeltis polypodioides var. *michauxianum*

135.   Angle-Vein Fern   Page 128
Polypodium triseriale

136.   Angle-Vein Fern   Page 128
Polypodium triseriale

137.   **Whisk-Fern**   Page 129
        Psilotum nudum

138.   **Coast Leather Fern**   Page 131
        Acrostichum aureum

140.   **Giant Leather Fern**   Page 132
        Acrostichum danaeifolium

139.   **Giant Leather Fern**   Page 132
        Acrostichum danaeifolium

141.   **Double-Edge Maidenhair**   Page 133
        Adiantum anceps

142.   Southern Maidenhair   Page 134
Adiantum capillus-veneris

143.   Trailing Maidenhair   Page 135
Adiantum caudatum

144.   Fragrant Maidenhair   Page 135
Adiantum melanoleucum

145.   Brittle Maidenhair   Page 136
Adiantum tenerum

146.   Woolly Maidenhair   Page 138
Adiantum villosum

147.   Hairy Lip Fern   Page 140
Cheilanthes lanosa

148.   Hairy Lip Fern   Page 140
         Cheilanthes lanosa

150.   Silverback Fern   Page 143
         Pityrogramma calomelanos

151.   Goldenrod Fern   Page 144
         Pityrogramma trifoliata

149.   Silverback Fern   Page 143
         Pityrogramma calomelanos

152.   Goldenrod Fern   Page 144
         Pityrogramma trifoliata

154.   Cretan Brake   Page 146
Pteris cretica

153.   Bahama Ladder Brake   Page 146
Pteris bahamensis

155.   Cretan Brake   Page 146
Pteris cretica

157.   Spider Brake   Page 147
Pteris multifida

156.   Long Brake   Page 145
Pteris grandifolia

158.   Spider Brake   Page 147
          Pteris multifida

159.   Giant Brake   Page 149
          Pteris tripartita

160.   Giant Brake   Page 149
          Pteris tripartita

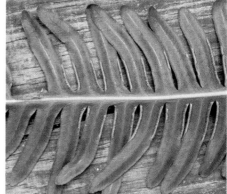

161.   Giant Brake   Page 149
          Pteris tripartita

162.   Chinese Ladder Brake Page 150
          Pteris vittata

163.   Chinese Ladder Brake Page 150
          Pteris vittata

164.   *Pteris X delchampsii*   Page 146

165.   Water Spangles   Page 151
Salvinia minima

166.   Ray Spiked Fern   Page 151
Actinostachys pennula

167.   Sand Spike-Moss   Page 155
Selaginella arenicola

168.   *Selaginella acanthonota*   Page 156

169.   Eaton's Spike-Moss   Page 156
Selaginella eatonii

170.   Gulf Spike-Moss   Page 156
Selaginella ludoviciana

171.   Blue Spike-Moss   Page 157
Selaginella uncinata

172.   Vine Spike-Moss   Page 158
Selaginella willdenovii

173.   Mariana Maiden Fern   Page 161
Macrothelypteris torresiana

175.   Mariana Maiden Fern   Page 161
Macrothelypteris torresiana

176.   Broad Beech Fern   Page 161
Phegopteris hexagonoptera

177.   Broad Beech Fern   Page 161
Phegopteris hexagonoptera

174.   Mariana Maiden Fern   Page 161
Macrothelypteris torresiana

178.   Abrupt-Tipped Maiden Fern   Page 162
Thelypteris augescens

179.   Downy Maiden Fern   Page 164
Thelypteris dentata

181.   Stately Maiden Fern   Page 164
Thelypteris grandis

180.   Downy Maiden Fern   Page 164
Thelypteris dentata

182.   Stately Maiden Fern   Page 164
Thelypteris grandis

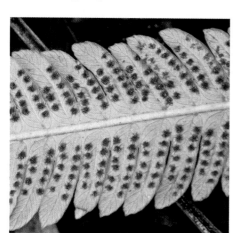

183.   Stately Maiden Fern   Page 164
Thelypteris grandis

184.   Variable Maiden Fern   Page 165
Thelypteris hispidula var. *versicolor*

185.   Hottentot Fern   Page 166
Thelypteris interrupta

186.   Hottentot Fern   Page 166
Thelypteris interrupta

187.   Southern Shield Fern   Page 167
Thelypteris kunthii

188.   Southern Shield Fern   Page 167
Thelypteris kunthii

189.   Jeweled Maiden Fern   Page 167
Thelypteris opulenta

190. **Jeweled Maiden Fern** Page 167
Thelypteris opulenta

191. **Ovate Maiden Fern** Page 168
Thelypteris ovata

192. **Marsh Fern** Page 169
Thelypteris palustris var. *pubescens*

194. **Grid-Scale Maiden Fern** Page 170
Thelypteris patens

193. **Grid-Scale Maiden Fern** Page 170
Thelypteris patens

195.   Grid-Scale Maiden Fern   Page 170
Thelypteris patens

198.   Lattice-Vein Fern   Page 172
Thelypteris reticulata

196.   Creeping Star-Hair Fern   Page 170
Thelypteris reptans

199.   Lattice-Vein Fern   Page 172
Thelypteris reticulata

197.   Glandular Maiden Fern   Page 171
Thelypteris resinifera

200. **Stiff Star-Hair Fern** Page 172
Thelypteris sclerophylla

201. **Dentate Lattice-Vein Fern** Page 173
Thelypteris serrata

203. **Shoestring Fern** Page 175
Vittaria lineata

202. **Free-Tip Star-Hair Fern** Page 174
Thelypteris tetragona

204. **Shoestring Fern** Page 175
Vittaria lineata

may be somewhat common. The form is distinguished by having at least some fronds with both fertile and sterile pinnae, the latter of which often occur on the upper portion of the frond, but may also occur near the base of the frond. According to many workers, this "interrupted cinnamon fern" is likely an environmentally induced variant resulting from disturbances such as mowing, fire, or late season frosts. Plants of this form sometimes have sterile pinnae at both the base and apex of the frond, which suggests a superficial resemblance to *Osmunda claytoniana* Linnaeus, a species that occurs north of Florida and is especially common in the northeastern United States. However, this latter species lacks the distinctive tufts of hairs at the base of the pinnae that characterize the cinnamon fern. In addition, specimens of forma *frondosa* typically display several types of fronds on the same plant, or in a single population of plants, a curiosity that is not true of *O. claytoniana*.

Synonyms: *Osmunda cinnamomea* var. *glandulosa* Waters

Royal Fern

Osmunda regalis Linnaeus var. *spectabilis* (Willdenow) A. Gray   **Photo 111**

Form: A large, conspicuous, tufted fern with leaves that are more reminiscent of a leguminous shrub or young tree than a pteridophyte; stem thick, sometimes stumplike or trunklike and arising slightly above the ground.

Fronds: 50 - 150 cm tall, green; dimorphic.

Petiole: Greenish to straw colored or pinkish, 10 - 75 cm long, typically with only a few scattered hairs at maturity.

Rachis: Green to straw colored, with a few scattered hairs.

Blade: Bipinnate with relatively large, short-stalked, lanceolate pinnules, to about 5 cm long.

Pinnae: Sterile pinnae closely alternate to nearly opposite along the rachis, lanceolate in overall shape, 6 - 28 cm long, to about 14 cm wide, with 5 to 13 pairs of alternately arranged pinnules; pinnule margins entire to minutely toothed; fertile pinnae contracted, without expanded tissue, covered with brownish sporangia and borne at the apex of the blade.

Habitat: Wet woods, wet flatwoods, creek swamps, cypress swamps, floodplains, calcareous hammocks, interdunal swales, streambanks, bogs.

Distribution: Throughout Florida.

Remarks: The very large, bipinnate leaves with relatively large pinnules set this species apart from all other of Florida's ferns; the conspicuous, dimorphic pinnae, the fertile ones of which lack leafy tissue at the tip and contain, instead, dense, brownish clusters of sporangia are diagnostic. Fibers from the stem of this species have been used in rope and net making, and as a growing medium for orchids. Other parts of the plant have been used medicinally to relieve sprains, treat wounds and broken bones, and to alleviate coughs and diarrhea. This species is listed as commercially exploited by the Florida Department of Agriculture.

Synonyms: *Osmunda spectabilis* Willdenow

PARKERIACEAE - WATER FERN OR WATER HORN FERN FAMILY

The Parkeriaceae family is composed primarily of short-lived, aquatic or semiaquatic species with erect, spongy stems. The family includes a single genus with only four species world-wide, two of which occur in Florida. The genus *Ceratopteris* has been variously included within other families including the Pteridaceae (Tryon and Tryon, 1982) and Ceratopteridaceae (Small, 1931 & 1938). It is a unique genus that has been difficult to relate to other fern genera. Hence, it is currently included within an isolated, monotypic family. The genus name derives from the Greek, *cerato,* which means horned, and *pteris,* or fern, and refers to the antlerlike appearance of the fertile blades. The floating habit of these species render the locations of known populations to be somewhat ephemeral.

Floating Water Fern, Floating Antler Fern

Ceratopteris pteridoides (Hooker) Hieronymus   **Photo 112, Page 115**

Form: A typically floating-leaved to sometimes rooted fern of swamps, bogs, and canals.

Fronds: Typically deltate to triangular in overall outline, of two types; fertile fronds to about 50 cm tall and wide, and with linear ultimate segments; sterile fronds shorter and with expanded blade tissue.

Petiole: Longitudinally ridged and furrowed; those of sterile fronds spongy, inflated (at least near the base), 1 - 19 cm long; those of fertile fronds spongy, to about 25 cm long.

Rachis: Similar to the petiole, inflated.

Blade: Sterile blades simple to pinnately or palmately lobed, often deeply pinnatifid, some-times bi- to quadripinnate, 5 - 33 cm long, 4 - 29 cm wide; fertile blades pinnate to quadrip-innate, with narrow, linear ultimate segments with strongly revolute margins.

Sori: Borne in crowded rows about equidistant between the midvein and the strongly inrolled leaf margins, often appearing encased by the leaf margins.

Habitat: Aquatic or semiaquatic in ponds and slow-moving rivers; sometimes in conjunction with masses of water-hyacinth *(Eichhornia crassipes* [Martius] Solms); usually floating but sometimes rooted in mud.

Distribution: Considered native to Florida and distributed nearly throughout the southern peninsula from Alachua County with increasing frequency southward.

Remarks: The expanded, mostly pinnately-lobed sterile leaves, inflated petioles (especially toward the base) that are mostly more than 10 mm wide, distinguish this species from *C. thal-ictroides.* It is otherwise easy to identify in aquatic habitats and not likely to be confused with other of Florida's ferns.

Synonyms: *Parkeria pteridoides* Hooker; *Ceratopteris lockhartii* (Hooker & Greville) Kunze

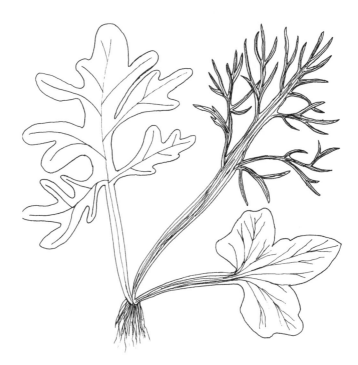

Figure 24.
Ceratopteris
pteridoides

Water Sprite

Ceratopteris thalictroides (Linnaeus) Brongniart   **Photo 113**

Form: An aquatic fern with rooted stem.

Fronds: Numerous, closely clustered, erect, to about 1 m tall or more, of two types; fertile ones with narrow, linear ultimate segments, sterile ones with expanded blade tissue.

Petioles: Green, longitudinally ridged and furrowed, spongy; those of fertile fronds 1 - 46 cm long, those of sterile fronds usually not exceeding about 31 cm in length.

Rachis: Similar to the petiole.

Blade: Fertile blades deeply bi-, tri- to quadripinnate-pinnatifid, lanceolate to narrowly triangular in overall outline, to about 45 cm long and 25 cm wide, ultimate pinnules linear, margins strongly revolute; sterile blades ovate to deltate in overall outline, pinnate to tripinnate, 2 - 41 cm long, 2 - 20 cm wide, margins deeply lobed.

Pinnae: Sterile pinnae ovate to triangular in outline, 5 - 25 cm long, 3 - 8 cm wide, divided into lobed pinnules.

Sori: Borne in one to three rows on the lower surface of fertile leaves; often enclosed and appearing encased by the strongly revolute leaf margins.

Habitat: Aquatic to semiaquatic in slow-moving rivers, ponds, and other slow-moving water.

Distribution: A non-native species that is not uncommon in the lower peninsula from about Citrus and Brevard Counties southward. It was reported as common on portions of the St. Johns River as early as 1879 (Curtiss, 1902).

115

Remarks: This is a pantropical species that is cultivated for use in home aquaria and has escaped and become established in Florida, Texas, and California. Its distinctive, divided fertile fronds and aquatic habit distinguish it from all but *C. pteridoides.* The latter species typically has simple to deeply-lobed sterile blades and inflated petioles, whereas the sterile blades of the current species has deeply bi- to tripinnately-divided blades, and noninflated petioles that do not normally exceed about 8 mm in width; but see remarks under *C. pteridoides.* Both Mickel (1979) and Wunderlin (1982) reported *C. richardii* Brongniart [=*C. deltoidea* Benedict] for Florida. However, it is now known that these names were misapplied to specimens of the present species (Wunderlin, 1998).

Synonyms: *Acrostichum thalictroides* Linnaeus

POLYPODIACEAE - POLYPODY FAMILY

The polypody family is a relatively large group of plants that generally have simple to deeply pinnatifid or pinnate blades. Most members of the family are small to medium size and many are epiphytic or epipetric. About 40 genera and approximately 500 species are known worldwide, depending upon the taxonomic classification used. Eight genera are represented in Florida. Nine of Florida's species are listed as endangered by the Florida Department of Agriculture.

The polypody family was formerly referred to as the "fern" or "true fern" family, and was once considered to include at least 171 genera and 7,227 species (Cobb, 1963), all of which share similarities in the structure of their spore cases (sporangia). In this inclusive interpretation, members of the family are characterized: 1) by having rounded, long-stalked sporangia; 2) by the annulus (the ring of cells that encircles the sporangia and serves in dispensing the spores), being vertical, interrupted by the sporangial stalk, and rupturing at about the four o'clock position to expel the ripened spores; 3) by the sporangia being collected into discrete, rounded, or elongated sori which are borne on the underside of the blade, sometimes under the rolled edges of the leaf segments; and 4) by the gametophyte being green, heart shaped, terrestrial, and bearing the sex organs on its lower surface. However, significant changes in the family's circumscription has occurred over the last several decades of the twentieth century (Weatherby, 1948; Smith, 1993a) and the significance of these sporangial characters for classification purposes has been diminished. As a result, a number of new families are now recognized from this once much larger group. In many previous works (see for example Clewell, 1985; Wunderlin, 1982), the Polypodiaceae were construed to also include many of the taxa which are included in this volume within the families Aspleniaceae, Dyropteridaceae, Pteridaceae, and Thelypteridaceae. Though some taxonomists disagree with these changes, these newly-defined groups will hopefully lead to a better understanding of phylogenetic affinities in the pteridophytes, as well as make it easier for fern enthusiasts to distinguish species of these families in the field.

Key to the Genera of the Polypodiaceae

1. Leaves simple, undivided.

  2. Sori borne in distinctive, conspicuous marginal lines or bands only on the distal (outermost) 1/3 to 1/2 of the blades, soral bands typically terminating just short of the tip of the frond . . . . *Neurodium*

  2. Sori rounded or oblong, distinct from each other and not joined as a single marginal line.

    3. Blades conspicuously scaly with two-colored scales, sori distinct from each other and oblong in shape . . . . *Pleopeltis*

    3. Blades lacking scales, or scales scattered, mostly on the midrib, and not two colored.

      4. Leaves with parallel lateral veins, these often conspicuous (less so in *Campyloneurum costatum*); stems 2 -10 mm in diameter, sori usually in two or more rows on either side of the midrib (some leaves of *Campyloneurum angustifolium* with only a single line) . . . . *Campyloneurum*

      4. Veins of the leaves not parallel, obscrue, forking and rejoining; stems less than 1.5 mm in diameter; sori borne in single rows on either side of the midvein . . . . *Microgramma*

1. Leaves pinnately divided or lobed.

  5. Blades densely covered with conspicuous, two-colored, dark-centered scales; plants forming dense populations on oaks, magnolias, and other hardwood trees . . . . *Pleopeltis*

  5. Blades lacking scales, or lower surfaces sparsely to moderately covered with inconspicuous, one-colored scales.

    6. Blades pinnate . . . . *Polypodium*

    6. Blades deeply pinnatifid to pectinate.

      7. Blades pectinate, less than 20 cm wide, with single-colored scales and/or hairs, blade segments linear in outline . . . . *Pecluma*

      7. Blades deeply pinnatifid or lobed, many greater than 25 cm wide, without hairs or scales.

        8. Stems usually greater than 8 mm in diameter, stem scales conspicuous, reddish to golden . . . . *Phlebodium*

        8. Stems usually less than 8 mm in diameter, stem scales brownish to blackish brown . . . . *Phymatosorus*

CAMPYLONEURUM

The strap fern genus takes its common name from the long, simple, straplike leaves of its member species. The genus name is derived from the Greek *kampylos,* or curved, and *neuron,* or nerve, and references the often curving central vein. The genus contains nearly 50 species, most of which are restricted to the tropics.

Four species of strap fern have been reported in the United States, all restricted to Florida. However, only three are likely to be, or to have ever been, extant in the flora. *C. latum* T. Moore was reportedly collected by J. J. Soar and A. A. Eaton in 1903 in Hattie Bauer Hammock in Dade County and was later reported by Eaton (1906) and Underwood (1906). But the validity of this collection is somewhat in doubt since it contained a mixture of leaves from both *C. latum* and *C. phyllitidis* (Wunderlin, *Flora of Florida,* in press). The species has not been collected in the state since. Previous authors have included it within our flora (Small, 1913; Long & Lakela, 1971; Lakela & Long, 1976), but more recent accounts (Lellinger, 1985; Nauman, 1993a; Keller, 1994; Wunderlin, 1998) have suggested that the plant is no longer present in the state (if, indeed, it ever was). Oddly, given its uncertain status, this species is listed as endangered on the state's Regulated Plant Index (see appendix 3). It may be distinguished from both *C. costatum* and *C. angustifolium* by its leaves being generally more than 6 cm wide, and from *C. phyllitidis* by its dark green, undulating, somewhat shorter and wider leaves, and by at least some petioles being more than 9 cm long. *C. latum* is not included in the descriptions below, but a cultivated specimen from Puerto Rico, which is now growing in south Florida, is pictured in photo 117 and 118.

Narrow Strap Fern

Campyloneurum angustifolium (Swartz) Fee   **Photos 114, 115**

Form: A narrow-leaved fern with arching, pendent fronds and a knotted, slender, short-creeping stem.

Fronds: Arching to pendent, to about 60 cm long.

Petiole: Very short to essentially absent, not exceeding about 8 cm long.

Blade: Linear, curving, tapering to both ends, dark green to yellowish, 30 - 60 cm long, to about 1.5 cm wide; margins sometimes inrolled; veins inconspicuous and slightly to strongly curved.

Sori: Round, borne in 1 - 2 conspicuous rows on either side of the central vein.

Habitat: Hammocks; epiphytic on bases of pond apples *(Annona glabra* Linnaeus), magnolias, and oaks.

Distribution: Collected in Dade, Monroe, and Collier Counties but now probably limited only to the latter, especially in Fakahatchee Strand State Preserve; more widely distributed in the West Indies, Mexico, and Central and South America. Eaton (1906) and Small (1918, 1931) report this species as occurring on live oaks *(Quercus virginiana* Miller) in Timm's hammock, near Homestead, where it is apparently no longer present. Darling (1961) reports having seen cultivated specimens that were taken from this location.

Remarks: The specific epithet of this species means "narrow leaved," a character that distinguishes it from others in its genus. It could perhaps be confused with the more widely distributed shoestring fern *(Vittaria lineata).* The latter differs from *C. angustifolium* by having narrower leaves with the sori borne in grooves near the blade margins. *C. angustifolium* is listed as endangered by the Florida Department of Agriculture.

Synonyms: *Polypodium angustifolium* Swartz

Tailed Strap Fern

Campyloneurum costatum (Kunze) C. Presl   **Photo 116**

Form: An arching to pendent epiphytic fern with a narrow, short-creeping stem.

Fronds: Strap-shaped, stiff, arching to pendulous, to about 50 cm long.

Petiole: Relatively long and distinct, to about 15 cm.

Blade: Narrowly elliptic, leathery, dark green, 20 - 40 cm long, 2 - 6 cm wide, long tapering to the base and pinched to a point at the apex; margins wavy to undulate; veins inconspicuous and slightly to strongly curved.

Sori: Round, borne in up to several rows on either side of the midvein.

Habitat: Hammocks and deep sloughs in Fakahatchee Strand and Big Cypress Swamp.

Distribution: Collected in Florida in both Dade and Collier Counties but now probably restricted to the latter and only in the Fakahatchee Strand and Big Cypress Swamp; somewhat more widely distributed in the West Indies and Central and South America.

Remarks: This is a rare species in the state and is listed as endangered by the Florida Department of Agriculture. It differs from *C. angustifolium* by having leaves that range 2 - 6 cm in width, and from *C. phyllitidis* by the blades having inconspicuous veins, and being acuminate, or pinched to a point, at the apices. Young specimens of this species usually have a distinct petiole, which helps distinguish them from those of *C. phyllitidis,* which usually do not. In addition, the present species is generally arching to pendulous with dark green leaves, whereas *C. phyllitidis* is more or less erect with lighter green leaves. The specific epithet, *costatum,* refers to the conspicuous costa, or midvein, of the leaf.

Synonyms: *Polypodium costatum* Kunze.

Long Strap Fern

Campyloneurum phyllitidis (Linnaeus) C. Presl   **Photos 119, 120**

Form: A relatively large, frequent, epiphytic fern with a relatively thick, short-creeping stem bearing few to many fronds.

Fronds: Erect to slightly arching, to about 1.4 m long.

Petiole: Absent or to a maximum of about 9 cm long and narrowly winged.

Blade: Narrowly elliptic to nearly linear, 24 - 140 cm long, 3 - 12 cm wide, leathery, yellowish green, long tapering to the base; margins entire to slightly wavy; veins conspicuous, parallel, straight to only slightly curved, angling-ascending from the midvein to the margins.

Sori: Round, borne in two parallel rows that lie between and parallel to the lateral veins; rows extending from the midvein to the blade margins.

Habitat: Hammocks and swamps; epiphytic on trees and sometimes epipetric on limestone in sinks.

Distribution: Fairly common throughout the central and southern peninsula from about Volusia, Lake, and Citrus Counties southward; also found on the Keys.

Remarks: The leaves of this species are generally wider and longer than those of *C. costatum* and have conspicuous rather than obscure lateral veins and long-tapering

apices, but see remarks for *C. costatum.*
Synonyms: *Polypodium phyllitidis* Linnaeus.

MICROGRAMMA

The genus *Microgramma* contains 20 to 30 tropical species distributed mostly in Africa, the West Indies, Mexico, and the Americas. A single species is represented in the United States and it is confined to southern Florida. The genus name derives from combining the Greek words *mikros* for small and *gramme* for line. The sori in the type species are elongate and borne in a linelike arrangement on the lower surfaces of the leaves.

Climbing Vine Fern

Microgramma heterophylla (Linnaeus) Wherry   **Photos 121, 122**

Form: An epiphytic, somewhat climbing fern with a slender, long-creeping stem with reddish to brown scales that are dark near the base (requires magnification).
Fronds: Erect, moderately spaced along the stem; sterile and fertile differing in appearance.
Petiole: Distinct, to about 2 cm long.
Blade: Fertile blades linear to narrowly lanceolate, 3 - 11 cm long, typically less than 1 cm wide, with short petioles; sterile blades typically lacking petioles, elliptic to oblanceolate, to about 4 cm long and 1.5 cm wide, shorter and wider than the fertile blades.
Sori: Round, borne in a single row on either side of the midvein and located about halfway between the midvein and margin.
Habitat: Tropical hammocks; epiphytic and climbing on smooth-barked trees and logs, also epipetric on limestone.
Distribution: Uncommon, scattered populations might exist in southernmost Florida in Collier, Monroe, and Dade counties, though it may be extant presently only in Collier County; also reported from Palm Beach County, but likely in error. Darling (1961) reported this species off the Loop Road south of the Tamiami Trail in 1942, Knappen (1929) reported it from Key Largo growing on the bark of milkbark trees *(Drypetes diversifolia* Krug & Urban), Eaton (1906) reported it from Hattie Bauer Hammock in Dade County, and Safford (1912) reported it as common on Key Largo in 1881, climbing over shrubs. Knappen commented that its stem was climbing "straight up, throwing out to one or both sides the closely appressed fronds. The ruddy tone from the hairs of the stem and the vivid green of the thin fronds [made] a striking contrast to the white bark" (p. 115). Where found, this plant tends to be plentiful, but it is not found in many locations.
Remarks: This is the single member of its genus in the United States. It is not common in Florida and is listed as endangered by the Florida Department of Agriculture. Its climbing habit, and relatively short, lanceolate leaves which are not hairy below, in combination with its single line of rounded, medial sori are usually enough to distinguish it from other Florida ferns. It is most similar to *Pleopeltis astrolepis* and *Neurodium lanceolatum.* However, the first of these two has stalked, star-shaped, two-colored scales that clothe the lower surfaces

of its leaves, and the second has sori that parallel portions of the blade margins. Though this species was found in Florida on Key Largo, where it still persists, as early as 1881, it was not found on the mainland until 1903.

Synonyms: *Polypodium heterophyllum* Linnaeus; *Phymatodes heterophyllum* (Linnaeus) Small.

NEURODIUM

The genus *Neurodium* was formerly called *Paltonium.* The genus is monotypic, meaning that it contains only a single species, and differs from all other genera of the Polypodiaceae by having the spores borne in linear, marginal clusters near the ends of the fronds rather than in rounded sori mostly between the margins and midribs throughout the length of the fronds.

The name for this genus is sometimes seen listed as *Nevrodium,* the name that was used when the genus was established in 1850 (see for example, Wunderlin, 1998). Though the latter name may actually be the better name, *Neurodium* is used here to maintain consistency with the *Flora of North America.* The name is derived from "neuron," or nerve, in reference to the fine veinlets.

Figure 25.
Neurodium lanceolatum

Ribbon Fern

Neurodium lanceolatum (Linnaeus) Fee   **Photo 123, Page 121**

Form: A tropical epiphyte with a slender, scaly, short-creeping stem and simple leaves.

Fronds: 1 - 4.5 dm long, erect to arching, borne in clusters of few to many.

Petiole: To about 4 cm long but often shorter, brownish in color, grooved toward the base.

Blade: Simple, narrowly lanceolate to nearly linear, 10 - 35 cm long, 1 - 4 cm wide, narrowly tapering toward the base; venation distinct, areoles toward the midrib much larger than those nearer the margins.

Sori: Borne in crowded, linear clusters along the margins of the apical 1/3 of the blade but terminating within about 5 mm of the blade apex.

Habitat: Epiphytic; hammocks and mangroves.

Distribution: Previously restricted to only a very few localities in southernmost Florida and collected in the state only in Dade and Monroe Counties, where it may no longer be extant; more generally distributed in the Bahamas, Jamaica, the Greater and Lesser Antilles, the Virgin Islands, Belize, Guatemala, Honduras, and French Guiana. It is most recently known in Florida from Key Largo, but was formerly also known from Elliott's Key, Old Rhodes Key, and on the shores of Biscayne Key at the eastern extremity of the Keys (Safford, 1912; Small, 1918, 1931).

Remarks: This species was formerly placed with the genus *Pteris* due to the position of its sori along the margins of the blades. It is associated with *Vittaria lineata* but is very rare in Florida, if it exists at all, and is easily distinguised from the latter species by its wider blades and distinctive marginal sori. It is also similar to *Microgramma heterophylla* and *Pleopeltis astrolepis.* However, its distinctive sori, as described above and pictured in figure 25 and photo 123 readily distinguish it from both of these latter species. It was first discovered in Florida in Dade County in 1881 and is listed as endangered by the Florida Department of Agriculture.

Synonyms: *Pteris lanceolata* Linnaeus; *Paltonium lanceolatum* (Linnaeus) C. Presl; *Nevrodium lanceolatum* (Linnaeus) Fee

PECLUMA

The genus *Pecluma* consists of 30 species worldwide, only three of which occur in Florida. Until the mid 1980s, members of the genus were included within the genus *Polypodium,* as were many species in the family Polypodiaceae. They were segregated (Price, 1983) based on a number of morphological and microscopic features, and may be distinguished from others in the family by combination of their short-creeping stems, deeply and narrowly cut (pinnatisect), comblike blades with more than 20 pairs of essentially linear pinnae, and round, ungrooved rachises. The name *Pecluma* results from combining the Latin words *pectinatus* and *plumula,* which mean "comblike" and "feathery," respectively, in reference to the deeply cut, mostly distichous or featherlike shape of the fronds.

Widespread Polypody

Pecluma dispersa (A. M. Evans) M. G. Price   **Photo 124**

Form: An epipetric to epiphytic, deeply cut polypody with a scaly, short-creeping stem.

Fronds: To about 3.5 dm tall, erect or arching, rather closely spaced along the stem.

Petiole: Black, 5 - 21 cm long.

Rachis: Black, scaly with narrowly lanceolate, brownish scales.

Blade: Deeply pinnatifid or pectinate, mostly lance shaped in overall outline, 17 - 70 cm long, 4.5 - 11 cm wide, deeply cut into more than 20 pairs of narrow segments; segments linear in overall shape, to about 5 mm wide or a little wider, finely hairy on the surfaces, rounded at the apices, with two-forked veins (requires 20x magnification and transmitted light).

Sori: Round, borne between the margins and midribs of the pinnae.

Habitat: Limestone outcrops and hammocks.

Distribution: Fairly common but sporadically distributed in limestone-rich areas from about Alachua County southward to about Martin and Hillsborough Counties, with outlier populations in Dade and Monroe Counties, including Pumpkin Key, where it was first collected by J. K. Small in 1915 and 1920, and later by A. M. Evans in 1963. The latter population is unique because of its tendency to remain in a juvenile, nonfertile stage (Evans, 1968).

Remarks: The epipetric to epiphytic habit, in combination with the mostly lance-shaped fronds, twice-forked veins, and conspicuous rachis scales distinguish this species from others in the genus. This plant was first described by Murray Evans (1968) from specimens collected in the historical fern grottoes in Citrus County, Florida. The specific epithet means widespread. It is listed as endangered by the Florida Department of Agriculture.

Synonyms: *Polypodium dispersum* A. M. Evans.

Plume Polypody

Pecluma plumula (Humboldt & Bonpland ex Willdenow)
M. G. Price   **Photos 125, 126**

Form: An epiphytic to sometimes epipetric fern with a brown-scaly stem; often curling and appearing to die during droughts or dry weather but appearing healthy again with rehydration, much as the resurrection fern *(Pleopeltis polypodioides)*.

Fronds: Closely set along the stem, pendent to erect, 15 - 50 cm long.

Petiole: Blackish, 3 - 15 cm long, thinly and minutely hairy.

Rachis: Black, scaly with lanceolate, whitish to brownish scales.

Blade: Deeply pinnatifid or pectinate, narrowly elliptic in overall outline and gradually tapering to both ends, typically 15 - 25 cm long but potentially twice this long, 3 - 7.5 cm wide, deeply cut into more than 20 pairs of linear, closely-set, bluntly-pointed segments; segments to about 3 mm wide, minutely hairy, veins obscure and once-forked.

Sori: Small, round, borne about halfway between the midribs and margins of the blade segments.

Habitat: Epiphytic on hammock trees.

Distribution: Fairly common throughout much of central Florida from about Duval to

Hillsborough, Polk, and Brevard Counties; also collected in Martin, Dade, and Monroe Counties. Reported by Small (1918) in the early part of the twentieth century as being present in south Florida only in hammocks of the Florida Keys.

Remarks: The once-forked veins, narrowly linear blade, conspicuous rachis scales, and predominantly (though not entirely) epiphytic habit distinguish this species from others in the genus. The specific epithet *plumula* means "plume like," a characterization of the distichous or featherlike fronds. This species is listed as endangered by the Florida Department of Agriculture.

Synonyms: *Polypodium plumula* Humboldt & Bonpland ex Willdenow.

Comb Polypody

Pecluma ptilodon (Kunze) M.G. Price var. *caespitosa*
(Jenman) Lellinger   **Photos 127, 128, 129**

Form: A mostly terrestrial (to occasionally epiphytic) polypody with a thick, black-scaly stem.
Fronds: Clustered along the stem, erect to arching, typically to about 8 dm tall but potentially taller.
Petiole: 3 - 15 cm long and dark, reddish brown.
Rachis: Sparsely scaly with filiform scales.
Blade: Deeply pinnatifid or pectinate, long elliptic to narrowly ovate in overall outline and conspicuously tapering to both base and apex, 27 - 90 cm long, 5 - 18 cm wide, deeply divided into linear, bluntly-pointed segments, the lowermost segments typically reduced to auricles; segments 4 - 8 mm wide with two- to four-forked veins.
Sori: Oval in shape, borne in a row between the midveins and margins of the blade segments.
Habitat: Mostly terrestrial in moist woods and hammocks; sometimes on limestone or rotten logs.
Distribution: Widely distributed across the Florida peninsula from about Duval County southward.
Remarks: The mostly terrestrial habit, two- to four-forked veins, and filiform to absent rachis scales distinguish this species from others in the genus. The varietal epithet means "growing in tufts" in reference to the tuftlike frond clusters. *Polypodium pectinatum* has also been reported for Florida by Small (1931, 1938). However, it has now been shown that this name was wrongly applied to the present species.

This species is listed as endangered by the Florida Department of Agriculture.
Synonyms: *Polypodium pectinatum* Linnaeus var. *caespitosum* Jenman; *P. ptilodon* Kunze var. *caespitosum* (Jenman) A. M. Evans.

Goldfoot Fern, Golden Polypody, Serpent-Fern

Phlebodium aureum (Linnaeus) J. Smith   **Photos 130, 131**

Form: An epiphyte on sabal palms *(Sabal palmetto* Loddiges), with long-creeping, thickened stems (to about 1.5 cm in diameter or more) that are densely clothed with rather large (to about 1 cm long), reddish brown to golden, narrowly lanceolate scales. Hence the common name goldfoot fern.

Fronds: Typically arching or pendent, 3 - 13 dm long, bright green, sometimes with a whitish cast.

Petiole: Rather long, from 12 - 50 cm, grooved, shiny dark brown to straw colored, without hairs but typically having a few scales toward the base.

Rachis: Shiny, similar to the petiole in color.

Blade: Deeply pinnatifid or pinnatisect, large and conspicuous, 1.5 - 8 dm long, 1 - 5 dm wide, divided into lanceolate segments, each segment 6 - 20 cm long, 1 - 4 cm wide with entire to slightly wavy margins, blade terminated by a long, terminal segment with a blunt apex.

Sori: Round, borne in conspicuous lines on either side of the axis of the blade segments.

Habitat: Epiphytic on trees and logs of hammocks and wet swamps; most often associated with old leaf bases of the sabal palm.

Distribution: Widespread across the New World tropics, including the West Indies, Mexico, and Central and South America; found in Florida mostly in the central and southern peninsula from about Nassau County southward along the east coast and Dixie and Alachua Counties southward along the west coast and central peninsula; a disjunct population, which was first collected in 1957 by the late ornithologist Dr. Henry M. Stevenson, occurs on St. Vincent Island National Wildlife Refuge along the Franklin County coast.

Remarks: The relatively large, deeply divided blades, distinctive rows of sori, and epiphytic habit distinguish this species in its habitat. It is not likely to be confused with any other Florida fern, with the possible exception of *Phymatosorus scolopendria* (Burman f.) Pichi-Sermolli (see photo 132, 133), a cultivated species from the Old World tropics first reported in Florida by Correll (1938). This latter species, whose common names include serpent fern and wart fern, has escaped in southern Florida and has been collected in both Dade (somewhat recently) and Manatee Counties. *P. scolopendria* is superficially similar to the present species, but has much narrower blade segments, a thinner stem (less than 8 mm in diameter), and blackish brown rather than reddish brown or golden stem scales.

Goldfoot fern is a well-loved plant that is often cultivated and for which a number of cultivars have been developed. Its genus name comes from the Greek word "phlebos," or veins, in reference to the species' prominent venation. The specific epithet means golden, an apt description of its colorful stem scales. One plant, which was collected from a fallen palm in a yard in Ormond Beach in Volusia County in the early 1980s, is still thriving as a potted plant in Panama City, Florida, on the remains of the original base. Though somewhat common throughout much of Florida, goldfoot fern is available in the trade and should not be taken from the wild.

Synonyms: *Polypodium aureum* Linnaeus.

PLEOPELTIS

Two species of the genus *Pleopeltis* occur in Florida. Both were formerly assigned to the genus *Polypodium*. The common name for the genus is shielded-sorus ferns. The genus's botanical name derives from the combination of the Greek words *pleos* or many, and *pelte,* or shield, a reference to the stalked (peltate) scales that cover and protect the young sori.

Star-Scaled Fern

Pleopeltis astrolepis (Liebmann) E. Fournier   **Page 127**

Form: An epiphytic fern with a slender, long-creeping, branched stem that is clothed with clusters of brown hairs and appressed, blackish scales.

Fronds: Undivided, narrowly lanceolate to nearly linear, to about 20 cm long and closely to well spaced along the stem.

Petiole: Very short when present, usually not exceeding about 2.5 cm long, dark colored, slightly to conspicuously flattened and sparsely scaly.

Blade: Simple, essentially linear in outline, 5 - 20 cm long, to about 2 cm wide, sparsely to moderately clothed with rounded, two-colored scales with dark centers and fringed margins (magnification required); scales more numerous on the lower surface.

Sori: Elongated or oval, borne on the terminal 2/3 of the blade in single rows on either side of the midrib.

Habitat: Swamps, epiphytic on pond apples *(Annona glabra* Linnaeus).

Distribution: This species is fairly common in the West Indies including Jamaica, Trinidad, Tobago, and the Greater and Lesser Antilles, as well as in continental tropical America from Mexico to Brazil and Bolivia. It has been documented in Florida only in Broward County, but the site of this report has now been destroyed and the species may no longer be extant in Florida. (This species has also been reported from Palm Beach County, but according to Keith Bradley [personal communication, 1999], this latter report was based on a mislabeled specimen from the Broward County station.)

Remarks: It is not clear how this species got its start in Florida but may have arrived by hurricane-driven spores. Whether it will persist or be found in other parts of the state is still to be seen. Its common name and specific epithet come from the stalked, two-colored, superficially star-shaped scales that clothe the leaf surfaces. It is most easily distinguished from other, simple-leaved members of the family by these scales in conjunction with the sori being elongated and borne on the terminal 2/3 of the leaves. *Microgramma heterophylla* is similar but lacks scales on the tissue of the lower surfaces of the leaves (but may have a few scales on the midrib), and its sori are rounded. *Neurodium lanceolatum* has sori lining the margins near the end of the blade rather than being borne between the midrib and the margins. *P. astrolepis* is listed as endangered by the Florida Department of Agriculture.

Synonyms: *Polypodium astrolepis* Liebmann; *Grammitis elongata* Swartz (not *Polypodium elongatum* Aiton); *G. lanceolata* Schkuhr; *G. revoluta* Sprengel ex. Willdenow; *Pleopeltis revoluta* (Sprengel ex. Willdenow) A. R. Smith.

Figure 26 .
Pleopeltis astrolepis

Resurrection Fern, Gray's Polypody, Gray Polypody, Scaly Polypody, Tree Polypody

Pleopeltis polypodioides (Linnaeus) E. G. Andrews & Windham var.
michauxiana (Weatherby) E. G. Andrews & Windham.   **Photo 134**

Form: An epiphytic fern with a slender, creeping, often exposed stem; often found growing on live oak *(Quercus virginiana* Miller) and southern magnolia *(Magnolia grandiflora* Linnaeus), but also on other species as well as roadside or clay embankments.

Fronds: 5 - 25 cm long, dark green when fresh; curled, brown, and appearing dead when dry.

Petiole: To about 8 cm long, grooved, round in cross-section, very scaly with overlapping scales, especially when young.

Rachis: Greenish and scaly.

Blade: Like an elongated triangle in overall shape, deeply pinnatifid, dark green and essentially without hairs and scales above, densely scaly below.

Pinnae: Oblong with blunt tips.

Sori: Round, distinct, so deeply set on the lower surfaces of the pinnae as to produce conspicuous,

127

raised bumps on the upper surfaces.

Habitat: Epiphytic on the trunks of rough-barked trees; also on rotting wood and old wooden shingles, clay embankments, limestone ledges.

Distribution: Throughout Florida.

Remarks: This is one of Florida's best known and most easily identified ferns and, like Spanish moss *(Tillandsia usneoides* [Linnaeus] Linnaeus), is a characteristic element of the southern flora. Its common name, resurrection fern, refers to the habit of its leaves, which become brown and appear dead during dry periods, but "resurrect" themselves after rains and rapidly become green and lush.

It is interesting to note that the dehydrated leaves of resurrection fern curl upward and inward rather than downward, a situation that encourages rather than discourages water loss since the lower surfaces of the leaves contain the stomata, microscopic openings in the epidermal tissue that allow for respiration. At first consideration, this propensity toward rapid moisture loss seems an odd adaptation that, in most plants, would encourage desiccation and death. However, in the resurrection fern, this rolling upward is an adaptation that insures rapid rehydration when rain returns. Unlike most other vascular plants, the resurrection fern can loose up to 97% of its water and still remain vital. Hence, during extended dry periods, plants of the species wither, but do not die. When rain returns, the scales on the lower, or exposed, surfaces of the leaves actually trap and direct water into the middle tissue of the blade, insuring quick and efficient rehydration. Thus, resurrection fern's adaptation facilitates rapid rehydration, rather than preventing dehydration. Were the leaves to curl downward, the leaves would rehydrate much more slowly (Pessin, 1924; Moran, 1998).

Resurrection fern has long been known and is most often seen listed by its scientific synonym, *Polypodium polypodioides.* Though it is quite similar in overall appearance to *P. virginianum,* a northern species that ranges as far south as the north Georgia mountains, it was reclassified into the genus *Pleopeltis* due to its densely scaly blade and petiole. Its specific epithet means "resembling *Polypodium.*"

A total of six varieties have been described for this species. Though Florida's specimens (as are those in the rest of its range in the southeastern United States) are thought to represent only the current variety, some populations in the lower peninsula are similar to the West Indian var. *polypodioides.* The two may be distinguished by the distribution of scales on the upper surfaces of the blades. Those of var. *michauxiana* are mostly without scales, except for a few on the rachis, while those of var. *polypodioides* usually have scattered scales (Wunderlin, *Flora of Florida,* in press).

Synonyms: *Polypodium polypodioides* (Linnaeus) Watt var. *michauxianum* Weatherby.

Angle-Vein Fern
Polypodium triseriale Swartz **Photos 135, 136**

Form: An epiphytic fern with a thickened, creeping, brown-scaly stem to about 1.5 cm in diameter.

Fronds: Arching to pendent, to about 1 m long, few in number, closely to well spaced along the stem.

Petiole: 10 - 35 cm long, reddish brown to straw colored, thin, lacking hairs.

Rachis: Without hairs.

Blade: Pinnate, large, 15 - 60 cm wide, terminating with a single pinna that is similar to the lateral pinnae, dull green in color and firmly herbaceous to slightly leathery to the touch.

Pinnae: Borne in 5 to 12 pairs, well spaced along the rachis, narrowly lanceolate in overall outline and typically less than 35 mm wide, terminating with a tapering point, sessile but widened at the base with tissue attaching directly to the rachis so as to have the superficial appearance of a winged stalk; margins entire or slightly wavy; venation netted, areoles often containing free veins.

Sori: Round, borne in one to three rows between the midrib and margins.

Habitat: Epiphytic in low, coastal hammocks.

Distribution: Widespread across tropical America and known from Jamaica, Puerto Rico, Lesser Antilles, Trinidad, and perhaps other locations in the West Indies, westward to southern Mexico and southward to Brazil and Bolivia; documented in Florida only in Collier County, where it may now be extirpated. It is sometimes seen in cultivation.

Remarks: This species is unlike any other member of its genus in Florida. It is immediately recognized by its rather large, pinnate (as opposed to pinnatifid) blades and mostly 2 - 3 rows of sori (its specific epithet literally means "three series," a description of the typically three rows of sori). It was discovered and collected in Florida in 1924 by J. K. Small and C. A. Mosier (Small, 1938), but has not been collected since and may be extirpated in Florida. It likely arrived in the state as wind-blown spores from the West Indies or continental tropical America.

Synonyms: *Goniophlebium triseriale* (Swartz) Pichi-Sermolli; *G. brasiliense* (Poiret) Farwell; *Polypodium brasiliense* Poiret.

PSILOTACEAE - WHISK-FERN FAMILY

The whisk-fern family includes two genera and up to eight species worldwide. Only a single genus and species occurs in the United States. Members of the family lack roots and are characterized by simple to branched, erect stems with reduced, leaflike or bractlike appendages rather than true leaves. The name for both the family and type genus derives from the Greek word *psilos,* which translates as naked and refers to the leafless aerial shoots.

Whisk-fern has been used medicinally in Hawaii (Hawkes & Degener, 1950). A tea derived from the plant was used as a remedy for thrush in children, as well as for a laxative or cathartic for adults. The spores were also given to babies as a remedy for diarrhea or used as a talcum powder to prevent chafing.

Whisk-Fern

Psilotum nudum (Linnaeus) Palisot de Beauvois   **Photo 137**

Form: A rootless fern with creeping, underground, fleshy, hairy, black, coral-like subterranium stems, and greenish aerial stems; having the appearance of a leafless twig or small, deciduous, leafless shrub.

Aerial Stem: Erect, greenish, 2 - 5 dm tall, several-branched, twiglike, bearing a few irregularly-spaced, tiny, scalelike appendages.

Sporangia: Yellowish to greenish yellow, 2 - 3 mm wide and often conspicuously thicker than the width of the stem, three-lobed, borne solitary on the upper parts of the green, aerial stem.

Habitat: Terrestrial in wet woods, swamps, mesic hammocks, on and around tree bases, commonly those of the sabal palm *(Sabal palmetto)*; also epiphytic on logs and in the forks of trees.

Distribution: From the central panhandle counties of Gulf, Leon, and Wakulla, eastward, southward and throughout the peninsula.

Remarks: No other fern has the "leafless twig" appearance of the whisk-fern, except, perhaps for the wedgelet fern *(Odontosoria clavata),* which grows mostly on rocky glades. The species was discovered in Florida in the late 1800s, but ranges throughout the tropics. It is also sporadically distributed along the eastern edge of the Southeastern Coastal Plain as far north as South Carolina. The specific epithet, *nudum,* which was originally conferred by Linnaeus, means bare and, like the genus name, refers to the plant's leafless stems.

This is one of several pteridophyte species that do not bear aboveground gametophytes. The tiny prothalli grow entirely underground, in crevices, or in decaying stumps or trunks of trees.

Synonyms: *Lycopodium nudum* Linnaeus

PTERIDACEAE - MAIDENHAIR FERN FAMILY

As treated here, the maidenhair fern family is represented in Florida by six genera, which include 22 species and one hybrid. Worldwide, however, the family includes about 40 genera and more than 1000 species. The scientific name for the family was given by Linnaeus and comes from the Greek word *pteris* for fern, which was derived from *pteron,* which means "wing" or "feather" in reference to the shape of the pinnae and fronds, respectively. *Pteris* is a common component in the names of many fern families, genera, and species.

As with some other large families of pteridophytes, the precise circumscription of the Pteridaceae is subject to controversy among botanists and pteridologists. Wunderlin (1998), for example, divides the Florida genera into the families Adiantaceae and Pteridaceae, and includes the genera *Adiantum, Cheilanthes, Pellaea,* and *Pityrogramma* in the former, and *Acrostichum* and *Pteris* in the latter. Lellinger (1985), on the other hand, who also includes the genera *Acrostichum* and *Pteris* within the Pteridaceae, treats the other four Florida genera (as well as several non-Florida genera) in the family Sinopteridaceae, a family which is not included here or in volume 2 of the *Flora of North America* (1993). Suffice it to say that future changes in the circumscription of this group are likely.

Keys to the Genera of Pteridaceae

1. Sporangia borne in solitary sori beneath the reflexed marginal lobes of ultimate segments; veins of leaves conspicuous . . . . *Adiantum*

1. Sporangia borne more less throughout the lower surfaces of the blades, or in more or less continuous lines along, and sometimes below, the curled blade margin, veins of the blades obscure.

   2. Sporangia completely covering the lower surface of fertile pinnae; fronds typically exceeding to much exceeding 1 m in length . . . . *Acrostichum*

   2. Sporangia scattered across the lower blade surfaces, but not completely covering the lower surface, or sporangia confined to the margins, often borne in more or less continuous lines along and sometimes below the curled blade margins; fronds typically less than 1 m tall.

      3. Sporangia scattered across the lower surfaces of the blade . . . . *Pityrogramma*

      3. Sporangia borne along the margins.

         4. Petioles longitudinally ridged, with two to three conspicuous grooves . . . . *Pteris*

         4. Petioles more or less rounded, not two to three grooved.

            5. Lower surfaces of blades distinctly hairy or glandular, fronds delicately cut, pinnules incised . . . . *Cheilanthes*

            5. Lower surfaces of blades essentially lacking hairs, fronds coarsely cut, pinnules oblong to lanceolate in outline, pinnules essentially entire . . . . *Pellaea*

ACROSTICHUM

In his 1938 treatise on the ferns of the southeastern United States, John K. Small remarks that the "leather-ferns are quite suggestive of primeval vegetation" (p. 67). Anyone who has visited a wetland rich with either species of *Acrostichum* will appreciate Small's assessment. None of Florida's pteridophytes are so large, luxuriant, or reminiscent of prehistoric verdure. Only two species of leather fern occur in Florida, and only a few more worldwide. The genus name comes from the Greek words *acros* and *stichos,* which mean tip and row respectively, and refer to the fact that only the uppermost pinnae of some species bear sporangia.

Coast Leather Fern, Golden Leather Fern, Leather Fern

Acrostichum aureum Linnaeus   **Photo 138**

Form: A robust, coarse, conspicuous fern with large, tufted fronds and creeping or ascending, often-branched stems.

Fronds: Arching, 1 - 3 m tall, to about 50 cm wide, borne in large, tufted crowns.

Petiole: Grooved, to about 1 cm in diameter and scaly near the base, without hairs above.

Rachis: Rounded below, conspicuously grooved above, often with short spines on the lower part.

Blade: Pinnate, longer than the petiole, 1 - 3 m long, with 12 to 20 pairs of alternate, typically well-spaced pinnae that do not overlap at the base.

Pinnae: Lanceolate to oblong, typically 10 - 30 cm long, sometimes longer, 1 - 7 cm wide, often less than 30 in number, only the upper five or fewer pairs of the fertile blades bearing sporangia, stalks of lowermost pinnae usually exceeding 2 cm long, midveins conspicuous, lateral veins netted and diverging from the midrib at an angle, areoles longer than wide; fertile pinnae brownish below and with inrolled margins, adjacent fertile pinnae usually well-spaced on the rachis, bases not overlapping.

Sori: Sporangia covering the lower surfaces of fertile pinnae and feltlike in appearance.

Habitat: Mangrove swamps, salt- and brackish marshes, low coastal hammocks.

Distribution: Along the western and southeasternmost coasts of southernmost Florida from about Pinellas to Dade Counties.

Remarks: This species may be most readily distinguished from *A. danaeifolium* by its well-spaced upper pinnae, only the uppermost five or less pairs of which are fertile on fertile blades, by the short spines on the lowermost part of the rachis when they are present, and by the stalks of the lower pinnae usually being up to 3 cm long (as opposed to 2 cm or less). With practice, the uppermost, fertile pinnae can be distinguished even when veiwed from the upper surface. *A. aureum* was first discovered in Florida by the French botanist Andre Michaux (1746-1802) in 1789 along what is now the Indian River. The specific epithet means golden yellow. It is listed as endangered by the Florida Department of Agriculture.

Giant Leather Fern, Inland Leather Fern

Acrostichum danaeifolium Langsdorff & Fischer   **Photos 139, 140**

Form: A relatively large, robust, coarse, conspicuous fern with an erect, stout, usually unbranched stem and fleshy roots.

Fronds: Tufted from a large crown, 1 - 5 m tall, 15 - 60 cm wide.

Petiole: Grooved, to nearly 2 cm in diameter and scaly near the base, otherwise without hairs.

Rachis: Distinctly grooved below with several shallow grooves, flattened to grooved above.

Blade: Pinnate, to about 5 m tall, leathery, with large pinnae.

Pinnae: Large, lanceolate, 7 - 30 cm long, 2 - 5 cm wide, usually 40 to 60 in number, borne alternately along the rachis, bases of upper one-third or so of adjacent pinnae often overlapping, stalks of lowermost pinnae usually less than 2 cm long; areoles longer than wide; all or most pinnae of fertile blades containing sporangia; veinlets on lower surface stiffly pubescent.

Sori: Sporangia covering the lower surfaces of fertile pinnae and feltlike in appearance; fertile pinnae distributed nearly throughout the length of the blade.

Habitat: Freshwater and brackish marshes, freshwater swamps, sinkholes in hammocks; more likely to be found inland than A. aureum.

Distribution: Throughout the peninsula from about Dixie and St. Johns Counties southward, more common in the southern counties.

Remarks: This species may be most readily distinguished from *A. aureum,* which is much less widespread or common, by nearly all of the pinnae on fertile fronds bearing sori, by its overlapping upper pinnae, and by the stalks of the lower pinnae usually not exceeding about 2 cm long. *A. danaeifolium* was first described from Brazil in 1810 and was first collected in Florida by Ferdinand Rugel (1806-1878) in 1843.

Synonyms: *Acrostichum lomarioides* Jenman.

ADIANTUM

Seven species of maidenhair ferns occur in Florida, four of which are escapes or introductions. The other three, including *A. capillus-veneris, A. melanoleucum,* and *A. tenerum,* were the only members of the genus listed by Small (1931) in his early work on Florida's ferns. An eighth species, *A. macrophyllum* Swartz, was reported as potentially naturalized in Florida in 1925 (Lellinger, 1985). This report was apparently based on a collection by J. K. Small at the Deering estate in Dade County. However, Small is known to have consulted with Deering's gardener, and Wunderlin (*Flora of Florida,* in press) suspects that this collection may have been from a cultivated specimen.

The genus name is from *adiantos,* an old Greek word that means "unwetted" and which refers to the hairless leaves that easily shed raindrops and appear to stay dry under water. Members of the genus are characterized by having the sporangia borne under the inrolled margins (false indusium) of the pinnules (see figure 27). Some taxonomists, including Wunderlin (1998), place this genus in the family Adiantaceae.

Figure 27. Characteristic Pinnule in the Genus *Adiantum,* Showing Curled Blade Edges Forming False Indusia

Double-Edge Maidenhair

Adiantum anceps Maxon & C. V. Morton   **Photo 141**

Form: A large, strictly tropical maidenhair fern with coarse blade tissue.

Fronds: Arching or weeping, 40 - 100 cm long.

Petiole: Blackish, erect, to about 2 dm tall.

Rachis: Thin, blackish, arching.

Blade: Bipinnate below, pinnate above, triangular in outline.

Pinnae: Segments long stalked, borne alternately along the rachis, pinnules 5 - 8 cm long, ovate with a long-tapering and pointed apex; margins toothed; blade tissue coarse; coloration of the stalk of the pinnule ending abruptly at its point of attachment with the pinnule.

Sori: Borne under inrolled flaps along all but the lower margin of the leaf segments.

Habitat: Known in Florida from the limestone sides of mosquito ditches.

Distribution: Native to Ecuador and Peru but cultivated in other areas; collected in Florida only in Dade County.

Remarks: This species can be confused with *A. trapeziforme,* another of Florida's rarely encountered, escaped introductions. The pinnae of the current species are generally longer than 5 cm while those of *A. trapeziforme* are usually shorter than 5 cm, and the marginal indusia of *A. trapeziforme* are typically produced primarily on two rather than three margins of the pinnules.

    A. anceps is cultivated in the tropics. Outside the tropics it is strictly a greenhouse plant and is very sensitive to cold. It does best in alkaline soil. Its specific epithet means "with two edges," in reference to the mostly ovate ultimate segments.

Southern Maidenhair, Venus's-Hair Fern

Adiantum capillus-veneris Linnaeus   **Photo 142**

Form: A delicate, rock-loving fern of limestone banks; with short-creeping stems bearing golden brown to brownish, or bronze colored scales.

Fronds: Pendent, 15 - 75 cm long, usually growing closely spaced along the stem.

Petiole: Thin, delicate, usually not exceeding about 1.5 mm in diameter, 5 - 25 cm long, purplish black to brownish, bearing scales but not hairs.

Rachis: Dark brown, slender, straight to somewhat flexuous, without hairs.

Blade: Pinnate above, more often bipinnate to tripinnate in the lower half of the blade, somewhat triangular to broadly lanceolate in overall shape, 8 - 45 cm long, 2.5 - 15 cm wide.

Pinnae: Widely alternate, simple to pinnate or bipinnate; pinnules typically fan shaped but variable in outline, 0.5 - 2.5 cm both long and wide, without hairs, borne on stalks 1 - 3 mm long, the brownish color of the stalks typically continuing onto the margin of the pinnule; margins of pinnules entire to toothed, apex lobed; veins ending in the teeth rather than in the sinuses between the teeth as is true for many other species of *Adiantum.*

Sori: Borne under the curled margins of the pinnae, a single sorus per segment lobe; hence covered, hidden, and protected by a "false indusium."

Habitat: Wet to moist limestone outcrops of sinks, rivers, and bluffs.

Distribution: Fairly common in the appropriate habitat in northern Florida, especially the panhandle, spottily distributed throughout the central peninsula. A Dade County population is escaped from cultivation. Unlike most members of this family in Florida, which are primarily tropical species, *A. capillus-veneris* is a temperate species that is widely distributed across much of the southern United States from Virginia to California and is long thought to be conspecific with the European maidenhair fern, which is distributed throughout the warmer parts of Europe, Africa, and Asia.

Remarks: This is the only maidenhair fern likely to be encountered in the panhandle. It is most similar to *A. tenerum,* the other species widespread in Florida, but distinguished by the dark color of the stalks extending onto, rather than stopping more or less abruptly at the base of, the pinnules. This species is widely used as an ornamental in both greenhouses and gardens and is relatively easy to establish on limestone boulders. Its specific eipthet, *capillus-veneris,* literally means "Venus's hair."

Synonyms: *Adiantum capillus-veneris* var. *modestum* (L. Underwood) Fernald; *A. capillus-veneris* var. *protrusum* Fernald; *A. capillus-veneris* var. *rimicola* (Slosson) Fernald.

Trailing Maidenhair

Adiantum caudatum Linnaeus   **Photo 143**

Form: A relatively long, trailing maidenhair fern with a short, erect, densely brown-scaly stem.

Fronds: Long, trailing, terminating in an elongated, essentially leafless, whiplike runner that sometimes reclines and roots at the apex to form new plants.

Petiole: 4 - 17 cm long, dark brown, densely covered with stiff, spreading, dark reddish hairs (requires magnification).

Rachis: Dark brown, covered with stiff, spreading hairs similar to those of the petiole.

Blade: Pinnate, 13 - 34 cm long, with numerous pinnae.

Pinnae: Unstalked to very short stalked, comblike by being relatively straight along the downward-facing margins, but conspicuously and somewhat deeply incised on the outward margins; both surfaces scarcely to somewhat short-hairy (requires magnification).

Sori: Borne under a marginal flap at the tips of the upward-facing margins of the pinnae.

Habitat: Hammocks.

Distribution: A nonnative species collected in Florida only in Dade County where it is now extirpated; native to the Old World tropics and distributed widely across Asia and Africa, including South China, India, Ceylon, Taiwan, the Philippines, and New Guinea. Likely to escape cultivation in Florida, but probably not destined to become weedy.

Remarks: The specific epithet, *caudatum,* means "with a taillike appendage" and refers to the whiplike stolon at the tip of the blade, one of the species' chief identifying characters. It is also distinguished among Florida's *Adiantum* by being mostly once divided (pinnate). This species is hardy and often cultivated in the tropics and subtropics but is quite sensitive to cold. In more temperate climes it is grown only in green houses.

Fragrant Maidenhair

Adiantum melanoleucum Willdenow   **Photo 144**

Form: A fragrant, branched maidenhair fern with a brown-scaly, short-creeping stem and clustered fronds.

Fronds: Erect to arching or spreading, 15 - 80 cm long.

Petiole: 8 - 60 cm long, to about 2 mm in diameter, grooved, dark reddish brown to blackish, roughly pubescent with minute hairs.

Rachis: Straight, roughly pubescent with minute hairs or without hairs.

Blade: Pinnate and somewhat linear to bi- or tripinnate, triangular or ovate in outline; 11 - 40 cm long, 8 - 35 cm wide.

Pinnae: Pinnate, lowermost pinnae often forked into two, nearly equal divisions; pinnules oblong, dull brownish green but shiny, to about 1.5 cm long, rectangular in outline, more or less straight or concave on the lower margins, unevenly toothed to narrowly lobed on the upper margins and apices, sometimes whitish below; coloration of the stalks of the pinnules extending a short distance onto the margin of the pinnule.

Sori: Borne below a dark brown flap at the margins of fertile pinnules.

Habitat: Rockland hammocks.

Distribution: Rare. Collected in Florida only in Dade County.

Remarks: The divided lower pinnae, roughened petiole and rachis, whitish color of the undersurface of the pinnules, and the coloration of the pinnule stalk extending a short distance onto the pinnule margin help distinguish this species from others in south Florida. The crushed leaves of this species are said to have the fragrance of sweet vernal grass (*Anthoxanthum ororatum* Linnaeus). However, the species is rare and is listed as endangered in Florida. Hence, it should not be disturbed. According to Small (1918a), it was first discovered in Florida in 1915. The specific epithet means "black and white."

Brittle Maidenhair

Adiantum tenerum Swartz   **Photo 145**

Form: A delicate, rock-loving fern with closely spaced fronds and a short creeping stem bearing two-colored scales with dark, reddish brown centers.

Fronds: Erect to pendent or arching, to about 1 m long.

Petiole: Typically about as long as the blade (though also both shorter and longer than the blade), 15 - 40 cm long, purplish black, without hairs, often with scales at the base that resemble those of the stem.

Rachis: Conspicuous, similar to the petiole, straight, without hairs.

Blade: Pinnate above, bi- to tripinnate below, deltate to ovate or broadly lanceolate in overall outline, 12 - 60 cm both long and wide, without hairs.

Pinnae: Pinnae and pinnules similar, typically fan shaped to diamond shaped, borne on dark-colored stalks to about 5 mm long, dark color of stalks ending more or less abruptly at the base of the supported segment, stalks joined to the segment at a slightly swollen joint; margins toothed and lobed at the apex.

Sori: Borne under the inrolled margins (false indusium) of the pinnules.

Habitat: Limestone outcrops along ledges, sinkhole walls, and grottoes.

Distribution: Mostly in the central peninsula in St. Johns, Alachua, Marion, Volusia, Citrus, Hernando, Hillsborough, and Pinellas Counties; also in Dade County.

Remarks: This species, which is listed as endangered in Florida, is very similar to *A. capillus-veneris,* the other widespread species in Florida, but may be distinguished from it by the coloration of the segment stalk ending more or less abruptly at the base of the pinnule rather than continuing onto the pinnule margins, and by the stalk attaching to the segment at a swollen joint, thus making the segment and stalk easy to separate (hence the common name brittle maidenhair). Its specific epithet means slender, in reference to its overall appearance.

Diamond Maidenhair

Adiantum trapeziforme Linnaeus   **Page 137**

Form: A dark green maidenhair fern with a stout, woody, creeping, scaly stem.

Fronds: Erect to spreading, 50 - 90 cm long or longer, closely to distantly spaced on the stem.

Petiole: Rounded to somewhat flattened, purplish black to black, shiny, 30 - 50 cm long, and usually as long as or longer than the blade.

Rachis: Rounded, similar to the petiole in color and diameter.

Blade: Triangular to ovate, tripinnate below, bipinnate toward the apex, with two to five pairs of pinnae.

Pinnae: Alternate on the rachis, stalked; pinnules also alternate, stalked, 2.5 - 5 cm long, one-sided in appearance, the dominant vein borne along one side of the pinnule, lower margins of lateral pinnae straight to slightly downcurved near the apex, upper margins toothed to deeply lobed; veins forked; coloration of the stalks of the pinnules ending abruptly at their point of attachment with the pinnule.

Sori: Elliptical in outline, 1 - 3.5 mm long, borne under a dark brown flap along the upper and outer leaf margins.

Habitat: Reported in Florida only from a Brazilian pepper *(Schinus terebinthifolius* Raddi) thicket near the Navy Wells Pineland Preserve near Florida City.

Distribution: Dade County.

Remarks: The trapezoidal pinnules, which are less than 5 cm long and have sori on the outer and upper margins, help distinguish this species, but see *A. anceps.* This plant was collected in 1980 by south Florida botanist George Avery. It is probably an escape or recent introduction. The specific epithet means "having the form of a trapezoid" and refers to the shape of the pinnules.

Synonyms: *Adiantum rhomboideum* Schkuhr.

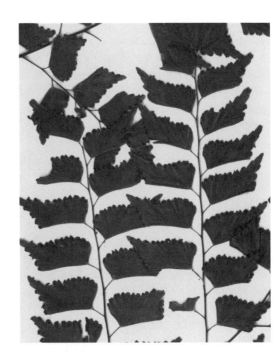

Figure 28.
*Adiantum trapezi-
forme*

Woolly Maidenhair

Adiantum villosum Linnaeus **Photo 146**

Form: A stiffly erect maiderhair fern with a short-creeping, brown-scaly stem.

Fronds: Borne closely in two ranks along the stem, ascending, potentially 50 - 100 cm tall throughout its range, but much shorter in its Florida location.

Petiole: Purplish black, angular, 35 - 60 cm long, clothed with brown, hairy, linear scales, hence the common name and specific epithet.

Rachis: Clothed with brown, hairy, linear scales like those of the petiole.

Blade: Bipinnate, ovate in outline, potentially 25 - 40 cm long, 25 - 50 cm wide, bearing two to six pairs of pinnae.

Pinnae: Alternate on the rachis, spreading, to about 25 cm long; pinnules 2 - 4 cm long, to about 1 cm wide; fertile pinnules mostly diamond shaped with pointed apices; margins of sterile pinnules doubly toothed; coloration of the stalks of the pinnules extending a short distance onto the margin of the pinnule.

Sori: Borne in a continuous or slightly interrupted line under a light brown marginal flap along the upward-facing margins of fertile pinnules.

Habitat: Rocky hammock.

Distribution: One location in Dade County.

Remarks: This species can be distinguished among the *Adiantum* by combination of the divided lower pinnae, the green coloration of the lower surfaces of the pinnules, and the coloration of the pinnule stalk extending a short distance onto the pinnule margin.

A. *villosum* is a recent introduction that was first recorded in Florida in 1988 by Alan Cressler and Carol Lippincott. Only a single population with a single plant is known. The species was misidentified as the very similar *Adiantum tetraphyllum* Willdenow when first discovered in the state and was, until recently, listed as such by the Florida Natural Areas Inventory. More recently, Cressler re-examined the specimen and determined the plant to be A. *villosum.* Some consider the plant a tropical waif that presumably arrived here by wind-blown spores and has persisted but not otherwise become established. Others consider it a rare, endangered species that is a natural part of our flora. It is not currently listed as endangered or threatened for Florida and is no longer tracked by the Florida Natural Areas Inventory.

Synonyms: *Adiantum falcatum* Swartz

CHEILANTHES

The lip ferns encompass about 150 species worldwide, most of which are found in the Western Hemisphere. Twenty-eight occur in North America, three rarely in Florida. Members of the genus are adapted to xeric (very dry) conditions and are generally found on rocky slopes or ledges. The three species reported from Florida, none of which have ever been common and two of which may no longer occur in the state, are all associated with limestone outcrops.

The genus *Cheilanthes* was established by Olaf Peter Swartz (1760-1818) in 1806. As a group, the various species within the genus have been difficult to classify, which has led to much taxonomic uncertainty. Tryon and Tryon (1982) point out that the group has a close relationship with several other genera, including *Adiantopsis, Bommeria, Doryopteris, Notholaena,* and *Pellaea,* only the latter of which is represented in Florida. Nevertheless, they have organized the genus into 11 more or less related groups. They caution, however:

> These ferns have evidently undergone strong divergent and convergent evolution as well as considerable extinction. Most species occur in xeric environments that have a mosaic distribution and such conditions would readily influence evolutionary change. The complexity of morphological patterns that have evolved is not amenable to classification into discrete subgenera and sections. (p. 250)

Both the common and scientific names for members of the genus come from the position of the sori, which are located near the margin, or "lip," of the pinnae segments. *Cheilos* is Greek for margin, and *anthus* for flower. This character is very helpful in recognizing members of the genus in Florida.

Alabama Lip Fern

Cheilanthes alabamensis (Buckley) Kunze

Form: A small, epipetric, somewhat lacy fern with thickened, short-creeping, brown-scaly stems which are 3 - 7 mm in diameter; stem scales very narrowly lanceolate.

Fronds: 5 - 50 cm tall and clustered along the stem.

Petiole: 3 - 23 cm long, blackish, hairy and sometimes scaly near the base, typically sparsely hairy above with long, whitish or yellowish hairs.

Rachis: Blackish with moderate to abundant, rusty to whitish hairs on the upper side, sometimes matted near the apex.

Blade: Bipinnate to bipinnate-pinnatifid, narrowly lanceolate to narrowly elliptic in overall outline, 3 - 31 cm long, to about 6 cm wide.

Pinnae: Lanceolate to oblong, sharp pointed at the apices, typically borne in 10 to 17 pairs, mostly without hairs or with only scattered hairs, midrib green above; pinnules mostly simple, occasionally pinnatifid, 2 - 7 mm long, oblong to lanceolate in outline.

Sori: Borne more or less continuously along the pinnule margin and covered continuously by the inrolled margin of the pinna.

Habitat: Limestone ledges and cliffs.

Distribution: Occurring in the United States generally north and west of Florida from about north Georgia westward through Alabama to Arizona, and northward to Virginia, Oklahoma, and Missouri; also occurring in northern Mexico and Jamaica; collected in Florida only near Indian River, presumably in Brevard County, by W. Faxon in 1875. A. H. Curtiss (1902) reported finding this species in 1901 at Cedar Grove in Washington County, a location he describes as being a few miles south of Chipley. Wherry (1964) also reports the species as occurring in Washington County, which may have been a reference to Curtiss's report, or may have been based on collections made in the same location by J. K. Small and Erdman West between 1934 and 1937. However, these collections have been found to be misidentifications of depauperate specimens of *C. microphylla* (Evans, 1975), and more recent searches by Bob Godfrey and Angus Gholson have not relocated the plant. Hence, the presence of this species in Washington County is now considered questionable (Wunderlin, 1998). Nevertheless, given the proximity of the range of *C. alabamensis* to Florida, it should probably be looked for in portions of the panhandle.

Remarks: This plant was first described as *Pteris alabamensis* in 1843 by Samuel Buckley (1809-1884) from rocks on the banks of the Tennessee River near Muscle Shoals, Alabama; hence, its common name and specific epithet. It differs from *C. microphylla* by its thicker stem and by the axis on the upper side of the pinnae being mostly green rather than mostly blackish. It differs from *C. lanosa* by the pinnae being mostly without hairs or having only scattered hairs rather than being conspicuously pubescent, and by the rachis and petiole being mostly blackish rather than purplish to reddish brown.

Synonyms: *Pteris alabamensis* Buckley, *Allosorus alabamensis* (Buckley) Kunze, *Pellaea alabamensis* (Buckley) Hooker.

Hairy Lip Fern

Cheilanthes lanosa (Michaux) D.C. Eaton   **Photos 147, 148**

Form: A small, erect to pendent, somewhat lacy, epipetric fern with a brown-scaly stem 4 - 8 mm in diameter.

Fronds: 7 - 50 cm tall, clustered along the stem.

Petiole: 3 - 18 cm long, purplish black to chestnut brown, with spreading hairs.

Rachis: Rounded on the upper side, purplish black to chestnut brown, hairy but without scales.

Blade: Bipinnate-pinnatifid to tripinnate, 4 - 24 cm long, to about 4.5 cm wide, narrowly elliptic to oblong in outline.

Pinnae: Lanceolate to long triangular in outline, sparsely clothed above, more densely clothed below with long, reddish hairs; pinnules oblong, lobed, with bluntly pointed apices.

Sori: Borne in clusters on the lateral lobes of the pinnules.

Habitat: Limestone ledges.

Distribution: Widely distributed and frequent across the eastern U.S.; documented in Florida only from Citrus County.

Remarks: This species takes its common and scientific names from its conspicuously pubescent leaves. The specific epithet *lanosa* means woolly. Though probably not quite as hairy as its name suggests, the abundance of the hairs on the upper surfaces of the pinnae help distinguish it from the two other species in Florida, each of which is likely to be only sparsely hairy above. The present species is most similar to *C. tomentosa* Link, another southern species whose range includes southern Alabama, but is not known to occur Florida.

  C. lanosa has been collected at least twice in Florida. The best documented collection is from Citrus County in 1934 and was collected by Robert P. St. John (Evans, 1975). The other specimen, which lacked location data, was collected in the 1840s by Ferdinand Rugel, who is known to have worked in Florida during this time period (Petrik-Ott & Ott, 1982).

Synonyms: *Nephrodium lanosum* Michaux; *Cheilanthes vestita* (Sprengel) Swartz.

Southern Lip Fern

Cheilanthes microphylla (Swartz) Swartz   **Page 142**

Form: A small to medium-size, somewhat lacy fern with a slender, long-creeping stem that is covered with narrow, brownish to orangish scales more or less appressed to the stem (requires magnification).

Fronds: 8 - 40 cm tall and scattered along the stem; not developing fiddleheads.

Petiole: Blackish, 4 - 21 cm long, rounded on the upper side, clothed with whistish to yellowish or orangish hairs.

Rachis: Rounded on the upper side, hairy.

Blade: Bipinnate-pinnatifid to tripinnate, oblong to narrowly lanceolate or elliptic in outline, 4 - 27 cm long, 1.5 - 6 cm wide.

Pinnae: Pinnate or pinnatifid, blunt tipped, axis of upper side black nearly throughout; slightly to not at all hairy.

Sori: Continuous to somewhat discontinuous along the margins or congested on lateral lobes of the pinnules.

Habitat: Limestone outcrops and shell mounds.

Distribution: Sporadically distributed in the Florida peninsula from about Duval County southward with a disjunct population reported from a single lime sink in Washington County; a tropical species restricted in the U. S. only to Florida. This species was reported by A. H. Curtiss as being present near the mouth of the St. John's River in the 1880s, but having been eliminated from this site by the early 1900s (Satchwell, 1916). Today it is listed as endangered by the Florida Department of Agriculture.

Remarks: This is the most likely species of lip fern to be found in Florida, and even it is uncommon and not widely reported. The blackish midrib on the upper surfaces of the pinnae, in conjunction with the only slightly hairy pinnae surfaces distinguish the species from the other members of its genus in Florida. The scientific epithet, *microphylla,* derives from the small, delicate pinnules.

Synonyms: *Adiantum microphyllum* Swartz

Purple Cliff Brake or Hairy Cliff Brake

Pellaea atropurpurea (Linnaeus) Link   **Page 142**

Form: A small, limestone-loving fern with a thickish, short-creeping to ascending stem with linear, reddish brown to tan scales.

Fronds: Tufted at the base, 5 - 50 cm tall, gray green in color and leathery to the touch, with hairy fiddleheads; fertile fronds generally longer and more divided than the sterile ones.

Petiole: Purplish red to blackish, shiny, lacking hairs.

Rachis: Purplish, shiny, lacking hairs.

Blade: Bi- to tripinnate, 5 - 30 cm tall, 3 - 18 cm wide.

Pinnae: Nearly opposite, often at right angles to and typically well spaced along the rachis, to about 8 cm long, hairy near the midrib below; uppermost pinnae simple and oblong in out-

Figure 29.
Cheilanthes microphylla

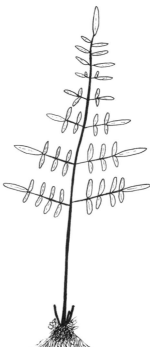

Figure 30.
Pellaea atropurpurea

line, lower pinnae divided into oblong segments.

Sori: Borne near to, continuous with, and protected by the pinnae margins.

Habitat: Limestone outcrops and crevices.

Distribution: Rare and perhaps no longer extant in Florida; widely distributed across much of the eastern U. S. and often cultivated in rock gardens. Collected in Florida only from Washington and Jackson Counties and listed as endangered by the Florida Department of Agriculture. The most recent collection was made in 1987 by Angus K. Gholson, Jr., in company with Robert Godfrey and W. Wilson Baker on private land south of Chipley. Only two plants were observed at this site.

Remarks: The distinctive form of this species makes it unlikely to be confused with any other Florida pteridophyte. The genus name likely refers to the grayish color of the blade tissue, and the specific epithet refers to the dark, purplish black petiole.

Synonyms: *Pteris atropurpurea* Linnaeus; *Pellaea atropurpurea* var. *cristata* Trelease.

PITYROGRAMMA

Pityrogramma is a genus of about 16 species worldwide, only two of which occur in Florida and North America. Its name derives from the Greek words *pityron,* for bran, and *gramme,* or line, in apparent reference to the lines of sori and powdery undersurfaces of the leaves. Species of the genus generally inhabit moist, open habitats and are sensitive to both drought and cold. The goldback fern, a common, rock-loving species of California and other western states was, until recently, known as *P. triangularis* (Kaulfuss) Maxon, but has now been transferred to the genus *Pentagramma* (Yaskievych et. al., 1993). In drought conditions its leaves curl up and expose their yellowish undersides, hence its common name.

Silverback Fern

Pityrogramma calomelanos (Linnaeus) Link var. *calomelanos*

Photo 149, 150

Form: A relatively large, conspicuous fern with a short, stout, erect to ascending stem that is clothed at the apex with shiny, dark golden brown, lanceolate scales.

Fronds: Tufted, to about 1.5 m tall.

Petiole: Shiny, reddish brown to dark purplish or blackish, scaly at the base, about as long as the blades.

Rachis: Similar to the petiole, grooved, tending toward brownish at the apex.

Blade: Bipinnate, bipinnate-pinnatifid, to tripinnate, leathery, dark green above, 20 - 95 cm long, 10 - 30 cm wide, narrowly deltate to somewhat lanceolate in outline, coated below with a whitish, waxy, mealy powder (farina).

Pinnae: Borne alternately to nearly opposite along the rachis, narrowly triangular in overall outline, pinnately divided into lanceolate or elliptic, sharp-pointed segments with toothed margins.

Sori: Numerous, sometimes nearly concealing the undersurface of fertile pinnules, often appearing embedded in the whitish powder on the lower surfaces of the pinnules.

Habitat: Ditches.

Distribution: Collected in Florida only in Polk, Hillsborough, and Manatee Counties. This is a species of the West Indies and tropical and subtropical America and Africa. It is often cultivated in greenhouses and is assumed to be escaped in Florida (Small, 1938; Wunderlin, 1982; Lellinger, 1985; Yatskievych & Windham, 1993). According to Small (1938), it was first collected in the state by W. A. Knight in 1931, who also considered it an escape. However, Mary Diddell (1956), an active Florida fern enthusiast during the first part of the twentieth century, questioned Small's assessment. She cites later work (Merrill, 1943) that claims that Constantine Samuel Rafinesque (1738-1840) collected the species in Florida prior to 1836 and, assuming it to be a new species, named it *Nesorus bicolor* Rafinesque. Diddell argues that the Florida interior was a wilderness during the years that Rafinesque made his collection, and that the introduction of tropical plants into the state did not begin until at least the 1880s. She also points out that species of *Pityrogramma* are quite susceptible to drought and cold, either of which will cause them to be killed back. She suggests that these conditions may explain the 100-year interim between the collections by Rafinesque and Knight. More recent authors, however, question whether the Rafinesque collection was, in fact, *P. calomelanos.* According to Yatskievych & Windham (1993), Rafinesque described his collection as having yellowish rather than whitish powder on the lower surfaces of the leaves. They hold, further, that since no type specimen for the plant can be located, and since Rafinesque's description lacks definitive precision, the collection cannot be equated to modern nomenclature. However, specimens of *P. calomelanos* with yellow farina have been reported (R. M. Tryon, 1962). Wunderlin (1998) treats it as native to the state.

Remarks: This species is most easily distinguished from all but *P. trifoliata* by the whitish powder that clothes the undersurfaces of the blades; distinguished from the latter by the terminalmost pinnae being distinctly lobed or divided rather than entire or merely toothed. Tryon (1962) reported several hybrids with this species, including one with the other Florida species, *P. trifoliata,* which has yellowish rather than whitish waxy powder on the lower surfaces of the pinnae. At least one additional variety of the present species is described as having yellow farina on the lower surfaces of the pinnae.

Synonyms: *Acrostichum calomelanos* Linnaeus.

Goldenrod Fern

Pityrogramma trifoliata (Linnaeus) R.M. Tyron   **Photos 151, 152**

Form: A rather large, conspicuous plant with a thick, brown-scaly, woody stem to about 2.5 cm in diameter; scales mostly dark brown along the edges and blackish in the center.

Fronds: 0.5 - 2 m tall.

Petiole: 10 - 35 cm long, rigid, grooved, shiny, dark reddish or purplish brown, scaly near the base.

Rachis: Similar to the petiole in color, typically without scales; occasionally with a few linear, hairlike scales.

Blade: Pinnate above, bipinnate below, narrowly lanceolate to almost linear in outline, to about 1.5 m long, 12 - 20 cm wide, sometimes clothed below with yellowish (sometimes whitish), waxy, mealy powder (farina).

Pinnae: Uppermost pinnae simple, lowermost palmately to pinnately divided into two to three segments; segments linear in outline, 8 - 15 cm long, to about 1 cm wide, with finely toothed margins.

Sori: Borne on the lower surfaces of the fertile pinnules and sometimes partially hidden by yellowish powder.

Habitat: Roadside ditches, canals.

Distribution: Occurring in Florida mostly in the southernmost peninsula from Palm Beach and Collier Counties southward; also reported from Hernando County; widely distributed across tropical America. There has also been some question about whether this species is native to the state. It is not often cultivated and is considered a natural part of our flora by Wunderlin (1998).

Remarks: This species is most easily distinguished from all but *P. calomelanos* by the yellowish to sometimes whitish powder that clothes the undersurfaces of the blades; distinguished from the latter by the terminalmost pinnae being entire or merely toothed rather than distinctly lobed or divided. The range of *P. trifoliata* seems to be expanding in Florida. Lellinger (1985) remarks that this species is easily overlooked due to its similarity to various members of the aster family.

This species is sometimes seen listed as *Trismeria trifoliata,* the single species in a monotypic genus. The characterization of the genus is based on this species' distinctive leaf division as well as characters of its spores.

Synonyms: *Acrostichum trifoliatum* Linnaeus; *Trismeria trifoliata* (Linnaeus) Diels.

PTERIS

The genus *Pteris* includes seven species in Florida (two of which are probably no longer extant in the state) and one hybrid, nearly all of which are nonnative species introduced for horticultural use. The species that occur in Florida are the only members of the genus that are present in North America.

Pteris grandifolia Linnaeus is often included in the state's flora but is only questionably native. It was originally discovered by Dr. Roy Woodbury near Cutler in 1952, and hence reported for Dade County by both Darling (1961) and Wherry (1964). However, it has not been found in more recent searches. Richard Wunderlin (personal communication, 1997) suggests that the species should probably be moved to Florida's "dubious" list. Keller (1994) lists the species as native to southern Florida, but extirpated in the wild. Its occurrence in Florida may have originated from specimens that escaped cultivation. The accompanying illustration (see photo 156) is of a cultivated specimen in southern Florida. The plant is easily recognized by its very large, arching, pinnate fronds, which are up to 2 m in length and superficially resemble those of the two species of *Acrostichum.*

Bahama Ladder Brake, Plumy Ladder Brake, Bahama Brake

Pteris bahamensis (J. Agardh) Fee   **Photo 153**

Form: An erect, terrestrial fern with a thin, short-creeping stem.

Fronds: 1 - 2 m tall and produced in clusters.

Petiole: 10 - 45 cm long, straw colored to greenish above, purplish black toward the base, without hairs or scales at maturity (sometimes sparsely scaly when young).

Rachis: Straw colored and lacking hairs or scales.

Blade: Pinnate, lanceolate to oblanceolate in overall shape, 25 - 60 cm tall, 3 - 16 cm wide.

Pinnae: Linear in shape, well separated on the rachis, terminal pinna long and conspicuous; mostly without hairs, sometimes with a few hairs on the central axis of the lower surface; lateral veins forked; margins entire to obscurely toothed.

Sori: Obscuring the blade tissue on the lower surfaces of the pinnae.

Habitat: Limestone outcrops and crevices in the Miami Rocklands and Big Pine Key pinelands; edges of hammocks.

Distribution: Southernmost Florida, from about Lake Okeechobee southward.

Remarks: *P. bahamensis* is similar in some respects to *P. vittata*. It may be distinguished from the latter by its petiole, which is much less scaly (scales are usually present only near the base of the petiole) and with dark brown rather than light-colored or reddish scales, and by its pinnae, which are typically sessile rather than short-stalked. A form with deeply divided pinnae is known from Dade County.

 P. bahamensis is often treated as *P. longifolia* var. *bahamensis* (Correll and Correll, 1996), as noted below. Nauman (1993b) suggests that the two species might well be conspecific but maintains the current taxon at the specific level due to differences in the amount of pubescence on the rachis, which is less dense on *P. bahamensis,* and the more heart-shaped base of the sterile pinnae of *P. longifolia*. This treatment is followed here.

 P. X *delchampsii* W. H. Wagner & C. E. Nauman, (see Photo 164) a hybrid between *P. bahamensis* and *P. vittata,* is also reported for southernmost Florida. The hybrid was discovered in the Coral Gables Canal by, and later named in honor of, the late C. E. Delchamps. In overall aspect it looks like a narrow form of *P. vittata,* but is more erect, less scaly on the rachis and petiole, the pinnae are stiffer and more separated, and the margins of the pinnae are less sharply toothed. Wagner and Nauman (1982) suggest that the plant may eventually develop a way to reproduce itself. It is currently known in Florida only from the southernmost tip of the state.

Synonyms: *P. diversifolia* Swartz var. *bahamensis* J. Agardh; *P. longifolia* Linnaeus var. *bahamensis* (J. Agardh) Hieronymus; *Pycnodoria bahamensis* (J. Agardh) Small; *Pycnodoria pinetorum* Small.

Cretan Brake

Pteris cretica Linnaeus var. *cretica*   **Photos 154, 155**

Form: A terrestrial or rock-loving species with a thin, creeping stem.

Fronds: To about 1 m long, borne in clusters.

Petiole: 10 - 50 cm and relatively long in proportion to the blade; straw colored to nearly whitish above, base reddish brown, darker, and sparsely scaly.

Rachis: Straw colored, not winged except for just below the terminal pinna.

Blade: Divided into several pinnae from a single, central point, 10 - 30 cm long, 6 - 25 cm wide.

Pinnae: Borne in one to three pairs, each to about 25 cm long and 0.5 - 1.5 cm wide, fertile pinnae narrow and usually not exceeding about 1 cm in width; remaining green throughout the year; margins distinctly toothed toward the apex, especially on fertile pinnae; lateral veins diverging at right angles to the midvein.

Sori: Borne in a conspicuous, narrow line along the margins on the lower side of the pinnae.

Habitat: Limestone sinks and outcrops in hammocks, river bluffs.

Distribution: A horticultural species now widely distributed worldwide; known in Florida from the central panhandle, especially near the Apalachicola River, and the central ridge of the north-central peninsula. The plant is often reported to be a naturalized addition to Florida's flora (Lakela & Long, 1976). However, Curtiss (1902) reports the species from the so-called Citrus County fern grottoes as early as 1881. In reviewing Curtiss's fern discoveries and describing his own visit to the Citrus County site, Harper (1916, p. 77) also lists *P. cretica* and comments that "it is inconceivable that an exotic plant could have been established at this locality at a time when there were no railroads or settlements near," and Small, in his 1938 Ferns of the Southeastern States, remarks: "Judging from the distribution in the state and the habitats there seems to be little doubt that it is indigenous" (p. 104). Wunderlin (1998) also treats it as native to the state.

Remarks: This species is most similar to *P. multifida.* It may be distinguished from the latter by its rachis being winged only on that portion just below the terminal pinna, as opposed to being winged throughout. A second variety, *P. cretica* Linnaeus var. *albolineata* Hooker, is also reported from Florida, primarily from Hernando County. It is rare in occurrence and may be easily distinguished from the current variety by the conspicuous, broad, white, central stripe running the length of the pinnae. *P. cretica* is a widely distributed fern and, including the variety mentioned above, is extremely common in cultivation. Whether the latter variety is also native, as opposed to introduced, is conjectural (Small 1938; Wherry 1964). The specific epithet, *cretica,* means "of Crete," in reference to the presumption that the species was first found on the island of Crete.

Synonyms: *Pycnodoria cretica* (Linnaeus) Small.

Spider Brake, Spider Fern, Chinese Brake, Huguenot Fern, Saw-Leaved Bracken

Pteris multifida Poiret in Lamarck **Photos 157, 158**

Form: A terrestrial or rock-loving fern with a slender, short-creeping, densely dark-scaly stem; remaining green throughout the winter due to the continuous production of new fronds.

Fronds: Clustered, 10 - 60 cm long.

Petiole: Pale to brownish, 5 - 30 cm long, scaly toward the base.

Rachis: Slightly but evenly winged throughout, narrowed above each pair of pinnae.

Blade: Pinnate with a long, terminal pinna; oblong to oblanceolate or narrowly triangular in overall shape, 10 - 40 cm long, 12 - 25 cm wide; appearing palmately compound with three pinnae when young, having several pairs of pinnae at maturity.

Pinnae: Borne oppositely in three to seven pairs, lowermost pinnae divided into relatively large pinnules, terminal pinnae not divided; margins of sterile pinnae entire to toothed throughout, toothing of fertile pinnae more often restricted to the terminal ends.

Sori: Borne along the edge of the pinnae and at least partially hidden by the inrolled margins.

Habitat: Cultivated in Florida and generally believed to be imported; found primarily in waste places, on masonry walls, and on calcareous substrates.

Distribution: Throughout the southeastern United States; rather spottily distributed in Florida, mostly in the panhandle and northern peninsula, but also collected in Dade County and likely to occur in almost any region.

Remarks: Easily distinguished from all but *Pteris cretica* by at least the lower pinnae usually being pinnatifid-lobed rather than unlobed, from *P. cretica,* which also has pinnatifid-lobed pinnae, by the rachis of the current species being winged throughout rather than just below the terminal pinna. Young specimens of the current species (those without spores) may be easily confused with *P. cretica.*

   P. multifida is native to Asia and was first discovered in the U. S. in 1868 in a Huguenot cemetery in Charlestown, South Carolina; hence, one of its common names, Huguenot fern. The common name "spider brake" is likely in reference to the spiderlike appearance of the deeply-divided leaves. The specific epithet, *multifida,* also means much divided.

Synonyms: *Pycnodoria multifida* (Poiret) Small

Striped Brake

Pteris plumula Desvaux

Form: A relatively large fern with erect to ascending, woody stems which are densely covered with dark brown scales.

Fronds: Spreading to nearly erect, to about 1.5 m long, densely clustered.

Petiole: As long as or longer than the blade, yellowish brown, grooved, scaly at the base but otherwise without hairs.

Rachis: Without hairs, smooth except for minute, hard protuberances in the axils of the pinnae.

Blade: Pinnate-pinnatifid but pinnatifid toward the apex, oblong to ovate in general outline, to about 50 cm wide and firm to the touch.

Pinnae: Those above the lower pair short-stalked, narrowly triangular to nearly linear, divided into linear to oblong segments, lower pair longer stalked and divided into two parts; pinnules 1 - 3 cm long, 3 - 6 mm wide; sharply awned at the point where the axis of the pinna joins the axes of the pinnules.

Sori: Borne under pale-colored indusia.

Habitat: Thickets and shady banks; the single Florida collection was in a cypress swamp.

Distribution: A horticultural species collected in Florida only once, in Palm Beach County; also distributed in the West Indies and perhaps continental tropical America.

Remarks: The two-parted lower pinnae help distinguish this species. The cultivar, *cv.*

Argyrae, which is known as silver brake due to the white band down the center of the blade, is occasionally cultivated in the U. S.

Synonyms: *P. pectinata* Desvaux; *P. felosma* John Smith; *P. quadriaurita* var. *affluentia* Jenman; *P. longipinnula* of Jenman; *P. quadriaurita* of numerous authors.

Giant Brake or Giant Bracken

Pteris tripartita Swartz   **Photos 159, 160, 161**

Form: A terrestrial fern with a stout, creeping to upcurved, densely scaly stem.

Fronds: 1 - 3 m tall.

Petiole: To about 1.25 m tall (about 1/3 the total length of the frond), straw colored to reddish brown, especially toward the base, somewhat scaly at the base, otherwise without hair or scales.

Rachis: Without wings, often with at least a few minute hairs (requires magnification).

Blade and Pinnae: 1 - 2 m wide, 1 - 2 m long, deltoid in overall shape, ultimately pinnate-pinnatifid, initially divided into three main parts or pinnae (hence the specific name) from a central point at the terminus of the petiole, each basal pinna further and repeatedly subdivided, ultimate segments numerous, margins of pinnules entire to finely toothed.

Sori: Borne along and under the inrolled portions of the margins on the lower sides of the pinnules.

Habitat: Escaped into wet glades and cypress and pond-apple wetlands.

Distribution: Introduced and escaped from about the central peninsula southward.

Remarks: Easily separated from other members of the genus by its multiply-divided fronds; superficially somewhat resembling bracken *(Pteridium aquilinum)* in general appearance (hence one of the common names), but much larger and occurring in wetlands rather than dry, sandy uplands.

According to Morton (1957), this plant is an Old World species that was likely introduced into cultivation by the Royal Palm Nurseries in Oneco, Florida through their 1896 catalog. It escaped cultivation and by 1928 was common in a number of places in Florida, especially near Pompano Beach. Morton reports that many plants sold from the nursery were the offspring of a single plant:

In the Royal Palm Nurseries, the original plant grew very large and was highly fertile; the method of propagation was merely to pick out the young sporelings, which came up throughout the greenhouses, often several hundred yards from the parent plant. The original plant was lost sometime around 1930. (Morton, 1957, pp. 12 - 13)

Good places to see specimens of this species include the Deering Estate in Miami, and along the boardwalk at the Daggerwing Nature Center in the South County Regional Park in Palm Beach County.

Synonyms: *Litobrochia tripartita* (Swartz) C. Presl

Chinese Ladder Brake, Ladder Brake, Chinese Brake

Pteris vittata Linnaeus   **Photos 162, 163**

Form: A terrestrial or rock-loving fern with a knotty, stout stem that is densely covered with pale brown to yellowish scales.

Fronds: Erect, clustered, 0.1 - 1 m tall.

Petiole: 1 - 30 cm long, green to pale brown, densely covered with fine scales.

Rachis: Sparsely to densely scaly, ridged and grooved, without wings.

Blade: Pinnate, 15 - 80 cm long, 6 - 35 cm wide, relatively narrow near the base, broadest above the middle, with a long, narrow, terminal pinna.

Pinnae: Borne oppositely along the rachis, those low on the rachis more widely spaced and shorter, those nearer the apex of the blade longer and more closely spaced, linear to narrowly lanceolate in overall shape, 2 - 18 cm long, less than 1 cm wide, margins finely toothed toward the apices, lateral veins diverging at right angles to the mid-vein and forked toward the margins.

Sori: Borne in elongated, dense clusters along the margins on the lower surfaces of the pinnae.

Habitat: Canal banks, hammocks, roadsides, culverts and bridges, brick buildings, disturbed sites, especially where concrete blocks and brick are present.

Distribution: A cultivated species, escaped at various locations throughout Florida, but more commonly so in the southern half of the peninsula; also established in Alabama and Louisiana.

Remarks: In his 1931 treatise on the ferns of Florida, J. K. Small lists this species as one of only three naturalized exotic ferns in Florida. Its common name, ladder brake, derives from the step-ladderlike appearance of its fronds; the specific epithet means striped or ribbonlike in reference to the pinnae. It is native to China where both its belowground stems and young fronds are sometimes used as food.

Synonyms: *Pycnodoria vittata* (Linnaeus) Small

SALVINIACEAE - FLOATING FERN OR WATER SPANGLE FAMILY

The family Salviniaceae includes a single genus with ten, floating-leaved, mostly tropical species. Only one species is widespread in Florida. The leaves of all species occur in threes. Two are conspicuous and float on the water surface while the third is greatly dissected and dangles rootlike below the other two. The larger, floating leaves are vested with four-pronged hairs that serve to redirect water droplets from the leaf surface. The orientation of the floating leaves is also unique in that the visible surface is actually the leaf's lower side.

This species is sometimes, though quite erroneously, identified as duckweed (*Lemna* sp.), a monocot that is unrelated to the pteridophytes. The confusion presumably comes from their floating habit. However, the two genera are not at all alike and are very unlikely to be confused except by uninformed observers who seem to lump all small-leaved, floating plants under the common name duckweed.

The family and genus are named for A. W. Salvini (1633-1720), an Italian botanist.

Water Spangles, Floating Fern

Salvinia minima Baker   **Photo 165**

Form: A floating-leaved species with brittle, rootless, hairy stems to about 6 cm long.
Leaves: 1 - 1.5 cm long, elliptic to almost round, sessile or with a very short petiole; leaves borne in threes along the stem, one of which is finely dissected and dangling, the other two heart-shaped at the base, bluish green above, with a distinctive midrib that makes them appear to be folded upward from the center; upward-facing surface of expanded leaves with stiff, four-pronged hairs, downward-facing surface brownish and with slender hairs.
Spores: Borne in sporocarps (hard, nutlike pods) on trailing, rootlike leaves that are submerged below the floating leaves.
Habitat: Floating on the surface of ponds, lakes, backwaters, canals, and slow-moving rivers; essentially confined to still waters but sometimes also on mud where water has receded.
Distribution: Throughout the state.
Remarks: Giant salvinia *(S. molesta* D. S. Mitchell), a closely related species, is a particularly invasive weed that is prohibited in the United States by federal law. It has become particularly troublesome in Texas, Louisiana, and South Carolina and might also prove to be a problem in Florida if not monitored carefully. It was reported from the southwest Florida coast in early 1999. Giant salvinia differs from *S. minima* by its larger leaves, which commonly measure about 2 cm long and 1.3 cm wide, and by the ends of the hairs on the upward-facing leaf surface being joined at their tips, thus resembling a miniature egg beater (those of *S. minima* are free at the tip). Accordin₂ o Small (1931), *S. minima* was first discovered in Florida in the St. Johns River in 1928, and was likely spread to other locations by wading birds. The same could happen with *S. molesta* if care is not taken.
Synonyms: Several names have been used but misapplied to this species. The most common of these in Florida is *S. rotundifolia* Willdenow.

SCHIZAEACEAE - CURLY-GRASS FERN FAMILY

This is a relatively small family with only three genera and about 30 species worldwide. A single genus and species is represented in Florida. The common name refers to the somewhat grasslike appearance of several of the species, some of which, especially those in the genus *Schizaea,* have leaves that are strongly reflexed or curling toward the apex. The botanical name for the family derives from the Greek *schizein,* which means "split" and refers to the narrow leaf lobes of some members of the family.

Ray Spiked Fern or Ray Fern

Actinostachys pennula (Swartz) Hooker   **Photo 166, Page 152**

Form: A grasslike, often loosely tufted fern with linear, atypical fern leaves and slender, erect to ascending stems with minute yellowish to brownish hairs (requires magnification).

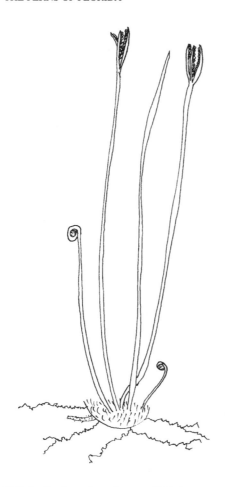

Figure 31.
Actinostachys pennula

Petiole: To about 2 cm long, reddish brown.

Leaves: Pale green, simple, narrowly linear, stiffly erect, to about 12 cm tall, without hairs, having the appearance of a petiole; apex of fertile leaves divided into up to six very narrow, brownish segments with minute yellowish to brownish hairs.

Sporangia: Fertile segment with two to three rows of crowded sporangia along one side.

Habitat: Hammocks, bay heads; reportedly epiphytic on rotten stumps, especially those of bay trees *(Persea* spp.), and in leaf litter; those in the single population still known in Florida occur mostly on the bases of clumps of royal fern *(Osmunda regalis* var. *spectabilis).*

Distribution: Rare. Collected in Florida only in Pinellas, Palm Beach, and Dade Counties and listed as endangered by the Florida Department of Agriculture; also occurring in the West Indies as well as Central and South America. The Pinellas population, which is apparently no longer extant, was discovered by John Beckner in 1952, but the population could not be found by Thomas Darling in 1958 (Darling, 1961). Eaton (1906) reported this species in tangled growth along the Miami River across the Alapattah, and Small (1918) reported that the species was known in the early parts of the twentieth century only from two locations in Florida: in hammocks at the headwaters of the Miami River and in Royal Palm Hammock. Few additional locations have been found in the intervening decades, indicating that this species has probably always been rare in the state. Known sites today include at least two protected populations on tree islands in remote locations of Loxahatchee National Wildlife Refuge in Palm Beach County (Alexander, et al.,1974; Keith Bradley, personal communication, 1998).

Remarks: Both the scientific and common names for this genus refer to the spikelike arrangement of the fertile leaf segments; *Actinostachys* comes from the Greek *aktis*, or ray, and *stachys*, or spike. The grasslike leaves and divided, terminal, spikelike fertile segments of this species distinguish it from all other pteridophytes in Florida.

A. pennula was long known as *Schizaea germanii* or *A. germanii*. However, Wagner (1993) reports that plants that were referred to this latter taxon are actually juvenile forms of this species. **Synonyms:** *Schizaea pennula* Swartz; *Actinostachys germanii* Fee; *Schizaea germanii* (Fee) Prantl.

SELAGINELLACEAE - SPIKE-MOSS FAMILY

The Selaginellaceae constitute a primitive collection of fern allies with creeping stems that are often spreading and mat-forming. The family is currently thought to consist of a single, worldwide genus with several subgenera and over 700 species, most of which occur in the tropics or subtropics. Thirty-eight species occur in North America, six (or perhaps seven) in Florida.

In addition to the six species treated below, A. W. Chapman collected a specimen labeled *Selaginella rupestris* (Linnaeus) Spring from Gadsden County, FL. Clausen (1946) dismissed this collection as having possibly originated elsewhere and having been mislabeled. He noted on the specimen's herbarium label (which is on deposit at the U. S. National Herbarium): "I doubt that these specimens belong with the data." In 1952 R. M. Tryon Jr. also indicated that the locality of this specimen was not accepted. Hence, the species has been discounted as part of Florida's flora. The site referenced by Chapman lies along a series of sandy ridges that now support a plantation of sand pine *(Pinus clausa* [Chapman ex Engelmann] Vasey ex Sargent). As might be expected from the habitat, two searches of Chapman's general area by the author, first with Angus K. Gholson and again with W. Wilson Baker, revealed abundant specimens of *S. arenico-la,* but no *S. rupestris.* However, *S. rupestris* is the most wide-ranging species of the genus and occurs across much of the eastern United States, but somewhat north of Florida. It is also sometimes reported as occurring in sandy soil. Snyder and Bruce (1986) report it from Coffee and Jeff Davis Counties, Georgia, less than 100 miles north of the Florida line, which represent somewhat disjunct populations at the southern extremity of the species' range. Since Gadsden and Jackson Counties, Florida, especially the regions between Chattahoochee and Marianna, and along the Apalachicola River, are well known for harboring a number of more northern species that are often found in populations that are disjunct from the main parts of their ranges, and since Chapman attributed the species to Florida in both the first and third editions of his *Flora of the Southern States,* it is not inconceivable that his label may have been correct. *S. rupestris* is similar to *S. areni-cola,* described below, but the aerial stem is decumbent or creeping with ascending branches, never erect or ascending like the latter species. It also roots along the decumbent stem, rather than only at the base of the stem as in *S. arenicola.*

It should also be noted that Long and Lakela (1976) included *S. plana* (Desvaux ex Poiret) Hieronymus, an erect species of the West Indies and Central America, as part of Florida's flora. However, this species, which is apparently closely related to *S. willdenovii,* has not been documented with a voucher for Florida and is not included in the descriptions below.

Earlier authors have sometimes segregated the family into at least four genera. Several of the species described below were once included within the genus *Diplostachyum,* which was distinguished by species with soft leaves "of two kinds, borne in two planes, the lateral ones the larger and two-ranked; blades not bristle-tipped; diffuse or prostrate plants with creeping stems and branches" (Small, 1938, p. 421). The same characters are useful today in segregating the Florida species into two working groups to aid in field identification. The first of these groups, subgenus *Tetragonostachys* (meaning "four-angled strobili"), which contains the *S. arenicola* complex, is characterized by squared strobili and rather thick, appressed to strongly ascending leaves. The other subgenus, *Stachygynandrum* (meaning "spikelike strobili"), contains the other of Florida's species and is characterized by cylindrical strobili and thin, spreading leaves. This latter subgenus includes those species which Small included within the genus *Diplostachyum.*

The family name derives from the root word *selago,* an ancient name for *Lycopodium,* a genus within which several of Florida's species were once included.

Meadow Spike-Moss

Selaginella apoda (Linnaeus) Spring

Form: An evergreen, prostrate to very low-growing, mat-forming fern ally, rooting all along the stem.
Leaves: Pale green in color, borne in four rows; lateral leaves distant from each other and conspicuous, ovate to lanceolate in overall outline, to about 2.25 mm long and 1.35 mm wide; medial leaves smaller, less conspicuous, appressed to the stem; margins toothed, green or with a very thin, pale edge.
Strobili: 1 - 2 cm long, somewhat flattened, borne in pairs at the tip of branchlets, sporophylls of two sizes.
Habitat: Hammocks, swamps, marshes, stream banks, moist lawns, pastures, meadows.
Distribution: Northern Florida southward to about Highlands County.
Remarks: This species is very similar to and difficult to distinguish from *S. ludoviciana* (pictured in photo 170). The two may be distinguished most easily by examining the leaf margins, counting the number of microphylls per centimeter, and noting the growth form (Buck & Lucansky, 1976). The leaves of *S. ludoviciana* have narrow, transparent to whitish margins about five cells in width while those of *S. apoda* have green margins, or exhibit only a very narrow transparent margin about one cell wide (this character requires 10x magnification and is sometimes more easily seen on the medial leaves). The number of microphylls (the small leaves appressed to the axis of the stem) in *S. apoda* ranges from 18 to 36 per cm, while the range is 10 to 20 per cm in *S. ludoviciana.* The growth habit for *S. apoda* is more or less prostrate and mat forming, unlike the

somewhat more erect habit of *S. ludoviciana.* To complicate matters, these species may also rarely hybridize to produce specimens with intermediate characters (Somers and Buck, 1975).

This species' specific epithet means "without feet," in reference to its mostly prostrate growth habit. **Synonyms:** *Lycopodium apodum* Linnaeus; *Diplostachyum apodum* (Linnaeus) Palisot de Beauvois; *Selaginella apus* (Linnaeus) Spring

Sand Spike-Moss
Selaginella arenicola L. Underwood subsp. *arenicola*   **Photo 167**

Form: An erect, low-growing fern ally with irregularly forked, belowground and aerial stems; aerial stems erect to ascending and borne in compact or spreading clumps to about 10 cm tall; plant exhibiting a superficially mosslike appeareance.

Leaves: Appressed to strongly ascending, overlapping on the aerial stem in about six rows, green to grayish green in color, triangular to somewhat lanceolate in overall outline, 2 - 3 mm long, to about 0.5 mm wide, minutely hairy at the base and along the margins, apex with a minute, whitish bristle.

Strobili: 1 - 3.5 cm long, larger in diameter than the vegetated aerial stems; sporophylls grooved, lanceolate, sometimes minutely hairy near the base and along the margins.

Habitat: Sandy soils of dry pinelands, scrub and coastal dunes.

Distribution: Ranging essentially throughout Florida and southern Georgia.

Remarks: This species can be most easily distinguished from other members of the genus in Florida by its erect, clump-forming habit, and dry, sandy habitat (but see the comments above concerning *S. rupestris,* and below concerning *S. acanthonota).* It specific epithet, which means "sand dweller," refers to this habitat.

The precise taxonomy of *S. arenicola* is somewhat unsettled. Small (1931, 1938) recognized two species for the taxon, *S. arenicola* L. Underwood and *S. acanthonota* L. Underwood, distinguishing between them on the basis of the relatively stiff, long (about as long as the blade), apical bristles on the leaves of the latter, and the shorter (about half as long as the blade), weaker, apical bristles of the former. Clausen (1946) also recognized both species, but questioned whether the two species might be physiological variants of a single species, and further noted that numerous specimens were intermediate between the two and thus difficult to classify (some of these intermediates were once recognized as *S. floridana).* In 1955 Tryon recognized *S. arenicola* as a single species with three subspecies: subsp. *arenicola,* subsp. *riddellii,* and subsp. *acanthonota,* the first and third of which are typically reported from Florida (plants of the second subspecies are generally reported from Texas to Alabama and Georgia). Lakela and Long (1976) followed Tryon's treatment, and Wunderlin (1982, 1998) mentioned subsp. *acanthonota* in synonymy with *S. arenicola.* Mickel (1979) mentioned only *S. arenicola* and subsp. *riddellii,* and Lellinger (1985) observed that the maintenance of these entities at even the subspecific level seems questionable. Valdespino (1993), on the other hand, writing in the *Flora of North America,* recognized both *S. arenicola* and *S. acanthonota* as full species, claiming that the two can be easily distinguished in the field. According to Valdespino, the former species displays mostly scalelike stem leaves on the underground stems, and has mostly belowground stems and glabrous leaf and sporophyll apices, whereas the underground stem leaves of the latter are not scalelike, the stems are mostly aerial, and the leaf and sporophyll apices are covered mostly with soft, inconspicuous hairs. The treatment here, in one of the few departures in this volume from the *Flora of North America,* does not recognize *S. acanthonota* for Florida, since the material I have seen from Florida is more closely similar to *S. arenicola* than the latter. However, photo 168, which seems to fit well the description and illustration of *S. acanthonota* found in Small (1938) and which was taken at Braxton Rocks, a Nature Conservancy Preserve in Coffee County, Georgia, shows a typical example of the latter species, which should probably be looked for in Florida. It appears more closely related to *S. rupestris* than to *S. arenicola.*

Synonyms: *Selaginella arenicola* L. Underwood subsp. *acanthonota* (L. Underwood) R. M. Tyson; *S. floridana* Maxon; *S. funiformis* Van Eseltine; *S. humifusa* Van Eseltine; *S. rupestris* (Linnaeus) Spring var. *acanthonota* (L. Underwood) Clute

Eaton's Spike-Moss, Pygmy Spike-Moss

Selaginella eatonii Hieronymus ex Small   **Photo 169**

Form: A small, low-growing, clump-forming species with creeping, few-branched to unbranched, flattened, stems; forming small, dense clumps less than 6 cm wide.

Leaves: Iridescent green in color, well-spaced to somewhat crowded on the stem; lateral leaves ovate, to about 1.5 mm long, and 1 mm wide; medial leaves lanceolate, smaller, to about 1.2 mm long, less than 0.5 mm wide, usually overlapping the stem; margins transparent and minutely toothed (requires magnification of at least 20x to see clearly); apex with a long bristle.

Strobili: Small, solitary, to about 2 mm long and wide.

Habitat: Rock hammocks, solution holes, limestone outcrops in pine rocklands.

Distribution: Dade County, Florida, and Cuba; first discovered in Florida in 1903 and first described by Small in his 1918 *Ferns of Tropical Florida.* Listed as endangered by the Florida Department of Agriculture.

Remarks: This plant's minute size, small, dense, matlike growth habit, and bristle-tipped, narrowly lanceolate medial leaves distinguish it from other members of the genus in its Florida range. Small named the species in honor of A. A. Eaton (1865-1908), a turn-of-the-century Florida fern collector and one of Small's field companions. Lakela and Long (1976) and others have treated this species under the name *S. armata* Baker, a West Indian species.

Synonyms: *Diplostachyum eatonii* (Hieronymus ex Small) Small

Gulf Spike-Moss, Louisiana Spike-Moss

Selaginella ludoviciana (A. Braun) A. Braun   **Photo 170**

Form: A prostrate to slightly erect, low-growing, mat-forming fern ally with slender roots all along the stem.

Leaves: Bright green with finely toothed margins; lateral leaves conspicuous, ovate to lanceolate, well-spaced along the stem, to about 2.7 mm long and 2 mm wide; medial leaves smaller, inconspicuous, to about 2 mm long and 1 mm wide, narrowly lanceolate, appressed to the stem; margins finely toothed and exhibiting a conspicuous, transparent to pale edge about five cells in width.

Strobili: To about 1.5 cm long, somewhat flattened, borne singly or in pairs.

Habitat: Swamp margins, moist slopes in rich woods, limestone ledges, ravine slopes.

Distribution: Northern Florida, sparingly southward to about Polk County.

Remarks: Very similar to *S. apoda.* See the remarks for the latter species for characters that distinguish the two.

This species was first described in 1860 by Alexander Braun who named it for Louisiana *(ludoviciana* means "of Louisiana"), the state in which it was first collected ten years earlier. In his *Ferns of Florida,* Small (1931) adopted Braun's name, but in his *Ferns of the Southeastern States* (1938) he assigned the species to the genus *Diplostachyum* with the new combination *D. ludoviciana* (A. Braun) Small. In more recent years several authors synonymized the species with the very similar *S. apoda,* a name by which it is still sometimes seen. Somers and Buck (1975) and Buck and Lucansky (1976), however, made convincing arguments for again raising the taxon to specific level and it is so treated by Valdespino (1993) and by Wunderlin (1998).

Synonyms: *Lycopodium ludovicianum* (A. Braun); *Diplostachyum ludovicianum* (A. Braun) Small

Blue Spike-Moss, Peacock Spike-Moss

Selaginella uncinata (Desvaux ex Poiret) Spring   **Photo 171**

Form: A prostrate, low-growing, mat-forming fern ally with a slender, straw-colored stem, and flat, divided lateral branches to about 5 cm long.

Leaves: Iridescent green to bluish green; lateral leaves well-spaced (especially along the main stem), generally ovate to oblong in overall shape, to about 4 mm long, 2.5 mm wide; medial leaves to about 3.5 mm long, 2 mm wide, appressed to the stem and slightly overlapping; margins pale, transparent, entire, without hairs.

Strobili: To about 1.5 cm long, borne singly at the tips of branchlets.

Habitat: Moist woods along streams and spring runs.

Distribution: Native to China; used horticulturally and naturalized at several locations in Florida, Georgia, and Louisiana; collected in Marion, Hillsborough, and Dade Counties, Florida and within 15 miles of the state line in Decatur and Thomas Counties, Georgia.

Remarks: The iridescent green color, entire leaves, and mat-forming habit help distinguish the species. It is vegetatively similar in appearance only to the closely related *S. willdenovii,* a high-climbing viny species with woodlike branches, but is well separated from it geographically. Its specific epithet means hooked or J-shaped, in reference to the earlike auricles at the base of the leaves.

Synonyms: *Lycopodium uncinatum* Desvaux ex Poiret

Vine Spike-Moss

Selaginella willdenovii (Desvaux ex Poiret) Baker   **Photo 172**

Form: A branching, high-climbing to scrambling, vinelike fern ally with woodlike stems to about 10 m long.

Leaves: Iridescent blue green in color; lateral leaves ovate to oblong, to about 4 mm long and 2 mm wide, rounded at the apices; medial leaves lanceolate, asymmetrical, less than 3 mm long, a little more than 1 mm wide, acutely to bluntly pointed at the apices; margins entire and transparent.

Strobili: Borne singly at the tips of the branchlets, to about 2 cm long.

Habitat: Hammocks.

Distribution: Native to Burma, Malaysia, Indonesia, and the Philippines; introduced to Florida and the West Indies and occurring mostly in Dade County, also collected in St. Lucie County.

Remarks: The high-climbing habit and long stems of this fern ally easily distinguish it from others in the genus. It is named for Carl Ludwig von Willdenow (1765-1812), who was director of the Berlin Botanical Garden.

Synonyms: *Lycopodium willdenowii* Desvaux ex Poiret

THELYPTERIDACEAE - MARSH FERN FAMILY

The genus name *Thelypteris,* from which the family name is derived, was first applied by Linnaeus and means "female fern," hence the common name "maiden fern" used for many species in the family. Previously, all of the ferns described below were included within the genus *Thelypteris,* which, itself, has been variously included, along with other genera, in the families Aspidiaceae and Polypodiaceae. To add to the taxonomic confusion, most of the species described below were also once included within the genus *Dryopteris,* a genus that is now included within the family Dryopoteridaceae. Suffice it to say that, depending upon the age of the reference consulted or the interpretation of its author, the species included here might be found under a variety of genera.

In the broad sense, the genus *Thelypteris* is one of the largest of the fern genera. Nearly 1,000 species are known worldwide, including at least 16 in Florida and 21 in North America. Many species of *Thelypteris* exhibit transparent, needlelike hairs on the blade tissue.

Many members of the marsh fern family, particularly those in the genus *Thelypteris,* are difficult to distinguish at first glance; some are even difficult to separate after close inspection. Many have similar fronds, pinnae, and pinnules that can only be distinguished from each other by venation patterns, the position of the sori on the pinnules, the type and amount of hairs on the blade tissue, or some other obscure character or combination of characters. Nevertheless, with diligence most specimens found in the field, especially the more common ones, can be assigned to species. The position of the lower lateral veins of adjacent pinnules is especially helpful in separating members of the *Thelypteris* into three distinctive categories. In one group, the basal lateral veins join together and run as one to the base of the sinus. In another group, the basal lateral veins join the pinnule margin at or above the sinus. In one species *(T.*

palustris) the veins are forked. Figure 32 illustrates these variations, and the following descriptions mention this character when it is important for identification purposes.

Species of *Thelypteris* typically grow in abundant and often showy populations that regularly include several members of the genus. They tend to be somewhat aggressive and a few species regularly hybridize with each other. As a result, they are not often used in gardens. Nevertheless, for relatively confined sites where a lush, relatively tall fernery is desired, such species as *Thelypteris dentata, T. kunthii, T. ovata,* and *Macrothelypteris torresiana* might prove to be worthy landscape candidates.

Key to the species of the Thelypteridaceae

1. Blades pinnatifid-pinnatifid, or blades bipinnate-pinnatifid to tripinnate.
    2. Blade pinnatifid, rachis with a conspicuous wing connecting adjacent pinnae . . . .
    . . . . *Phegopteris hexagonoptera*
    2. Blade bipinnate-pinnatifid to tripinnate . . . . *Macrothelypteris torresiana*
1. Blades pinnate or pinnate-pinnatifid.
    3. Blades pinnate.
        4. Margins of pinnae sharply toothed, at least toward the tips . . . . *T. serrata*
        4. Margins entire, undulate, or with blunt, more or less rounded teeth . . . .
        . . . . *T. reticulata*
    3. Blades pinnate-pinnatifid.
        5. Basal lateral veins of adjacent pinnules joining the margin of the pinnule at or
        above the base of the sinus.
            6. Lateral veins of the pinnules forked toward the tip (seen only with 10x magnification) and having the form of tiny tuning forks . . . . *T. palustris*
            6. Lateral veins of the pinnules not forked.
                7. Lower pair of pinnules of the pinnae absent or reduced in size, giving the pinnae
                an overall lanceolate appearance . . . . *T. grandis*
                7. Lower pair of pinnules of the pinnae equal to or longer than those above.
                    8. Lower surfaces of blades vested with conspicuous sulphur yellow or reddish
                    glands.
                        9. Lower surfaces of blades vested with sulphur yellow glands. . . . .
                        . . . . *T. opulenta*
                        9. Lower surfaces of blades with reddish glands . . . . *T. resinifera*
                    8. Lower surfaces without glands, or with only inconpsicuous reddish glands that
                    require magnification to see clearly.
                        10. Stem erect to suberect, lower pinnules of the pinnae enlarged, often paralleling the rachis and sometimes incised, scales at the base of the petioles ovate
                        in shape and without hairs . . . . *T. patens*
                        10. Stem creeping, scales of the lower petiole lanceolate and usually hairy.
                            11. Upper surfaces of the pinnae hairy, at least on the veins . . . .
                            . . . . *T. kunthii*
                            11. Upper surfaces of the pinnae without hairs, or with only a very few, very

short hairs, these confined to the midvein.

    12. Blade abruptly tapering toward the tip, apical pinna typically narrow throughout and similar in appearance to the lateral pinnae, lateral pinnae typically less than 1.5 cm wide . . . . *T. augescens*

    12. Blade not or only slightly abruptly tapering toward the tip, apical pinna different in appearance from lateral pinnae, at least the medial lateral pinnae typically greater than 1.5 cm wide . . . . *T. ovata*

5. Basal veins of the pinnules joining together below and running as a single vein to the base of the sinus.

  13. Plant typically growing on limestone, blades usually arching, pendent, often vine like or runnerlike at the tip and sometimes rooting at the apex, pinnae much reduced in size near the apex . . . . *T. reptans*

  13. Plant terrestrial, not vinelike, not rooting at the apex.

    14. Plant with branched, star-shaped (stellate) hairs, especially on the rachis, but also often on other parts.

      15. Blade typically exceeding 15 cm wide, apical pinnae typically well-separated from lateral pinnae and appearing somewhat like them . . . . *T. tetragona*

      15. Blades less than 15 cm wide, apex of blade gradually tapering into the terminal pinna . . . . *T. sclerophylla*

    14. Plants with simple hairs, or without hairs.

      16. Blades lacking hairs, sori marginal and appearing to connect from pinnule to pinnule in a continuous line throughout each pinna . . . . *T. interrupta*

      16. Blades hairy.

        17. Lower surfaces of blades vested with sulphur yellow glands . . . . *T. opulenta*

        17. Lower surfaces of blades lacking sulphur yellow glands.

          18. Lowermost lateral veins of adjacent pinnules joining together below the sinus to form a single vein at least 2 mm long . . . . *T. dentata*

          18. Lowermost lateral veins of adjacent pinnules joining together below the sinus to form a single vein that usually does not exceed 1 mm long . . . . *T. hispidula*

Mariana Maiden Fern, Torres's Fern

Macrothelypteris torresiana (Gaudichaud-Beaupre) Ching

Photo 173, 174, 175

Form: A medium-size, erect to arching, lacy, finely divided, evergreen (at least in central and southern Florida) fern.

Fronds: 6 - 150 cm tall, often somewhat arching or spreading; borne in clusters from the base; fertile and sterile similar in appearance.

Petiole: 15 - 75 cm long, pale to whitish, stout when mature, relatively thin and wiry when young; grooved.

Rachis: Whitish, thin on young fronds to thickish on mature fronds.

Blade: Bipinnate-pinnatifid to tripinnate, triangular in overall shape, 25 - 85 cm long, 25 - 50 cm wide.

Pinnae: To about 35 cm long and 10 cm wide; pinnules 2 - 8 cm long, to about 2.5 cm wide, their margins dentate to pinnatifid; both upper and lower surfaces vested with needlelike hairs.

Sori: Round, borne along the midribs of the pinnules; often without indusia; typically without hairs, but sometimes glandular.

Habitat: Escaped from cultivation, established in wet woods, under bridges, and along moist roadsides and streams.

Distribution: Statewide.

Remarks: The lacy, bipinnate-pinnatifid leaves make this plant easy to distinguish from all other members of its family, and from most other Florida ferns. It could, perhaps, be confused with *Athyrium felix-femina,* but may be distinguished at a glance by the lower pinnae of the current species being longer rather than shorter than those above, and nearly opposite, rather than mostly alternate (sometimes widely so) on the rachis.

M. torresiana was for a long time referred to as *Dryopteris setigera,* a name which has been determined to have been misapplied to the species (Morton, 1941; Smith, 1993b; Leonard, 1972). Leonard, in particular, points out that the "true *D. setigera* is a rare Asian species, probably not cultivated nor naturalized in the New World" (1972, p. 97).

Mariana maiden fern was first collected in the United States in Florida in 1904 or 1906 (Small, 1938; Leonard, 1972). It is an alien species that is native to the Mariana Islands (hence, the common name), but has been used extensively for cultivation in the southeastern United States. It is widely naturalized in Florida. Its genus name means "large female fern," and its specific epithet is in honor of Luis de Torres, the governor of Guam in 1820.

Synonyms: *Polystichum torresianum* Gaudichaud-Beaupre; *Dryopteris uliginosa* (Kunze) C. Christensen; *Thelypteris torresiana* (Gaudichaud-Beaupre) Alston; *T. uliginosa* (Kunze) Ching.

Broad Beech Fern, Southern Beech Fern

Phegopteris hexagonoptera (Michaux) Fee   **Photos 176, 177**

Form: A small- to medium-size, deciduous fern with a winged rachis and slender, long-creeping stem.

Fronds: 25 - 75 cm tall, easily broken, dull green in color, dying back in winter; fertile and sterile similar in appearance but fertile appearing late in the season.

Petiole: Straw colored, sometimes darker toward the base, 20 - 45 cm long.

Rachis: Green in color, conspicuously winged throughout its extent.

Blade: Bipinnatifid, triangular or deltoid in overall shape; 15 - 33 cm long, about as broad at the widest point; lowermost pinnae inclined forward or downward.

Pinnae: Pinnatifid, 7 - 20 cm long, long-pointed at the tip.

Sori: Round, small, borne near the margins of the pinnule, near the end of a vein.

Habitat: Rich, well-drained woods, shaded slopes and ravines, hammocks.

Distribution: North-central panhandle, including Washington, Jackson, Gadsden, Liberty, and Leon counties.

Remarks: The winged rachis, triangular shape of the blade, and inclined lower pinnae help distinguish this species. This plant ranges widely across the eastern United States and is often found in woodlands dominated by American beech trees *(Fagus grandifolia* Ehrhart), hence its common name. It is a species of shady woodlands and dies back in winter as well as when it receives too much sun. Hence, it does best under cultivation only when planted in deep shade. The specific epithet means "six-angled wing" and refers to the plant's winged rachis. The plant was first discovered in 1803 and described by Andre Michaux (1746-1802), a European botanist who explored much of North America and whose name is encountered frequently among the names and authorities of American plants.

Synonyms: *Polypodium hexagonopterum* Michaux; *Dryopteris hexagonoptera* (Michaux) C. Christensen; *Thelypteris hexagonoptera* (Michaux) Nieuwland.

Abrupt-Tipped Maiden Fern

Thelypteris augescens (Link) Munz & I.M. Johnson   **Photo 178**

Form: A relatively tall, robust, evergreen fern with a scaly, long-creeping stem that is 4 - 8 mm in diameter.

Fronds: Evergreen, 65 - 140 cm long; sterile and fertile fronds similar.

Petiole: Straw colored, 15 - 70 cm long, 2 - 9 mm in diameter; base with tan to brownish, linear-lanceolate scales with marginal hairs.

Rachis: Straw colored, hairy.

Blade: Pinnate-pinnatifid, 30 - 70 cm long, abruptly narrowed to a long, pinnatifid tip.

Pinnae: Narrow, lowermost 10 - 22 cm long, to about 1.5 cm wide, uppermost much shorter; segments curved and with revolute margins; hairy below, without hairs on the midveins and lateral veins above.

Sori: Round, medial, hairy.

Habitat: Limestone banks.

Distribution: Southernmost Florida, including both Dade and Collier Counties; also collected in Levy County.

Remarks: Similar in many respects to *T. ovata* by lacking hairs on the lateral and midveins on the upper surfaces of the pinnules, distinguished from it by the pinnae always being less than 2 cm wide. The abruptly-narrowed blade is often a very good character for distinguishing this species. Though

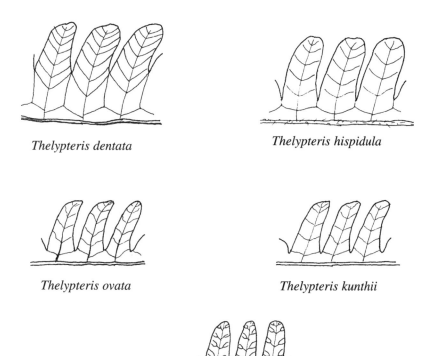

Thelypteris dentata

Thelypteris hispidula

Thelypteris ovata

Thelypteris kunthii

Thelypteris palustris

Figure 32. Typical Pinnule Venation in *Thelypteris*

not all blades exhibit this character in its extreme form, and a few other species, most notably *T. kunthii,* have similar, though less dramatically-tapered blades, this character is present often enough to make it useful in field identification. However, *T. augescens* is known to hybridize with both *T. kunthii* and *T. ovata,* making intermediate specimens very difficult to identify. Small (1931) reported this species as new to Florida as of 1915. The specific epithet, *augescens,* derives from the Greek word *augesco,* which means to increase or grow, perhaps in reference to its long-creeping stem. This species is listed as threatened by the Florida Department of Agriculture.

Synonyms: *Aspidium augescens* Link; *Christella augescens* (Link) Pichi-Sermolli; *Dryopteris augescens* (Link) C. Christensen.

Downy Maiden Fern, Downy Shield Fern, Tapering Tri-Vein Fern

Thelypteris dentata (Forsskal) E.P. St. John   **Photos 179, 180**

Form: A medium-size, evergreen (in central and southern Florida, dying back in northern Florida) fern with a stout, short-creeping stem.

Fronds: 40 - 150 cm tall, fertile fronds with longer petioles and more contracted and wider pinnae.

Petiole: Purplish brown, especially nearer the base, 15 - 50 cm long, with stout hairs, and brown, hairy scales, the latter more numerous near the base.

Rachis: Purplish and hairy.

Blade: Pinnate-pinnatifid, 20 - 100 cm long, to about 25 cm wide, with several pairs of the lower pinnae steadily decreasing in length toward the base.

Pinnae: 7 - 17 cm long, to about 3 cm wide, shallowly cut into squarish, blunt lobes with broadly rounded apices; basal veins of adjacent pinnae joining together 2 - 4 mm below the sinus and running directly to it (requires magnification); both upper and lower surfaces vested with short hairs.

Sori: Rounded to kidney shaped, small, borne nearly equidistant between the midvein and margins of the pinnules.

Habitat: Floodplains, under bridges, roadsides, moist woods, rocky hammocks.

Distribution: Throughout Florida. Small (1931) implies that this species arrived in Florida from the tropics by natural means, then later died out in the southern parts of the state. However, it is more likely that it was introduced from the tropics and has now become well established. It is often found in disturbed sites and is regarded as a greenhouse weed.

Remarks: Distinguished from other members of the genus by the combination of decreasing length of pinnae toward the base, blunt pinnules, and by the veins of adjoining pinnules joining together 2 - 4 mm below the sinus.

Synonyms: *Polypodium dentatum* Forsskal; *Christella dentata* (Forsskal) Brownsey & Jermy; *Cyclosorus dentatus* (Forsskal) Ching; *Dryopteris dentata* (Forsskal) C. Christensen; *D. mollis* (Swartz) Hieronymus; *Thelypteris reducta* Small.

Stately Maiden Fern

Thelypteris grandis A.R. Smith var. *grandis*   **Photos 181, 182, 183**

Form: A relatively large, evergreen fern with a stout, scaly, long-creeping stem to about 1 cm in diameter.

Fronds: Potentially to about 3 m tall (but probably not exceeding about 1.5 m in Florida), to 50 cm wide, borne several centimeters apart along the rhizome.

Petiole: Straw colored above, base brownish and sparsely vested with hairy scales, 1 - 1.3 m tall, to about 1.2 cm in diameter.

Rachis: Straw colored, with minute hairs (requires magnification).

Blade: Pinnate below, tapering to a pinnatifid apex; approaching 2 m in length, 45 - 90 cm wide; widest nearest the base.

Pinnae: Pinnatifid, 15 - 45 cm long, 2 - 4.8 cm wide, straight to ascending, pinnules some-what curved; hairy on the veins below, but hairs lacking on the midveins and lateral veins on the upper surfaces of the pinnules, and on the blade tissue throughout; lowest pair of veins from adjacent pinnules joining at the base of the sinus rather than below it; first few pinnules on the lowest pinnae often reduced in size or missing.

Sori: Round, borne about equidistant between the midvein and margins of the pinnules.

Habitat: Wet swamps.

Distribution: Collected in Florida only in Collier County.

Remarks: This rare species may be distinguished by a combination of its large size, stout petioles, and, most importantly, by the reduced size of the pinnules on the lower pinnae as described above. The species was first discovered in Florida by Dan Austin and Clifton Nauman in November 1978 as part of a survey of the flora of Fakahatchee Strand in Big Cypress National Preserve (Nauman, 1979a). This population remains healthy, but is con-fined to an old tram road and is apparently not spreading. This species is listed as endangered by the Florida Department of Agriculture.

Synonyms: *Nephrodium paucijugum* Jenman.

Variable Maiden Fern, St. John's Shield Fern

Thelypteris hispidula (Decaisne) C. F. Reed var. *versicolor*
(R. P. St. John) Lellinger **Photo 184**

Form: A relatively tall, conspicuous, evergreen (in central and southern Florida) woods fern with a stout, creeping to erect stem.

Fronds: Borne in clusters from the base, 40 - 95 cm long; fertile and sterile fronds similar.

Petiole: Straw colored, to about 40 cm long, hairy, with brown, hairy scales at the base.

Rachis: Straw colored to pale greenish; hairy.

Blade: Pinnate-pinnatifid, lower one to two pairs of pinnae often reduced, sometimes signif-icantly so; upper and lower surfaces of blade tissue and veins hairy.

Pinnae: Pinnatifid, 4 - 14 cm long, to about 2 cm wide, hairy above and below, basal veins of adjacent pinnae often joining together 1 - 2 mm below the sinus, then running as one to the base of the sinus (may require 10x magnification to see clearly).

Sori: Borne in a row between the margin and central axis of fertile pinnae, with a hairy, kid-ney-shaped, peltate indusium.

Habitat: Streamsides, hammocks, limestone sinks and outcrops, moist woodlands, seep-age areas.

Distribution: Statewide.

Remarks: This is one of three widespread members of this genus that are similar in appear-ance and difficult to distinguish at a glance. The present species is most similar in general appearance to *T. kunthii* and *T. ovata*. The present species may be distinguished from the other two by examining the lowest lateral veins of adjacent pinnules with a 10x hand lens. Many (but not all) of those of the present species join each other approximately 1 - 2 mm below the sinus and then run directly to the sinus. Those of *T. kunthii* and *T. ovata,* if they join at all, do so at the base of the sinus; more often they join the margin of the pinnule above the base of the sinus. *T. hispidula* is further distinguished from *T. ovata* by the pinnules being hairy above rather than glabrous or vested with only a few short hairs. *T. hispidula* was originally described in 1938 by Robert Porter St. John, and was first introduced to science under the synonym *T. versicolor* in Small's *Ferns of the Southeastern States*. The type specimen for the species was collected by R. P. St. John near Brooksville, Hernando County, Florida.

Synonyms: *Thelypteris versicolor* R. P. St. John in Small; *Dryopteris versicolor* (R. P. St. John) Broun; *Thelypteris macilenta* E. P. St. John; *T. quadrangularis* (Fee) Schelpe var. *versicolor* (R. P. St. John) A. R. Smith.

Hottentot Fern, Willdenow's Fern, Spready Tri-Vein Fern

Thelypteris interrupta (Willdenow) K. Iwatsuki   **Photos 185, 186**

Form: A robust, mostly erect, evergreen fern with a long-creeping, cordlike stem and widely-spaced fronds; stem black except for a green tip.

Fronds: 0.5 - 2 m tall or taller, to about 30 cm wide, borne 3 - 7 cm apart along the rhizome.

Petiole: 20 - 125 cm long, 3 - 6 mm in diameter; straw colored to tan above, blackish near the base; without hairs or scales.

Rachis: Straw colored to pale purplish.

Blade: Pinnate-pinnatifid, 30 - 125 cm tall, widest at the base and tapering to a pinnatifid apex.

Pinnae: 7 - 30 cm long, 1 - 2 cm wide; shiny green above; lower surface of main axis vested with tan scales, tissue and veins most often lacking hairs, though sometimes with very short (less than 0.3 mm long) needleshaped hairs; pinnules deltate in shape; lowest lateral veins from adjacent pinnules joining together below and leading to the sinus.

Sori: Round, borne near the margins of the pinnule and appearing to form a single line that is seemingly connected from pinnule to pinnule.

Habitat: Marshes, low hammocks, swamps, cypress heads, creek beds, open woods, wet roadside ditches.

Distribution: Generally common from about Marion County southward; also collected in Liberty and Franklin Counties and along the Suwannee River.

Remarks: *T. interrupta* may be distinguished from other Florida *Thelypteris* by the combination of 1) the lowest lateral veins of adjacent pinnules joining below and running as a single vein to the sinus (requires magnification), 2) by the absence or near-absence of hairs on the blade tissue, and 3) by the distinctive sori, which appear to be connected in a single line along the margins of the pinnules. The latter of these is by far the most easily-seen character and is diagnostic among Florida's species of *Thelypteris*.

   T. interrupta is sometimes treated as *T. totta* (Thundberg) Schelpe, a species attributed to both South and North America as well as South Africa (see Lellinger, 1985). Lellinger argues that the name used here should be reserved for specimens from India until cytological work is completed to determine whether the two taxa are conspecific. The specific epithet comes from the continuous line of sori, interrupted only by the base of the sinus.

Synonyms: *Pteris interrupta* Willdenow; *Cyclosorus gongylodes* (Schkuhr) Link; *C. interruptus* (Willdenow) H. Ito; *C. tottus* (Thunburg) Pichi-Sermolli; *Dryopteris gongylodes*

(Schkuhr) Kuntze; *Thelypteris gongylodes* (Schkuhr) Small; *T. totta* (Thunburg) Schelpe.

Southern Shield Fern, Widespread Maiden Fern

Thelypteris kunthii (Desvaux) C.V. Morton   **Photos 187, 188**

Form: A relatively tall, robust, evergreen (sometimes dying back in cold winters in north Florida) fern with a stout (to 8 mm diameter), short- to long-creeping stem and erect to arching fronds.

Fronds: Coarse, 50 - 160 cm tall, to about 40 cm wide at the base; fertile and sterile similar in appearance.

Petiole: Straw colored above, shading to dark, reddish brown below; scaly at the base.

Rachis: Straw colored.

Blade: Pinnate-pinnatifid, triangular to lanceolate in overall form; 15 - 80 cm long.

Pinnae: Pinnatifid, 8 - 20 cm long, to about 2.5 cm wide, hairy on the lateral and midveins both above and below; tissue of pinnules typically hairy below, sometimes without hairs on the tissue above; basal veins of adjacent pinnules occasionally joining each other at the base of the sinus, more typically joining the margin of the pinnule above the base of the sinus.

Sori: With hairy, peltate, kidney-shaped indusia; borne between the margins and central veins of the pinnules.

Habitat: Limestone sinks and outcrops, streamsides, ditches, under bridges, roadsides, woodlands.

Distribution: Statewide.

Remarks: This is one of the state's more common *Thelypteris*. It is similar in overall aspect to *T. hispidula,* but is distinguished by basal veins of adjacent pinnules not joining together below the sinus. It is distinguished from *T. ovata* by the upper surfaces of the pinnules being hairy on the veins and axes, but also see remarks for *T. augescens.* To make identification even more challenging, *T. kunthii* is known to hybridize with and produce intermediates between *T. augescens, T. hispidula* var. *versicolor,* and *T. ovata.* See the key to species above for help in distinguishing this species from others in the genus.

Synonyms: *Nephrodium kunthii* Desvaux; *Christella normalis* (C. Christensen) Holttum; *Dryopteris normalis* C. Christensen; *Thelypteris macrorhizoma* R. P. St. John; *T. normalis* (C. Christensen) Moxley; *T. saxatilis* R. P. St. John; *T. unca* R. P. St. John.

Jeweled Maiden Fern

Thelypteris opulenta (Kaulfuss) Fosberg   **Photos 189, 190**

Form: A medium-size marsh fern with a short-creeping stem that is clothed with dark brown, hairy scales.

Fronds: Slightly dimorphic, to about 1.5 m tall.

Petiole: Dark purplish brown toward the base, 50 - 70 cm tall, vested with minute, glandular hairs (requires 20x magnification to see clearly).

Rachis: Similar to the petiole in color.

Blade: 50 - 90 cm tall, 25 - 50 cm wide, generally ovate in outline and abruptly tapered at the apex, vested throughout with minute, stalked, colorless glands (requires high magnification).

Pinnae: To about 30 cm long, 1.5 - 2.5 cm wide, borne alternately along the rachis; axis and veins of the lower surface vested with minute, globular, sulfur yellow glands (requires magnification); lowermost lateral veins of adjacent pinnules various, sometimes meeting the margin above the base of the sinus, sometimes at the base of the sinus, sometimes meeting each other and joining as one below the sinus; fertile pinnules often with inrolled margins.

Sori: Borne near the pinnule margin (or apparently so due to inrolled margins) within glandular indusia.

Habitat: Shaded hammocks, in association with strangler fig *(Ficus aurea* Nuttall) in its Florida station.

Distribution: Collected in Florida only in Dade County; last collected in 1993, likely escaped from cultivation.

Remarks: This species is very restricted in distribution in Florida. It was last collected in a Dade County hammock that has now been developed into a subdivision. It is most easily distinguished from other members of its genus by the minute, globular, sulfur yellow glands on the axis and veins of the lower surfaces of the leaves.

Synonyms: *Aspidium opulentum* Kaulfuss, *Amphineuron opulentum* (Kaulfuss) Holttum.

Ovate Maiden Fern

Thelypteris ovata R. P. St. John var. *ovata*   **Photo 191**

Form: A moderately tall, often arching, evergreen (but dying back in cold winters in northern Florida) woods fern with a moderately slender, branching stem.

Fronds: 35 - 165 cm long, fertile and sterile similar.

Petiole: Straw colored above, shading to reddish brown below, 10 - 80 cm long.

Rachis: Straw colored, sparsely to densely hairy.

Blade: 15 - 75 cm long, to about 40 cm wide, pinnate-pinnatifid, egg-shaped in general outline (hence the specific epithet), often abruptly tapered to a pinnatifid apex.

Pinnae: Pinnatifid, hairy to somewhat hairy below, moderately shiny and lacking hairs above (or with only sparse hairs on the axis above, these generally not exceeding about 0.2 mm long); basal veins of adjacent pinnae joining the margin of the pinnule at or, more typically, above the base of the sinus, but sometimes joining together below and running as one to the base of the sinus.

Sori: Small, round, borne near the margins of the pinnules; indusia kidney shaped and sparsely hairy.

Habitat: Limestone sinks and outcrops, calcareous hammocks, moist woods.

Distribution: Statewide.

Remarks: Roland M. Harper, a well-known southern geologist, botanist, and naturalist, first discovered this species in 1902 in Georgia, where it is not common. It was not officially named and described until 1938 when it appeared in J. K. Small's *Ferns of the Southeastern States.* It is most easily confused with *T. hispidula* and *T. kunthii,* but may be distinguished from both by being more lustrous above and by lacking hairs (or having only a few very small hairs less than 0.2 mm long) on the veins and axes on the upper sides of the pinnules (see the key to species, above). There are several large and conspicuous populations of this species along the trails at Florida Caverns State Park, near Marianna.

Marsh Fern

Thelypteris palustris Schott var. *pubescens* (Lawson) Fernald   **Photo 192**

Form: A relatively narrow *Thelypteris* with a black, relatively thin, creeping stem.

Fronds: 20 - 90 cm tall, dying back in winter; sterile and fertile fronds similar; sometimes with fertile fronds that are narrower, more erect, and with inrolled segments that often appear more contracted than those on sterile fronds.

Petiole: Straw colored to darkened (especially at the base), typically 9 - 45 cm long (sometimes longer), to about 3 mm in diameter, base with tan, ovate, glabrous scales.

Rachis: Straw colored to greenish, with short, very fine hairs which require magnification to see clearly.

Blade: Pinnate-pinnatifid, 10 - 40 cm long (occasionally longer), to about 16 cm wide at the widest point, narrowly oval to narrowly elliptic in overall outline, tapering to an acute, pinnatifid tip; wider at the base than at the tip.

Pinnae: Pinnatifid, mostly alternate on the rachis, 2 - 10 cm long, to about 2 cm wide; individual pinnules entire and linear to oblong; lateral veins of the pinnules forked toward the margins (requires magnification).

Sori: Round, medial, at least partially concealed by the inrolled margins of the leaf segments.

Habitat: Wet, open woods, marshes, swamps.

Distribution: Throughout Florida.

Remarks: The lateral veins on the pinnules are forked toward the tip, a characteristic that easily distinguishes this species from others in the family. Its specific epithet refers to its preference for marshy habitats.

T. palustris is the type species of the genus and is one of the few fern species complexes that occurs on all of the world's large continents; though it is absent from Australia, it does occur in New Zealand (A. F. Tryon, et. al, 1980). This species was once thought to contain at least four varieties, and has been thought by some to be possibly conspecific with *T. confluens* (Thundberg) Morton, a species of Africa, Madagascar, southern India, New Zealand, and South America (Proctor, 1985). A. F. Tryon and others (1980) have shown there to be only two varieties (var. *palustris* and var. *pubescens*), and that the current species and *T. confluens* may be reliably distinguished by differences in the surfaces of their spores. All of Florida specimens are referred to var. *pubescens*.

Synonyms: *Lastrea thelypteris* (Linnaeus) Bory var. *pubescens* Lawson; *Dryopteris thelypteris* (Linnaeus) A. Gray var. *pubescens* (Lawson) Weatherby; *Thelypteris palustris* var. *haleana* Fernald

Grid-Scale Maiden Fern

Thelypteris patens (Swartz) Small var. *patens*   **Photos 193, 194, 195**

Form: An evergreen fern with a very stout, erect to suberect stem that on some plants is trunk-like and extends 30 cm or more above the ground.

Fronds: 15 - 200 cm tall, clustered at the ground, sterile and fertile similar.

Petiole: Stout, to about 1 cm in diameter or a little more, 5 - 50 cm long (or sometimes up to twice this long), conspicuously brown scaly at the base.

Rachis: Straw colored, grooved, very hairy with translucent hairs.

Blade: Pinnate-pinnatifid, 25 - 100 cm long, broadest near the base and tapering to a pinnatifid apex.

Pinnae: 3 - 32 cm long, 1 - 4 cm wide, lowest pair of veins from adjacent pinnules joining the pinnule margins at the base of the sinus or just above it; lowermost pinnules of the pinnae often enlarged, sometimes incised, and running parallel with the rachis.

Sori: Round, borne equidistant or nearly so between the midvein and margins of the pinnules.

Habitat: Rocky hammocks, especially eroded limestone.

Distribution: Dade County.

Remarks: *T. patens* is distinguished from other members of the genus by the combination of erect to suberect stems, glabrous and ovately shaped scales at the base of the petioles, and the basal veins from adjacent pinnae running together at or just above the base of the sinus. The enlarged lower pinnules paralleling the rachis, which sometimes have incised margins, also help distinguish the species.

Lellinger (1985) suggested that this species be removed from the United States's fern flora because, at the time his manual was published, the last known collection for the taxon was made in 1905 by A. A. Eaton in the Miami area. It had also previously been reported in 1881 "on the shores of Biscayne Bay, at the eastern extremity of the Keys" (Safford, 1912, p. 6). However, the plant has more recently been collected, in 1993 by Alan Cressler who discovered approximately 41 plants in a rockland hammock in Miami (Keith Bradley, personal communication, 1998). Hence, it is included here. *T. patens* is currently known in Florida from this small population. The species is a West Indian plant that was first collected and described from Jamaica in the late 1700s. It is listed as endangered by the Florida Department of Agriculture.

Creeping Star-Hair Fern,
Creeping Fern, Walking Wood Fern

Thelypteris reptans (J. F. Gmelin) C. V. Morton   **Photo 196**

Form: A reclining, evergreen fern with a creeping to slightly erect stem.

Fronds: 10 - 55 cm long, sterile leaves lax, reclining to prostrate and often rooting at the apices or along the rachis, tip of frond often vinelike or runnerlike; fertile leaves somewhat more erect and not rooting.

Petiole: 1 - 25 cm long, green, with star-shaped hairs and vested at the base with brownish, hairy scales.

Rachis: Greenish, vested with star-shaped hairs.

Blade: Pinnate, except pinnatifid toward the apex, 3 - 32 cm long; often hanging pendently, sometimes vinelike, creeping, and rooting at the apex.

Pinnae: Well spaced along the rachis, especially toward the base, 1 - 5 cm long, 0.3 - 2.5 cm wide, decreasing in size toward the base and apex of the blade; margins sometimes entire, more often with rounded teeth, or shallowly lobed; veins and tissue hairy, a few hairs star shaped; basal veins of adjacent pinnules joining together well below and running as one to the sinus.

Sori: Round, more often closer to the pinnule midvein than the margin.

Habitat: Limestone sinks and outcrops, grottoes, rocky walls.

Distribution: Known from the sinkhole region of west-central Florida to include Hernando, Citrus, Levy, Marion, and Alachua Counties; also collected in Dade, Broward, and Collier Counties. In her 1929, 2,000-mile fern field trip in Florida, Knappen (1929) reported seeing this species at Snapper Creek and Hattie Bauer Hammocks in Dade County, and in the fern grottoes near both Pineola and Gainesville.

Remarks: No other member of the genus has reclining fronds that sometimes root at the apices and along the rachises. This is one of the few members of the genus that is often used in fern gardens. It is particularly appropriate for rock gardens and rock walls in the more tropical parts of the state. Its specific epithet means "creeping," in reference to its elongated leaf tips. This species is listed as endangered by the Florida Department of Agriculture.

Synonyms: *Polypodium reptans* J. F. Gmelin; *Dryopteris reptans* (J. F. Gmelin) C. Christensen; *Goniopteris reptans* (J. F. Gmelin) C. Presl.

Glandular Maiden Fern, Wax-Dot Maiden Fern

Thelypteris resinifera (Desvaux) Proctor   **Photo 197**

Form: A medium-size to relatively large, graceful, evergreen fern with an erect stem potentially to more than 1 cm in diameter.

Fronds: 0.15 to 1.3 m tall, evergreen, often borne in clusters; sterile and fertile fronds similar in appearance.

Petiole: Straw colored, darker toward the base, 3 - 25 cm long, to about 4 mm in diameter, with brownish, ovate-lanceolate scales, especially near the base.

Rachis: Brownish at the base, yellowish to straw colored above; sparsely hairy.

Blade: Long elliptic in overall outline and tapering to both base and apex; pinnate-pinnatifid, to about 1.1 m long, apex pinnatifid.

Pinnae: Borne nearly all the way to the base of the frond, 2 - 20 cm long, to about 2.5 cm wide, deeply cut, narrow in appearance, those toward the base of the blade much reduced in length and more widely spaced than those at midfrond or nearer the apex, lower pair of pinnules often conspicuously larger than those above; with rounded, reddish glands on the tissue of the lower surfaces (requires magnification), hence the specific epithet and common names.

Sori: Rounded, often few in number and widely spaced, mostly about equidistant between the midvein and margins of the pinnules, but tending toward the margins on some pinnules; with tan, sparsely hairy indusia.

Habitat: Wet hammocks.

Distribution: Uncommon, west central Florida in the vicinity of Hillsborough, Polk, Pasco, and DeSoto Counties.

Remarks: Most easily distinguished from other Florida marsh ferns by the combination of its erect fronds with sharply reduced lower pinnae, erect rhizomes, and the rounded, reddish glands on the lower surfaces of the blades.

Synonyms: *Polypodium resiniferum* Desvaux; *Amauropelta resinifera* (Desvaux) Pichi-Sermolli; *Dryopteris panamensis* (C. Presl) C. Christensen; *Thelypteris panamensis* (C. Presl) E. P. St. John.

Lattice-Vein Fern

Thelypteris reticulata (Linnaeus) Proctor   **Photo 198, 199**

Form: A large, evergreen fern with a short-creeping stem.

Fronds: To about 2 m tall or more, fertile and sterile only slightly different in appearance.

Petiole: Stout, to about 1 m tall, 1 cm in diameter, longer on fertile leaves, tan in color, fine-scaly to lacking scales near the base, essentially without hairs or scales above.

Rachis: Tan.

Blade: Pinnate, 50 - 120 cm tall.

Pinnae: Well spaced along the rachis, in 20 or more pairs, 20 - 30 cm long, 1.7 - 6 cm wide, widest at the base and tapering to a long-pointed apex, somewhat similar in shape to the leaves of a willow tree, with 12 to 20 rows of areoles between the midvein and the pinna margin, hence the specific epithet *reticulata*; margins entire or finely toothed with rounded teeth.

Sori: Elongate to curved, appearing as lines perpendicular to the lateral veins and lying along V-shaped veins that connect the lateral veins.

Habitat: Swampy hammocks in deep shade, old logging trams.

Distribution: Rare and restricted primarily to the southern tip of the state from about Lee, Collier, and Broward Counties southward.

Remarks: The rows of areoles evident on the lower surfaces of the pinnae, in conjunction with the pinnae margins being entire or only finely round-toothed distinguish this species from other members of the genus. Very similar to *T. serrata,* which has more sharply toothed pinnae. This species is listed as endangered by the Florida Department of Agriculture.

Synonyms: *Polypodium reticulatum* Linnaeus; *Dryopteris reticulata* (Linnaeus) Urban; *Meniscium reticulatum* (Linnaeus) Swartz.

Stiff Star-Hair Fern

Thelypteris sclerophylla (Poeppig ex Sprengel) C.V. Morton

Photo 200

Form: A medium-size, evergreen fern with a short-creeping to nearly erect stem.

Fronds: Typically 20 - 55 cm tall, but sometimes taller, borne in clusters, sterile and fertile fronds similar in overall appearance.

Petiole: Thin, 5 - 25 cm long, straw colored above, reddish brown at the base, vested throughout with star-shaped hairs and near the base with hairy, brown scales.

Rachis: Straw colored and hairy with minute star-shaped hairs.

Blade: Pinnate-pinnatifid, gradually narrowing to a pinnatifid tip, 15 - 55 cm long, 5 - 10 cm wide, somewhat narrow and long-elliptic in overall shape and tapering to both the base and apex.

Pinnae: 2 - 8 cm long, 1 - 2 cm wide, deeply lobed with rounded pinnules, and with star-shaped hairs on the veins, midveins, and blade tissue; basal veins of adjacent pinnules joining together and running as one to the sinus.

Sori: Rounded, borne about equidistant between the midvein and margins of the pinnae segments.

Habitat: Oolitic limestone hammocks.

Distribution: Dade County.

Remarks: This is a rare fern that is distinguished among the species of *Thelypteris* by the combination of its narrow, elongated blade that tapers to both ends; its deeply toothed pinnae; and the minute, nearly sessile, star-shaped hairs on its veins and blade tissue (seeing the star-shaped hairs requires magnification). This species is listed as endangered by the Florida Department of Agriculture.

Synonyms: *Aspidium sclerophyllum* Poeppig ex Sprengel; *Dryopteris sclerophylla* (Poeppig ex Sprengel) C. Christensen; *Goniopteris sclerophylla* (Poeppig ex Sprengel) Wherry.

Dentate Lattice-Vein Fern or Toothed Lattice-Vein Fern

Thelypteris serrata (Cavanilles) Alston   **Photo 201**

Form: A rather large, evergreen fern with a short-creeping stem.

Fronds: Pinnate, 0.65 - 2 m tall or more.

Petiole: Stout, to about 1 cm in diameter at the base but often less than half of this, 25 - 120 cm tall, light brown to tan in color, hairy, finely scaly to scaleless at the base.

Rachis: Brownish to tan colored.

Blade: Pinnate, lanceolate in overall shape, 40 - 100 cm tall.

Pinnae: Lanceolate to broadly linear, 10 - 25 cm long, 1.5 - 4.5 cm wide, somewhat similar in shape to the leaves of a willow tree, with 10 to 30 rows of areoles between the midvein and margins; margins with hooked teeth; main axis and veins hairy.

Sori: Elongated, appearing as lines perpendicular to the lateral veins and lying along V-shaped veins that connect the lateral veins.

Habitat: Cypress sloughs, swamps, river banks.

Distribution: Uncommon but reported from several counties in south-central and south Florida, including Dade, Palm Beach, Martin, Highlands, DeSoto, and Polk. Small (1931) described this species as common in deep swamps of the Lake Okeechobee region.

Remarks: The rows of areoles evident on the lower surfaces of the pinnae, in conjunction with the sharply toothed pinnae margins, distinguish this species from other members of the genus. Very similar to *T. reticulata,* which has finely, round-toothed pinnae margins. According to Small (1931), *T. serrata* was discovered in Florida in 1912, nearly 12 years after the discovery of *T. reticulata.* It is now listed as endangered by the Florida Department of Agriculture.

Synonyms: *Meniscium serratum* Cavanilles; *Dryopteris serrata* (Cavanilles) C. Christensen.

Free-Tip Star-Hair Fern

Thelypteris tetragona (Swartz) Small   **Photo 202**

Form: A medium-size, evergreen fern with with a short-creeping stem.

Fronds: To about 1.1 m tall and with long petioles.

Petiole: Straw colored above, darker at the base, 10 - 60 cm long, sometimes with minute star-shaped hairs.

Rachis: Straw colored, four-angled, hairy, sometimes with forked or star-shaped hairs.

Blade: Pinnate-pinnatifid, broadly lanceolate in overall shape, 15 - 45 cm long, 10 - 30 cm wide, not tapered at the base.

Pinnae: 7 - 18 cm long, 2 - 3 cm wide, lower pair often reflexed downward; lower pair of veins of adjacent pinnules joining together and running as one to the sinus; terminal pinna similar in form to lateral pinnae, and not joined with the uppermost lateral pinnae.

Sori: Rounded, borne slightly closer to the midvein than to the margins of the pinnae segments.

Habitat: Moist to damp woods, hammocks, lime sinks.

Distribution: West-central Florida; Marion, Citrus, and Hernando Counties; also distributed in Mexico, the West Indies, and Central and South America.

Remarks: This species is probably most similar to and is sometimes confused with *T. dentata*. The latter species sometimes appears to have the well-separated terminal pinna, but its pinnae are often more closely spaced and its terminal pinna is more lanceolate in shape rather than being of more uniform width as in *T. tetragona*.

Synonyms: *Polypodium tetragonum* Swartz; *Dryopteris tetragona* (Swartz) Urban; *Goniopteris tetragona* (Swartz) C. Presl.

VITTARIACEAE - SHOESTRING FERN FAMILY

This is a family of primarily epiphytic ferns with simple, entire leaves. The family contains approximately ten genera and 100 species worldwide; only the genus *Vittaria* is present in North America and only a single species, *Vittaria lineata,* occurs in Florida. Members of the family are known for their abundant root hairs which trap water and debris that provide nutrients to the plant. The genus name comes from the Latin *vitta,* which means ribbon, band, or stripe, in reference to the linear shape of the leaves.

A second species, *V. graminifolia* Kaulf., was reported for Florida by Wherry (1964), based upon a collection made in what is now the Fakahatchee Strand State Preserve. However, after extensive review of the site and circumstances of this collection, and after determining that the specimen on which the report was found was actually a depauperate specimen of *V. lineata,* Gastony (1980) recommended deleting the species from Florida's fern flora.

It is also interesting to note that *Vittaria* gametophytes have been found across much of the unglaciated Appalachian Plateau, Blue Ridge, Ridge and Valley, and Upland Piedmont of eastern north America, as well as in Ohio and Pennsylvania (Cusick, 1983). Now named *V. appalachiana* Farrar & Mickel, these plants coat rock surfaces in sheltered, mostly mountain habitats and seldom develop sporophytes. In the few cases where sporophytes are produced, the leaves are less than 5 mm long. In addition, a number of gametophytes as well as sporophytes, presumably of *V. lineata,* also occur on sandstone outcrops at Braxton Rocks, a Nature Conservancy Preserve, in Coffee County in south-central Georgia (see photo 204).

Shoestring Fern, Grass Fern, Beard Fern

Vittaria lineata (Linnaeus) Smith   **Photo 203. 204**

Form: An epiphytic species with clustered, pendent, linear, grasslike leaves (hence the specific epithet), and densely brown-scaly, and hairy stems.

Fronds: Dark green, thick, shiny, 0.3 - 1 m long, 1 - 3 mm wide, pendent, essentially without petioles.

Sori: Borne in submarginal grooves; inconspicuous and covered by the inrolled margins of the blades.

Habitat: Moist hammocks, in Florida epiphytic mostly on sabal palms *(Sabal palmetto* Loddiges); sometimes found on rock north of Florida.

Distribution: Throughout the peninsula, eastward and southward of an imaginary line connecting Levy and Duval Counties; common in the more southern counties.

Remarks: The narrow, linear, inrolled leaves hanging pendently from the trunks of sabal palms generally make this an easy-to-identify species. The only species with which it might be confused is the narrow strap fern *(Campyloneurum angustifolium)*, a rare species found mainly in the Fakahatchee Strand. The latter differs by its fronds mostly exceeding 4 mm wide, and by its sori being borne in rows of distinct dots on the lower surface of the frond. Shoestring fern often grows in association with goldfoot fern *(Phlebodium aureum).*

Synonyms: *Pteris lineata* Linnaeus

Appendix 1. Checklist of Florida Pteridophytes Included in the Current Volume

Species	Origin	FDAC	FNAI	EPPC
ANEMIACEAE (2 taxa)				
Anemia adiantifolia	N			
Anemia wrightii	N	E	S1	
ASPLENIACEAE (16 taxa)				
Asplenium abscissum	N			
Asplenium auritum	N	E	S2	
Asplenium cristatum	N			
Asplenium heterochroum	N			
[a]*Asplenium monanthes*	N	E	S1	
Asplenium playtneuron	N			
Asplenium pumilum	N	E	S1	
Asplenium resiliens	N			
Asplenium serratum	N	E	S1	
[a]*Asplenium trichomanes*	N			
Asplenium trichomanes-dentatum	N	E	S1S2	
Asplenium verecundum	N	E		
Asplenium X *biscaynianum*	D		S1	
Asplenium X *curtissii*	D		S1	
Asplenium X *heteroresiliens*	N		S1S2	
Asplenium X *plenum*	D		S1	
AZOLLACEAE (1 taxon)				
Azolla caroliniana	N			
BLECHNACEAE (6 taxa)				
Blechnum occidentale	N	E	S1	
Blechnum serrulatum	N			
Stenochlaena tenuifolia	X			
Woodwardia areolata	N			
Woodwardia radicans	X			
Woodwardia virginica	N			
DENNSTAEDTIACEAE (6 taxa)				
Dennstaedtia bipinnata	N	E	S1	
Hypolepis repens	N			
Odontosoria clavata	N	E	S2S3	
Pteridium aquilinum var. *caudatum*	N			
Pteridium aquilinum var. *latiusculum*	N			

Species	Origin	FDAC	FNAI	EPPC
Pteridium aqulinium var. *pseudocaudatum*	N			
DRYOPTERIDACEAE (24 taxa)				
Athyrium filix-femina subsp. *asplenioides*	N	T		
Ctenitis sloanei	N	E		
Ctenitis submarginalis	N	E		
Cyrtomium falcatum	X			
Cystopteris protrusa	Nx			
Deparia petersenii	X			
Diplazium esculentum	X			
Dryopteris ludoviciana	N			
Lomariopsis kunzeana	N	E	S2S3	
Nephrolepis biserrata	N	T		
Nephrolepis cordifolia	X			1
Nephrolepis exaltata	N			
Nephrolepis multiflora	X			1
Nephrolepis X averyi	N			
Onoclea sensibilis	N			
Polystichum acrostichoides	N			
*Polystichum tsussimense	X			
Rumohra adiantiformis	X			
Tectaria coriandrifolia	Nx	E	SX	
Tectaria fimbriata	N	E	S2	
Tectaria heracleifolia	N	T		
Tectaria incisa	X			1
Tectaria X amesiana	Nx		SX	
Woodsia obtusa	Nx		S2S4	
EQUISETACEAE (2 taxa)				
Equisetum hyemale var. *affine*	N			
Equisetum ramosissimum subsp. *ramosissimum*	X			
GLEICHENIACEAE (1 taxon)				
Dicranopteris flexuosa	N			
HYMENOPHYLLACEAE (5 taxa)				
Trichomanes holopterum	N	E	S1	
Trichomanes krausii	N	E	S1S2	

Species	Origin	FDAC	FNAI	EPPC
Trichomanes lineolatum	Nx	E		
Trichomanes petersii	N		S1S2	
Trichomanes punctatum				
subsp. *floridanum*	D	E	S1	
ISOETACEAE (4 taxa)				
Isoetes appalachiana	N			
-a*Isoetes boomii*				
Isoetes flaccida	N			
Isoetes hyemalis	N			
LYCOPODIACEAE (8 taxa)				
Lycopodiella alopecuroides	N			
Lycopodiella appressa	N			
Lycopodiella prostrata	N			
*Lycopodiella X *brucei*	N			
*Lycopodiella X *copelandii*	N			
Palhinhaea cernua	N	C		
Phlegmariurus dichotomus	N	E	S1	
Pseudolycopodiella caroliniana	N			
LYGODIACEAE (3 taxa)				
Lygodium japonicum	X			1
Lygodium microphyllum	X			1
Lygodium palmatum	?			
MARSILEACEAE (5 taxa)				
Marsilea ancylopoda	X			
*Marsilea hirsuta	X			
Marsilea macropoda	X			
Marsilea minuta	X			
Marsilea vestita	X			
OPHIOGLOSSACEAE (11 taxa)				
Botrychium biternatum	N			
Botrychium dissectum	N			
Botrychium jenmanii	N			
Botrychium lunarioides	N		S1	
Botrychium virginianum	N			
Cheiroglossa palmata	N	E	S2	
-**Ophioderma pendula*	X			

Species	Origin	FDAC	FNAI	EPPC
Ophioglossum crotalophoroides	N			
Ophioglossum engelmannii	N			
Ophioglossum nudicaule	N			
Ophioglossum petiolatum	X?			
OSMUNDACEAE (2 taxa)				
Osmunda cinnamomea	N	C		
Osmunda regalis var. *spectabilis*	N	C		
PARKERIACEAE (2 taxa)				
Ceratopteris pteridoides	N			
Ceratopteris thalictroides	X			
POLYPODIACEAE (14 taxa)				
Campyloneurum angustifolium	N	E	S1	
Campyloneurum costatum	N	E	S1	
-*Campyloneurum latum*	?	E		
Campyloneurum phyllitidis	N			
Microgramma heterophylla	N	E	S2S3	
Neurodium lanceolatum	N	E	S1S2	
Pecluma dispersa	N	E		
Pecluma plumula	N	E		
Pecluma ptilodon var. *caespitosa*	N	E		
Phlebodium aureum	N			
Phymatosorus scolopendria	X			
Pleopeltis astrolepis	Nx	E	SX	
Pleopeltis polypodioides var. *michauxianum*	N			
Polypodium triseriale	N			
PSILOTACEAE (1 taxon)				
Psilotum nudum	N			
PTERIDACEAE (23 taxa)				
Acrostichum aureum	N	T	S3	
Acrostichum danaeifolium	N			
Adiantum anceps	X			
Adiantum capillus-veneris	N			
Adiantum caudatum	X			
Adiantum melanoleucum	N	E	S1	
Adiantum tenerum	N	E	S3	

Species	Origin	FDAC	FNAI	EPPC
Adiantum trapeziforme	X			
Adiantum villosum	N			
Cheilanthes alabamensis	Nx			
Cheilanthes lanosa	Nx			
Cheilanthes microphylla	N	E	S3	
Pellaea atropurpurea	Nx	E	S1S2	
Pityrogramma calomelanos	N			
Pityrogramma trifoliata	N			
Pteris bahamensis	N	T	S3	
Pteris cretica	N			
Pteris grandifolia	X			
Pteris multifida	X			
Pteris plumula	X			
Pteris tripartita	X			
Pteris vittata	X			2
Pteris X delchampsii	N			
SALVINIACEAE (2 taxa)				
Salvinia minima	N			
-Salvinia molesta	X			
SCHIZAEACEAE (1 taxon)				
Actinostachys pennula	N	E	S1	
SELAGINELLACEAE (6 taxa)				
Selaginella apoda	N			
Selaginella arenicola	N			
Selaginella eatonii	N	E	S2	
Selaginella ludoviciana	N			
Selaginella uncinata	X			
Selaginella willdenovii	X			
THELYPTERIDACEAE (18 taxa)				
Macrothelypteris torresiana	X			
Phegopteris hexagonoptera	X			
Thelypteris augescens	X	T		
Thelypteris dentata	X			
Thelypteris grandis	N	E		
Thelypteris hispidula var.versicolor	N			
Thelypteris interrupta	N			
Thelypteris kunthii	N			

Species	Origin	FDAC	FNAI	EPPC
*Thelypteris opulenta	X			
Thelypteris ovata	N			
Thelypteris palustris var.*pubescens*	N			
Thelypteris patens	N	E		
Thelypteris reptans	N	E		
Thelypteris resinifera	N			
Thelypteris reticulata	N	E		
Thelypteris sclerophylla	N	E	S1	
Thelypteris serrata	N	E		
Thelypteris tetragona	N			
VITTARIACEAE (1 taxon)				
Vittaria lineata	N			

Marginal Marks
* not included in the *Flora of North America* Volume 2, but known to occur in Florida (11 taxa)
a included in the *Flora of North America* Volume 2, but not shown as occurring in Florida (3 taxa)
- not included in Wunderlin (1998) (4 taxa)

Origin - Native, Endemic, or Alien (Exotic)
N Native to Florida (123 taxa, including Nx and D)
Nx Native to Florida but likely no longer extant in the state due to extirpation or extinction (9 taxa)
D Endemic to Florida (4 taxa)
X Alien (exotic) to, but naturalized or escaped in Florida (38 taxa, includes X?)
X? Perhaps native in part (1 taxon)
? Status undetermined, likely never to have occurred naturally in Florida (2 taxa)

FDAC - Florida Department of Agriculture, Regulated Plant Index
E Endangered (42 taxa)
T Threatened (6 taxa)
C Commercially Exploited (3 taxa)

FNAI - Florida Natural Areas Inventory State Ranks
S1 Critically imperiled in Florida, extreme rarity
S2 Imperiled in Florida, rare
S3 Very rare and local throughout range
SX Believed to be extinct in Florida

EPPC - Florida Exotic Pest Plant Council
1 Alien to but naturalized or escaped in Florida and listed as a Category I exotic pest plant in the state (5 taxa)
2 Alien to but naturalized or escaped in Florida and listed as a Category II exotic pest plant in the state (1 taxon)

(Category 1 & 2 pest plants also included with the 37 alien species, above. Category 1 plants are those known to be currently invading and displacing native flora in native habitats, and Category 2 plants are those with the potential to do so.)

Appendix 2. Florida Pteridophytes According to Wunderlin (1998)

ADIANTACEAE
Adiantum anceps
Adiantum capillus-veneris
Adiantum caudatum
Adiantum melanoleucum
Adiantum tenerum
Adiantum trapeziforme
Adiantum villosum
Cheilanthes alabamensis
Cheilanthes lanosa
Cheilanthes microphylla
Pellaea atropurpurea
Pityrogramma calomelanos
Pityrogramma trifoliata

ASPLENIACEAE
Asplenium abscissum
Asplenium auritum
Asplenium cristatum
Asplenium dentatum
Asplenium heterochroum
*Asplenium monanthes
Asplenium playtneuron
Asplenium pumilum
Asplenium resiliens
Asplenium serratum
Asplenium trichomanes
Asplenium verecundum
Asplenium X biscaynianum
Asplenium X curtissii
Asplenium X heteroresiliens
Asplenium X plenum

AZOLLACEAE
Azolla caroliniana

BLECHNACEAE
Blechnum occidentale
Blechnum serrulatum
Stenochlaena tenuifolia

Woodwardia areolata
Woodwardia radicans
Woodwardia virginica

DENNSTAEDTIACEAE
Dennstaedtia bipinnata
Hypolepis repens
Odontosoria clavata
Pteridium aquilinum var. caudatum
Pteridium aquilinum var. latiusculum
Pteridium aqulinium var. pseudocaudatum

DRYOPTERIDACEAE
Ctenitis sloanei
Ctenitis submarginalis
Cyrtomium falcatum
Dryopteris ludoviciana
Polystichum acrostichoides
Polystichum tsussimense
Rumohra adiantiformis
Tectaria coriandrifolia
Tectaria fimbriata
Tectaria heracleifolia
Tectaria incisa
Tectaria X amesiana

EQUISETACEAE
Equisetum hyemale var. affine
Equisetum ramosissimum

GLEICHENIACEAE
Dicranopteris flexuosa

HYMENOPHYLLACEAE
Trichomanes holopterum
Trichomanes krausii
Trichomanes lineolatum
Trichomanes petersii
Trichomanes punctatum subsp. floridanum

ISOETACEAE
Isoetes appalachiana
Isoetes flaccida
Isoetes hyemalis

LOMARIOPSIDACEAE
Lomariopsis kunzeana

LYCOPODIACEAE
Huperzia dichotoma
Lycopodiella alopecuroides
Lycopodiella appressa
Lycopodiella caroliniana
Lycopodiella cernua
Lycopodiella prostrata
*Lycopodiella X brucei
*Lycopodiella X copelandii

MARSILEACEAE
Marsilea ancylopoda
*Marsilea hirsuta
Marsilea macropoda
Marsilea minuta
Marsilea vestita

NEPHROLEPIDACEAE
Nephrolepis biserrata
Nephrolepis cordifolia
Nephrolepis exaltata
Nephrolepis multiflora
Nephrolepis X averyi

OPHIOGLOSSACEAE
Botrychium biternatum
Botrychium dissectum
Botrychium jenmanii
Botrychium lunarioides
Botrychium virginianum
Ophioglossum crotalophoroides
Ophioglossum engelmannii
Ophioglossum nudicaule
Ophioglossum palmatum
Ophioglossum petiolatum

OSMUNDACEAE
Osmunda cinnamomea
Osmunda regalis var.*spectabilis*

PARKERIACEAE
Ceratopteris pteridoides
Ceratopteris thalictroides

POLYPODIACEAE
Campyloneurum angustifolium
Campyloneurum costatum
Campyloneurum phyllitidis
Microgramma heterophylla
Nevrodium lanceolatum
Pecluma dispersa
Pecluma plumula
Pecluma ptilodon var. *caespitosa*
Phlebodium aureum
Phymatosorus scolopendria
Pleopeltis astrolepis
Pleopeltis polypodioides var. *michauxianum*
Polypodium triseriale

PSILOTACEAE
Psilotum nudum

PTERIDACEAE
Acrostichum aureum
Acrostichum danaeifolium
Pteris bahamensis
Pteris cretica
Pteris grandifolia
Pteris multifida
*Pteris plumula
Pteris tripartita
Pteris vittata
Pteris X delchampsii

SALVINIACEAE
Salvinia minima

SCHIZAEACEAE
Actinostachys pennula
Anemia adiantifolia
Anemia wrightii

Lygodium japonicum
Lygodium microphyllum
Lygodium palmatum

SELAGINELLACEAE

Selaginella apoda
Selaginella arenicola
Selaginella eatonii
Selaginella ludoviciana
Selaginella uncinata
Selaginella willdenovii

THELYPTERIDACEAE

Macrothelypteris torresiana
Phegopteris hexagonoptera
Thelypteris augescens
Thelypteris dentata
Thelypteris grandis
Thelypteris hispidula var.*versicolor*
Thelypteris interrupta
Thelypteris kunthii
**Thelypteris opulenta*

Thelypteris ovata
Thelypteris palustris var. *pubescens*
Thelypteris patens
Thelypteris reptans
Thelypteris resinifera
Thelypteris reticulata
Thelypteris sclerophylla
Thelypteris serrata
Thelypteris tetragona

VITTARIACEAE
Vittaria lineata

WOODSIACEAE
Athyrium filix-femina subsp. *asplenioides*
Cystopteris protrusa
Deparia petersenii
Diplazium esculentum
Onoclea sensibilis
Woodsia obtusa

*not included in the *Flora of North America* Volume 2
[a]included in the *Flora of North America* Volume 2 but not shown as occurring in Florida

Appendix 3. Pteridophytes Included on Florida's Regulated Plant Index

Name	Federal Status*	State Status*
ANEMIACEAE		
Anemia wrightii	N	E
ASPLENIACEAE		
Asplenium auritum	N	E
Asplenium monanthes	N	E
Asplenium pumilum	N	E
Asplenium serratum	N	E
Asplenium trichomanes-dentatum	N	E
Asplenium verecundum	N	E
BLECHNACEAE		
Blechnum occidentale	N	E
DENNSTAEDTIACEAE		
Dennstaedtia bipinnata	N	E
Odontosoria clavata	N	E
DRYOPTERIDACEAE		
Athyrium filix-femina subsp. *asplenioides*	N	T
Ctenitis sloanei	N	E
Ctenitis submarginalis	N	E
Lomariopsis kunzeana	N	E
Nephrolepis biserrata	N	T
Tectaria coriandrifolia	N	E
Tectaria fimbriata	N	E
Tectaria heracleifolia	N	T
HYMENOPHYLLACEAE		
Trichomanes holopterum	N	E
Trichomanes krausii	N	E
Trichomanes lineolatum	N	E
Trichomanes punctatum subsp. *floridanum*	N	E
ISOETACEAE		
*Isoetes engelmannii***	N	E
LYCOPODIACEAE		
Palhinhaea cernua	N	C

Name	Federal Status*	State Status*
Phlegmariurus dichotomus	N	E
OPHIOGLOSSACEAE		
Cheiroglossa palmata	N	E
Osmunda cinnamomea	N	C
Osmunda regalis var. *spectabilis*	N	C
POLYPODIACEAE		
Campyloneurum angustifolium	N	E
Campyloneurum costatum	N	E
Campyloneurum latum	N	E
Microgramma heterophylla	N	E
Neurodium lanceolatum	N	E
Pecluma dispersa	N	E
Pecluma plumula	N	E
Pecluma ptilodon	N	E
Pleopeltis astrolepis	N	E
PTERIDACEAE		
Acrostichum aureum	N	T
Adiantum melanoleucum	N	E
Adiantum tenerum	N	E
Cheilanthes microphylla	N	E
Pellaea atropurpurea	N	E
Pteris bahamensis	N	T
SCHIZAEACEAE		
Actinostachys pennula	N	E
SELAGINELLACEAE		
Selaginella eatonii	N	E
THELYPTERIDACEAE		
Thelypteris augescens	N	T
Thelypteris grandis	N	E
Thelypteris patens	N	E
Thelypteris reptans	N	E
Thelypteris reticulata	N	E
Thelypteris sclerophylla	N	E
Thelypteris serrata	N	E

*E=endangered (43 species) T=threatened (7 species) C=commercially exploited (3 species)
N=not listed

*****Isoetes engelmannii* has been shown not to occur in Florida. However, three species of *Isoetes* found in Florida, including *I. boomii, I. hyemalis* and *I. appalachiana,* the latter of which is the one that has been previously misidentified as *I. engelmannii,* should probably also be included on the Regulated Plant Index.

It should be noted that several additional taxa are tracked by the Florida Natural Areas Inventory which do not appear on the Regulated Plant Index. Four *(Asplenium* X *curtissii, Asplenium* X *heteroresiliens, Asplenium* X *plenum, Tectaria* X *amesiana)* are hybrids, which are not accepted on the state list, while three *(Woodsia obtusa, Botrychium lunari- oides, Trichomanes petersii)* are sufficiently uncommon or poorly documented to warrant concern about their status.

Appendix 4. Where to Find Ferns in Florida

Floridians and visitors are blessed with an outstanding assortment of preserved natural and seminatural areas, many of which provide abundant opportunity for studying the state's native ferns. Following is a brief listing of some the more important of these parks, forests, refuges, and preserves. Though the following list is not exhaustive, it will provide an excellent starting point for your fern explorations. However, one note of caution and conservation bears mention. None of Florida's public lands allow collecting and many populations of the state's ferns cannot tolerate disturbance. Enjoyment of these beautiful plants should be restricted to observing them in their natural habitats.

State Parks, County and Local Parks, State Forests

Florida's park system encompasses over 100 installations with a variety of outdoor recreation opportunities. While most of these parks preserve at least some small part of the state's natural environment, those that follow should be on the trip list for anyone interested in learning Florida's ferns. For further information about these, or any of Florida's state parks, write to the Department of Natural Resources, Division of Recreation and Parks, 3900 Commonwealth Blvd., Tallahassee, FL 32399-3000. In addition to the state parks, many Florida counties and cities have local parks that are equally appealing to fern lovers. A few of these are highlighted below.

Florida Caverns State Park. This is one of the panhandle's most important and well-known botanical treasures. Located just north of Marianna on Florida Highway 167, it includes several outstanding nature trails that wind through the park, and its limestone outcrops and calcareous soils offer plenty of opportunity for fern study. Look especially for several species of *Thelypteris* and rock-loving spleenworts (including Morzenti's spleenwort), royal fern, sensitive fern, grapefern, and Cretan brake.

Torreya State Park. This park encompasses one of Florida's most unique and interesting plant communities. It is located north of Bristol on Liberty County Road 1641, off Florida 12. A number of fern species can be found here, including bracken, Christmas fern, several species of spleenworts and *Thelypteris,* southern maiden-hair fern, southern lady fern, sensitive fern, broad beech fern, southern wood fern, Cretan brake, at least two species of grapefern, two species of adder's-tongue, and horsetail.

Withlacoochee State Forest. Florida supports several state forests. The Withlacoochee State Forest (WSF), located in the west-central peninsula northeast of Tampa and southeast and east of Brooksville, is one of the best for ferns. WSF encompasses the northern edge of the central Florida lime-sink region that was once one of Florida's finest areas for fern botany. Though much of the area that previously contained these ferneries has now been converted to agricultural use, there is still some excellent terrain for finding at least two species of *Pecluma,* as well as royal fern, cinnamon fern, both chain ferns, and some of the state's rarest spleenworts and filmy ferns. Only a few locations are known for the rarest of these species, but others may turn up with diligent searching.

Gold Head Branch State Park. The deep ravine at this fascinating park is excellent for ferns. One of the state's best populations of creeping bramble fern is found here, as are several species of *Thelypteris,* both chain ferns, and shoestring fern. The sandy uplands also support populations of sand spike-moss. The park is located northeast of

Keystone Heights in the north-central peninsula.

Ravine State Gardens. This state garden is located in Palatka. Its central feature is a huge natural ravine that contains numerous native and exotic plants, including numerous ferns from cinnamon and royal fern to Mariana maiden fern. The pool along the roadside has a large population of *Azolla.*

Highlands Hammock State Park. Located just west of Sebring in the heart of Florida's white sand scrub, Highlands Hammock offers one of the best varieties of ferns of any of the state parks. At least 29 species can be found here, including shoestring fern, whisk fern, long strap fern, goldfoot fern, comb polypody, sword fern, sand spike-moss, creeping bramble fern, both netted and Virginia chain fern, *Ceratopteris,* water spangles, several species of *Thelypteris,* swamp fern, and several club-mosses.

Collier-Seminole State Park. In some ways this park marks the beginning of Florida's subtropical plant community as one drives along the west coast south from Naples and east along the Tamiami Trail. It is best known for its dense tangle of mangroves but also offers an interesting trail with a number of ferns. Both of the state's leather ferns can be seen here, as well as goldfoot fern, swamp fern, and long strap fern, as well as several additional common species.

Fakahatchee Strand State Preserve. Fakahatchee Strand State Preserve is, without equal, Florida's finest fern locality. At least 36 pteridophyte species are known to occur here, including several of the state's rarest and most geographically restricted. Common ferns include several species of *Nephrolepis,* as well as swamp fern, long strap fern, giant leather fern, cinnamon fern, and royal fern. Less common, but regularly encountered, species include eared spleenwort and whisk fern. Specialties include lattice-vein fern and dentate lattice-vein fern, birdnest fern, both the narrow and tailed strap ferns, hand fern, Florida tree fern, brown-hair comb fern, and the state's only known populations of hanging fir-moss and stately maiden fern. It should be noted that the best ferneries in the Fakahatchee are off the beaten track, deep in the swamp's interior. Such locations can be challenging to visit, but reward observers with an outstanding array of native species.

Daggerwing Nature Center. This nature center in Palm Beach County's South Regional County Park is located west of Boca Raton, west of U.S. 441, and south of Yamato Road. In addition to a visitor center, it also has a boardwalk trail through an interesting hammock that supports a number of ferns. From the boardwalk it is easy to see giant leather fern, giant brake, and swamp fern. Both broad and incised halberd ferns are also reported here.

Fern Forest Nature Center. This is a Broward County park located at 201 Lyons Rd., South, Pompano Beach. It contains more than 250 acres with ten plant communities and over 20 species of ferns, including water spangles, eastern mosquito fern, giant leather fern, long strap fern, goldfoot fern, hand fern, broad halberd fern, giant sword fern, birdnest fern, Florida tree fern, and several species of *Thelypteris.*

National Parks, Forests, and Wildlife Refuges

Few people don't know about **Everglades National Park.** For those attempting to learn Florida's tropical and subtropical ferns, a visit to this outstanding natural resource is a must. The pine rocklands within and near the park support pine fern, wedgelet fern, bahama ladder brake, and the pineland edges often support exceptionally large specimens of bracken. Giant sword fern and giant leather fern are also common here.

In addition to its one-of-a-kind national park, Florida also encompasses three national forests: the Apalachicola, Osceola, and Ocala. All offer a mosaic of native plant communities and are productive places to search for Florida's ferns. The **Apalachicola National Forest,** in particular, which is located southwest of Tallahassee, offers many opportunities for fern study, especially along creeks and under and near the many highway bridges. Netted chain fern, sensitive fern, cinnamon fern, royal fern, and several species of *Thelypteris* are easily observed. **The Osceola National Forest**, located in the north-central part of the state northeast of Lake City, is vegetatively similar to the Apalachicola and has similar fern species. **The Ocala National Forest** harbors about a dozen fern species, including an inland population of giant leather fern. The Ocala is located in the north-central peninsula along Highways 19 and 40. There is an excellent map for each of Florida's national forests. Information may be obtained by writing: National Forests in Florida, 325 John Knox Rd., Tallahassee, FL 32303.

Florida Native Plant Society and Fern Clubs

The Florida Native Plant Society (FNPS) is a statewide organization dedicated to the preservation, conservation, and restoration of Florida's native plants. The organization supports about two dozen local chapters that offer guided field trips to some of the locations mentioned above as well as to a variety of Florida's other special places. FNPS also publishes *The Palmetto,* a quarterly journal that focuses on Florida's native plants as well as activities of the association. Information about FNPS may be obtained by writing the society headquarters at P.O. Box 690278, Vero Beach, FL 32969-0278.

In addition to FNPS, at least two regions of the state are served by fern clubs. The Tampa Bay Fern Club, which is active in central Florida, publishes a monthly newsletter, offers monthly meetings, and may be reached by writing Tampa Bay Fern Club, c/o Strohmenger, P.O. Box 17716, Tampa, FL 33682-7716. The Miami area is served by the South Florida Fern Society, which can be reached care of John Corrigan, Fairchild Tropical Gardens, 10901 Old Cutler Rd., Miami, FL 33156.

BIBLIOGRAPHY

Adams, David C. and P. B. Tomlinson. 1979. Acrostichum in Florida. *American Fern Journal.* 69(2):42-46.

Alexander, Taylor R. and Alan G. Crook. 1974. Schizaea germanii Rediscovered in Florida. *American Fern Journal.* 64:30.

Anderson, Loran C. 1986. Noteworthy Plants from North Florida, II. *Sida.* 11(4):379-384.

Austin, Daniel F., Julie L. Jones, and Bradley C. Bennett. 1990. Vascular Plants of Fakahatchee Strand State Preserve. *Florida Scientist.* 53(2):89-117.

Beckner, John. 1968. Lygodium microphyllum, Another Fern Escaped in Florida. *American Fern Journal.* 58:93-94.

Benedict, R. C. 1911. Botrychium Jenmanii in Cuba. *American Fern Journal.* 1(3):98-99.

Benedict, R. C. 1916. The Origin of New Varieties of Nephrolepis by Othogenetic Saltation, I. Progressive Variations. *Bulletin of the Torrey Botanical Club.* 43:207-234.

Bentham, George and Sir Joseph D. Hooker. 1862-1883. Genera Plantarum. London.

Bierhorst, David W. 1977. The Systematic Position of Psilotum and Tmesipteris. *Brittonia.* 29:3-13.

Boom, Brian M. 1982. Synopsis of *Isoetes* in the Southeastern United States. *Castanea.* 47:38-59.

Boom, Brian M. 1983. Chapman's Quillwort Reconsidered. *American Fern Journal.* 73(2):39-41.

Broun, Maurice. 1936a. Pteris multifida Poir. Naturalized in West-Central Florida. *American Fern Journal.* 26(1):21.

Broun, Maurice. 1936b. Some Impressions of the "Land of Ferns," and a Florida Fern Garden. *American Fern Journal.* 26:55-59.

Bruce, James G. 1976. Comparative Studies in the Biology of Lycopodium carolinianum. *American Fern Journal.* 66(4):125-137.

Brunton, Daniel F. and Donald M. Britton. 1996a. The Status, Distribution, and Identification of Georgia Quillwort *(Isoetes georgiana;* Isoetaceae). *American Fern Journal.* 86(4):105-113.

Brunton, Daniel F. and Donald M. Britton. 1996b. Alabama and Georgia. *Castanea.* 61(4):61-62.

Brunton, Daniel F. and Donald M. Britton. 1997. Appalachian Quillwort *(Isoetes appalachiana,* sp. nov.; Isoetaceae), A New Pteridophyte from the Eastern United States. *Rhodora.* 99:118-133.

Brunton, Daniel F., Donald M. Britton, and W. Carl Taylor. 1994. *Isoetes hyemalis,* sp. nov. (Isoetaceae): A New Quillwort from the Southeastern United States. *Castanea.* 59(1):12-21.

Buck, William R. and Terry W. Lucansky. 1976. An Anatomical and Morphological Comparison of *Selaginella apoda* and *Selaginella ludoviciana. Bulletin of the Torrey Botanical Club.* 103(1):9-16.

Burkhalter, J. R. 1980. Three Additions to the Pteridophyte Flora of Escambia County, Florida. *American Fern Journal.* 70(2):112.

Burkhalter, J. R. 1985. A New Station for *Dicranopteris flexuosa* in Bay County, Florida. *American Fern Journal.* 75:79.

Burkhalter, J. R. 1995. *Marsilea minuta* (Marsileaceae): New to Florida and North America. *Sida.* 16(3):545-549.

Carter, Richard and Wayne R. Faircloth. 1986. *Osmunda cinnamomea* forma *frondosa* in the Coastal Plain of Georgia and Florida. *American Fern Journal.* 76(4):189.

Chapman, A. W. 1860. *Flora of the Southern United States.* New York: Ivison, Phinney, & Co.

Chapman, A. W. 1884 [1883]. *Flora of the Southern United States,* 2nd Edition. New York: Ivison, Blakeman, Taylor & Co.

Chapman, A. W. 1897. *Flora of the Southern United States,* 3rd Edition. Cambridge, Mass.: Cambridge Botanical Supply Co.

Chrysler, M. A. 1941. The Structure and Development of Ophioglossum palmatum. *Bulletin of the Torrey Botanical Club.* 68:1-19.

Clausen, Robert T. 1938a. Ophioglossum petiolatum Hooker. *American Fern Journal.* 28(1):1-10.

Clausen, Robert T. 1938b. A Monograph of the Ophioglossaceae. *Memoirs of the Torrey Botanical Club.* 19(2):1-171.

Clausen, Robert T. 1942. Ophioglossum vulgatum on the Inner Coastal Plain of Alabama. *American Fern Journal.* 32(3):105-108.

Clausen, Robert T. 1946. Selaginella, subgenus Euselaginella, in the Southeastern United States. *American Fern Journal.* 36(3):65-82.

Clewell, Andre F. 1985. Guide to the Vascular Plants of the Florida Panhandle. Gainesville, FL: University Presses of Florida.

Cobb, Boughton. 1963. *A Field Guide to the Ferns.* Boston: Houghton Mifflin Co.

Correll, D. S. 1938. A County Check-List of Florida Ferns and Fern Allies. *American Fern Journal.* 28:11-16;46-54;91-100.

Correll, D. S. and H. B. Correll. 1996 (reprint). *Flora of the Bahama Archipelago.* Vaduz, Germany: A. R. G. Gantner Verlag.

Cranfill, Ray. 1980. *Ferns and Fern Allies of Kentucky.* Kentucky Nature Preserves Commission Scientific and Technical Series, Number 1.

Cranfill, Raymond B. 1981. Bog Clubmosses (Lycopodiella) in Kentucky. *American Fern Journal.* 71:97-100.

Cranfill, Raymond B. 1993. Blechnaceae. *Flora of North America, Vol 2, Pteridophytes and Gymnosperms.* New York: Oxford University Press.

Cronquist, Arthur. 1981. *An Integrated System of Classification of Flowering Plants.* New York: Columbia University Press.

Cronquist, Arthur. 1988. *The Evolution and Classification of Flowering Plants.* 2nd Ed. Bronx: New York Botanical Garden.

Cronquist, Arthur, Armen Takhtajan, and Walter Zimmermann. 1966. On the Higher Taxa of Embryobionta. *Taxon.* 15(4):129-134.

Curtiss, A. H. 1902. Among Florida Ferns. *The Plant World.* 5(4):66-72 and 5(5):91-92.

Cusick, Allison W. 1983. Vittaria Gametophytes Discovered in a New Physiographic Province. *American Fern Journal.* 73(2):33-38.

Darling, Thomas Jr. 1961. Florida Rarities. *American Fern Journal.* 51(1):1-15.

Darling, Thomas Jr. 1982. The Deletion of Nephrolepis pectinata From the Flora of Florida. *American Fern Journal.* 72(2):63.

Darwin, Charles. 1859. *On the Origin of Species.*

DeVol, Charles E. 1957. The Geographic Distribution of Ceratopteris pteridoides. *American Fern Journal.* 47(2):67-72.

Diddell, Mary. 1936. Growing Florida Ferns. *American Fern Journal.* 26(1):1-10.

Diddell, Mary. 1941. New Stations for Florida Pteridophytes. *American Fern Journal.* 31(2):48-52.

Diddell, Mary. 1948. Diplazium esculentum in Florida. *American Fern Journal.* 38:16-19.

Diddell, Mary. 1956. The Status of Pityrogramma calomelanos in Florida. *American Fern Journal.* 46(1):22-28.

Diego Gomez, Luis. 1976. A Note on the Young Fronds of Ophioglossum palmatum. *American Fern Journal.* 66:27.

Dunbar, Lin. 1989. *Ferns of the Coastal Plain: Their Lore, Legends, and Uses.* Columbia, SC: University of South Carolina Press.

Eaton, A. A. 1906. Pteridophytes Observed During Three Excursions into Southern Florida. *Bulletin of the Torrey Botanical Club.* 33:455-486.

Eaton, D. C. 1872. Note 20. Marsilea quadrifolia L. *Bulletin of the Torrey Botanical Club.* 3:19.

Eaton, D. C. 1878. New or Little-Known Ferns of the United States. No. 5. *Bulletin of the Torrey Botanical Club.* 1(46):263-265.

Evans, A. Murray. 1968. The Polypodium pectinatum-plumula Complex in Florida. *American Fern Journal.* 8:169-175.

Evans, A. Murray. 1975. Cheilanthes in Florida. *American Fern Journal.* 65(1):1-2.

Faircloth, Wayne R. and Mary Norsworthy. 1975. Notes on Some Ophioglossaceae in the Georgia Coastal Plain. *American Fern Journal.* 65:28.

Fernald, M. L. 1950. Adiantum capillus-veneris in the United States. *Rhodora.* 52:201-208.

Flora of Taiwan. 1975. Taipei: Epoch Publishing.

Foster, F. Gordon. 1984. *Ferns to Know and Grow.* Portland, OR: Timber Press.

Gastony, Gerald J. 1980. The Deletion of Vittaria graminifolia from the Flora of Florida. *American Fern Journal.* 70(1):12-14.

Gastony, Gerald J. 1986. Electrophoretic Evidence for the Origin of Fern Species by Unreduced Spores. *American Journal of Botany.* 73(11):1563-1569.

Gastony, Gerald J. and Michael D. Windham. 1989. Species Concepts in Pteridophytes: The Treatment and Definition of Agamosporous Species. *American Fern Journal.* 79(2):65-77.

Gillis, W. T. and G. R. Proctor. 1975. Additions and Corrections to the Bahama Flora—II. *Sida.* 6:52-62.

Gledhill, D. 1989. *The Names of Plants.* 2nd ed. Cambridge: Cambridge University Press.

Goudey, Christopher J. 1988. *A Handbook of Ferns for Australia and New Zealand.* Melbourne: Lothian Publishing Co.

Graham, Douglas A. and Warren H. Wagner, Jr. 1991. An Exceptional Leaf of *Botrychium dissectum. American Fern Journal.* 82(3):103-106.

Gruber, C. L. 1937. A Fern Collector's Notes. *American Fern Journal.* 27(1):24-27.

Harper, Roland M. 1916. The Fern Grottoes of Citrus County, Florida. *American Fern Journal.* 6(3):68-81.

Hauke, Richard L. 1979. Equisetum ramosissimum in North America. *American Fern Journal.* 69(1):1-5.

Hauke, Richard L. 1984. Equisetum ramosissimum in Louisiana. *American Fern Journal.* 74(2):61.

Hauke, Richard L. 1992. Revisiting Equisetum ramosissimum. *American Fern Journal.* 82:83-84.

Hawkes, Alex D. and Otto Degener. 1950. The Upright Psilotum. *American Fern Journal.* 40(2):207-210.

Holttum, R. E. 1971. The Family Names of Ferns. *Taxon.* 20(4):527-531.

Holub, J. 1964. Lyocopodiella, novy rod radu Lycopodiales. *Preslia.* 36:16-22.

Horner, Harry T. and Howard J. Arnott. 1963. Sporangial Arrangement in North American Species of Selaginella. *Botanical Gazette.* 124(5):371-383.

House, H. D. 1933. Additions to the Fern Flora of New York State. *American Fern Journal.* 23(1):1-7.

Jeffrey, C. 1982. *An Introduction to Plant Taxonomy.* Cambridge: Cambridge University Press.

Jones, David L. 1987. *Encyclopedia of Ferns.* Portland, OR: Timber Press.

Jones, Samuel B., Jr. and Arlene E. Luchsinger. 1979. *Plant Systematics.* New York: McGraw-Hill.

Kato, Masahiro. 1993. Diplazium. *Flora of North America, Vol 2, Pteridophytes and Gymnosperms.* New York: Oxford University Press.

Keller, Don. 1994. *Checklist of Ferns and Fern Allies of South Florida.* Unpublished list prepared by the author.

Kittredge, E. M. 1941. An Osmunda cinnamomea Variant. *American Fern Journal.* 31:71-72.

Knappen, Nellie. 1929. Round About Florida for Ferns. *American Fern Journal.* 19(4):113-119.

Lakela, Olga and Robert W. Long. 1976. *Ferns of Florida: An Illustrated Manual and Identification Guide.* Miami: Banyan Books.

Landry, Garrie P. and William D. Reese. 1991. *Ctenitis submarginalis* (Langsd. & Fisch.) Copel. New to Louisiana: First Record in the U.S. Outside of Florida. *American Fern Journal.* 81(3):105-106.

Lawrence, George H. M. 1955. *An Introduction to Plant Taxonomy.* New York: Macmillan Publishing Co.

Lellinger, David B. 1981. Notes on North American Ferns. *American Fern Journal.* 71(3):90-94.

Lellinger, David B. 1984. Notes on North American Ferns, II. *American Fern Journal.* 74(2):62-63.

Lellinger, David B. 1985. *A Field Manual of the Ferns & Fern-Allies of the United States & Canada.* Washington, D.C.: Smithsonian Institution Press.

Leonard, Steve W. 1972. The Distribution of Thelypteris torresiana in the Southeastern United States. *American Fern Journal.* 62(4):97-99.

Long, Robert W. and Olga Lakela. 1971. *A Flora of Tropical Florida: A Manual of the Seed Plants and Ferns of Southern Peninsular Florida.* Miami: University of Miami Press.

Lucansky, Terry W. 1981. *Chain Ferns of Florida. American Fern Journal.* 71(4):101-108.

Luebke, Neil T. 1992. Three New Species of Isoetes for the Southeastern United States. *American Fern Journal.* 82(1):23-26.

Malone, C. R. and V. W. Proctor. 1965. Dispersal of *Marsilea mucronata* by Water Birds. *American Fern Journal.* 55:167-170.

Meeuse, A. D. J. 1961. Marsileales and Salviniales—"Living Fossils?" *Acta Botanica Neerlandica.* 10:257-260.

Merrill, E. D. 1943. New Names for Ferns and Fern Allies Proposed by C. S. Rafinesque, 1806-1838. *American Fern Journal.* 33(2):41-56.

Mesler, Michael R. 1973. Sexual Reproduction in Ophioglossum crotalophoroides. *American Fern Journal.* 63(2):28-33.

Mesler, Michael R. 1974. The Natural History of Ophioglossum palmatum in South Florida. *American Fern Journal.* 64(2):33-39.

Mickel, John T. 1979. *How to Know the Ferns and Fern Allies.* Dubuque, Iowa: Wm. C. Brown Co., Publishers.

Mickel, John T. 1993. *Flora of North America, Vol 2, Pteridophytes and Gymnosperms.* New York: Oxford University Press.

Mickel, John T. 1994. *Ferns for American Gardens.* New York: Macmillan Publishing Co.

Mohr, Charles. 1901. *Contributions from the U. S. National Herbarium Volume VI: Plant Life of Alabama.* Washington: Government Printing Office.

Moran, Robbin C. 1981. An Unusual Record of Asplenium trichomanes from Northeastern Florida. *American Fern Journal.* 71(3):95.

Moran, Robbin C. 1993. Ctenitis. *Flora of North America, Vol 2, Pteridophytes and Gymnosperms.* New York: Oxford University Press.

Moran, Robbin C. 1997. The Little Nitrogen Factories. *Fiddlehead Forum.* 24(2):9,12-14.

Moran, Robbin C. 1998. Palea-botany. *Fiddlehead Forum.* 25(3):19,21-23.

Morton, C. V. 1941. On the Florida Fern Known as Dryopteris setigera. *American Fern Journal.* 31(1):12-14.

Morton, C. V. 1950. Notes On the Ferns of the Eastern United States. *American Fern Journal.* 40:241-252.

Morton, C. V. 1957. Observations on Cultivated Ferns. I. *American Fern Journal.* 47:7-14.

Morton, C. V. 1958. Observations on Cultivated Ferns. V. The Species and Forms of Nephrolepis. *American Fern Journal.* 48(1):18-28.

Morton, C. V. 1960. Observations on Cultivated Ferns VI. The Ferns Currently Known as Rumohra. *American Fern Journal.* 50:145-155.

Morton, C. V. 1969. New Combinations in Cyathea, Ctenitis, and Asplenium. *American Fern Journal.* 59:65-67.

Morton, C. V. and Robert K. Godfrey. 1958. *Diplazium japonicum* naturalized in Florida. *American Fern Journal.* 48:28-30.

Morton, C. V. and D. B. Lellinger. 1966. The Polypodiaceae Subfamily Asplenioideae in Venezuela. *Memoirs of the New York Botanical Garden.* 15:1-49.

Morton, C. V. and Charles Neidorf. 1956. The Virginia Chain Fern. *American Fern Journal.* 46(1):28-30.

Morzenti, Virginia M. 1967. Asplenium plenum: A Fern Which Suggests an Unusual Method of Species Formation. *American Journal of Botany.* 54(9):1061-1068.

Moyroud, R. and C. E. Nauman. 1989. A New Station for *Dicranopteris flexuosa* in Florida. *American Fern Journal.* 79:155.

Nash, George V. 1895. Notes on Some Florida Plants. *Bulletin of the Torrey Botanical Club.* 22(4):141-161.

Nauman, Clifton E. 1979a. A Thelypteris New to Florida. *American Fern Journal.* 69(2):64.

Nauman, Clifton E. 1979b. A New Nephrolepis Hybrid From Florida. *American Fern Journal.* 69(3):65-70.

Nauman, Clifton E. 1981. The Genus Nephrolepis in Florida. *American Fern Journal.* 71(2):35-40.

Nauman, Clifton E. 1986. The Ferns of Florida. *The Palmetto.* 6(3):4-5.

Nauman, Clifton E. 1993a. Campyloneurum. *Flora of North America, Vol 2, Pteridophytes and Gymnosperms.* New York: Oxford University Press.

Nauman, Clifton E. 1993b. Pteris. *Flora of North America, Vol 2, Pteridophytes and Gymnosperms.* New York: Oxford University Press.

Nauman, Clifton E. 1993c. Gleicheniaceae C. Presl. *Flora of North America, Vol 2, Pteridophytes and Gymnosperms.* New York: Oxford University Press.

Nauman, Clifton E. and Daniel F. Austin. 1978. Spread of the Exotic Fern Lygodium microphyllum in Florida. *American Fern Journal.* 68(2):65-66.

Nauman, Clifton E. and Richard Moyroud. 1986. A New Substrate for Ophioglossum palmatum in Florida. *American Fern Journal.* 76(2):1986.

Nelson, Gil. 1998. A New Station for *Dicranopteris flexuosa* in Franklin County, Florida. *American Fern Journal.* 88(3):143.

Noble, M. A. 1914. Fern Hunting in Florida, in the Phosphate Country. *American Fern Journal.* 4:65.66.

Noble, M. A. 1916. Fern Hunting in Florida in the Phosphate Country. *American Fern Journal,* 6:42-44.

Ohwi, Jisaburo. 1965. *Flora of Japan.* Washington, D.C.: Smithsonian Institution.

Palmer, Ernest J. 1932. Notes on Ophioglossum engelmanii. *American Fern Journal.* 22(2):43-47.

Pember, F. T. 1911. A Fern Collector in Florida. *American Fern Journal.* 1(3):45-48.

Pemberton, Robert W. 1998. The Potential of Biological Control to Manage Old World Climbing Fern *(Lygodium microphyllum)*, an Invasive Weed in Florida. *American Fern Journal.* 88(4):176-182.

Pemberton, Robert W. and Amy P. Ferriter. 1998. Old World Climbing Fern *(Lygodium microphyllum)*, a Dangerous Invasive Weed in Florida. *American Fern Journal.* 88(4):165-175.

Pessin, Louis J. 1924. A Physiological and Anatomical Study of the Leaves of *Polypodium polypodioides. American Journal of Botany.* 11:370-381.

Petrik-Ott, Aleta Jo, and Franklyn D. Ott. 1982. Cheilanthes lanosa and Cystopteris protrusa in Florida. *American Fern Journal.* 72(1):31.

Pfeiffer, N. E. 1922. Monograph of the Isoetaceae. *Annals of the Missouri Botanical Garden.* 9:79-233.

Prado, Jefferson, and Monica Palacios-Rios. 1998. Taxonomy and Distribution of Adiantum trapeziforme and A. pentadactylon. *American Fern Journal*. 88(4):145-149.

Price, Michael G. 1983. Pecluma, A New Tropical American Fern Genus. *American Fern Journal*. 73(3):109-116.

Proctor, George R. 1985. *Ferns of Jamaica: A Guide to the Pteridophytes*. London: British Museum (Natural History).

Radford, Albert E. 1986. *Fundamentals of Plant Systematics*. New York: Harper & Row.

Safford, William Edwin. 1912. Notes of a naturalist Afloat—II. *American Fern Journal*. 2(1):1-12.

St. John, Edward P. 1936a. Rare Ferns of Central Florida. *American Fern Journal*. 26(2):41-50.

St. John, Edward P. 1936b. New Ferns of Central Florida. *American Fern Journal*. 26(2):50-55.

St. John, Edward P. 1941. Habitats and Distribution of Ophioglossum in Florida. *American Fern Journal*. 31(4):143-148.

St. John, Edward P. 1949 (1950). The Evolution of the Ophioglossaceae of the Eastern United States. *The Quarterly Journal of the Florida Academy of Sciences*. 12(4):207-219.

St. John, Edward P. 1952. The Evolution of the Ophioglossaceae of the Eastern United States, III—The Evolution of the Leaf. *The Quarterly Journal of the Florida Academy of Sciences*. 15(1):1-19.

St. John, Edward P. and Robert P. St. John 1935. Fern Study in Central Florida. *American Fern Journal*. 25(2):33-44.

Satchwell, M. W. 1916. Ferns of Duval County, Florida. *American Fern Journal*. 6:39-42.

Shurtleff, Rosamond. 1938. Botrychium dissectum. *American Fern Journal*. 28(1):25-28.

Singletary, Mary L. 1950. The Net Fern in Florida. *American Fern Journal*. 40(2):176-177.

Small, John K. 1913. Flora of the Southeastern United States. 2nd Edition. New York: Published by the Author.

Small, J. K. 1918a. *Ferns of Tropical Florida*. New York: Published by the Author (reprinted by Micanopy Publishing Co., Micanopy, FL).

Small, J. K. 1918b. *Ferns of Royal Palm Hammock. New York:* Published By The Author (reprinted by Micanopy Publishing Co., Micanopy, FL).

Small, J. K. 1920. Of Grottoes and Ancient Dunes, A Record of Exploration in Florida in December 1918. *Journal of The New York Botanical Garden*. 21(242):25-54.

Small, J. K. 1931. *Ferns of Florida*. New York: The Science Press.

Small, J. K. 1938. *Ferns of the Southeastern United States: Descriptions of the Fern-Plants Growing Naturally in the States South of the Virginia-Kentucky State Line and East of the Mississippi River.* 1964 facsimile edition. New York: Hafner Publishing Co.

Small, J. K. 1939. The Identity of Aspidium ludovicianum. *American Fern Journal*. 29(2):41-45.

Smith, Alan R. 1993a. Polypodiaceae. *Flora of North America, Vol 2, Pteridophytes and Gymnosperms*. New York: Oxford University Press.

Smith, Alan R. 1993b. Thelypteridaceae. *Flora of North America, Vol 2, Pteridophytes and Gymnosperms*. New York: Oxford University Press.

Smith, John Donnell. 1911. A Collecting Trip in Southern Florida. *American Fern Journal*. 1(3):51-53.

Snyder, Lloyd H., Jr. and James G. Bruce. 1986. *Field Guide to the Ferns and Other Pteridophytes of Georgia*. Athens, GA: University of Georgia Press.

Somers, Paul and William R. Buck. 1975. Selaginella ludoviciana, S. apoda and Their

Hybrids in the Southeastern United States. *American Fern Journal.* 65(3):76-82.

Spurr, Stephen H. 1941. Factors Determining the Distribution of Florida Ferns. *American Fern Journal.* 31(3):91-97.

Thieret, John W. 1980. *Louisiana Ferns and Fern Allies.* Lafayette, LA: Lafayette Natural History Museum.

Thomas, R. Dale. 1978. Lycopodium cernuum in Louisiana. *American Fern Journal.* 68:96.

Thorne, Robert F. 1968. Synopsis of a Putatively Phylogenetic Classification of the Flowering Plants. *Aliso.* 6(4):57-66.

Thorne, Robert F. 1992. An Updated Phylogenetic Classification of the Flowering Plants. *Aliso.* 13:365-389.

Tryon, Alice F. and Robbin C. Moran. 1997. *The Ferns and Allied Plants of New England.* Lincoln, MA: Center for Biological Consevation, Massachusetts Audubon Society.

Tryon, Alice F., Rolla Tryon, and Frederic Badre. 1980. Classification, Spores, and Nomenclature of the Marsh Fern. *Rhodora.* 82:461-474.

Tryon, Rolla M. 1936. Botrychium dissectum and Forma obliquum. *American Fern Journal.* 26(1):26-30.

Tryon, Rolla M. 1941. A Revision of the Genus *Pteridium. Rhodora.* 43:1-31, 37-67.

Tryon, Rolla M. 1955. *Selaginella rupestris* and Its Allies. *Annals of the Missouri Botanical Garden.* 42:1-99.

Tryon, Rolla M. 1962. Taxonomic Fern Notes. II. Pityrogramma (including Trismeria) and Anogramma. *Contributions from the Gray Herbarium of Harvard University.* Cambridge, Mass.

Tryon, Rolla and Alice F. Tryon. 1982. *Ferns and Allied Plants With Special Reference to Tropical America.* New York: Springer-Verlag New York, Inc.

Underwood, Lucien Marcus. 1891 [1892]. Distribution of Tropical Ferns in Peninsular Florida. *Proceedings of the Indiana Academy of Sciences.* 1:83-89.

Underwood, Lucien Marcus. 1900. *Our Native Ferns and Their Allies with Synoptical Descriptions of the American Pteridophyta North of Mexico,* ed. 6. New York.

Underwood, Lucien Marcus. 1906. Species Added to the Flora of the United States from 1900 to 1905. *Bulletin of the Torrey Botanical Club.* 33:189-205.

Valdespino, Ivan A. 1993. Selaginellaceae. *Flora of North America, Vol 2, Pteridophytes and Gymnosperms.* New York: Oxford University Press.

Valier, Kathy. 1995. *Ferns of Hawai'i.* Honolulu: University of Hawai'i Press.

Wagner, Florence S. 1992. Cytological Problems in *Lycopodium* Sens. Lat. *Annals of the Missouri Botanical Garden.* 79:718-729.

Wagner, W. H. Jr. 1960. Evergreen Grapeferns and the Meanings of Infraspecific Categories as Used in North American Pteridophytes. *American Fern Journal.* 50(1):32-45.

Wagner, W. H. Jr. 1963. A Biosystematic Survey of United States Ferns—Preliminary Abstract. *American Fern Journal.* 53(1):1-16.

Wagner, W. H. Jr. 1966. Two New Species of Ferns from the United States. *American Fern Journal.* 56:3-17.

Wagner, W. H. Jr. 1977. Systematic Implications of the Psilotaceae. *Brittonia.* 29:54-63.

Wagner, W. H. Jr. 1992. *Hiemobotrychium,* a New Section of *Botrychium* Subgenus *Sceptridium* from the Southeastern United States. *Novon.* 2:267-268.

Wagner, W. H. Jr. 1993. Schizaeaceae. *Flora of North America, Vol 2, Pteridophytes and Gymnosperms.* New York: Oxford University Press.

Wagner, W. H. Jr. and Joseph M. Beitel. 1992. Generic Classification of Modern North American Lycopodiaceae. *Annals of the Missouri Botanical Garden.* 79:675-696.

Wagner, Warren H. Jr. and Clifton E. Nauman. 1982. Pteris X delchampsii, a Spontaneous Fern Hybrid from Southern Florida. *American Fern Journal.* 72(4):97-102.

Wagner, Warren H. Jr. and Alan R. Smith. 1993. *Pteridophytes. Flora of North America, Vol 1, Introduction.* New York: Oxford University Press.

Wagner, W. H. Jr. and Florence S. Wagner. 1983. Genus Communities as a Systematic Tool in the Study of New World *Botrychium* (Ophioglossaceae). *Taxon.* 32(1):51-63.

Wagner, W. H. Jr. and Florence S. Wagner. 1993. Ophioglossaceae. *Flora of North America, Vol 2, Pteridophytes and Gymnosperms.* New York: Oxford University Press.

Wagner, W. H. Jr., Florence S. Wagner, S. W. Leonard, M. R. Mesler. 1981. A Reinterpretation of Ophioglossum dendroneuron E. P. St. John. *Castanea.* 46:311-322.

Walker, Trevor G. 1962. The *Anemia adiantifolia* Complex in Jamaica. *The New Phytologist.* 61(3):291-298.

Ward, Daniel B. and David W. Hall. 1976. Re-introduction of Marsilea vestita into Florida. *American Fern Journal.* 66(4):113-115.

Weatherby, C. A. 1948. Reclassification of the Polypodiaceae. *American Fern Journal.* 38(1):6-12.

Werth, Charles R., Melanie L. Haskins, Akke Hulburt. 1985. *Osmunda cinnamomea* forma *frondosa* at Mountain Lake, Virginia *American Fern Journal.* 75:128-132.

Whitehead, Charles. 1941. Beware of "Lycopodium." *American Fern Journal.* 31(3):100-102.

Wherry, Edgar T. 1964. *The Southern Fern Guide. Southeastern and South-Midland United States.* Garden City, NJ: Doubleday and Co.

Wunderlin, Richard P. 1982. *Guide to the Vascular Plants of Central Florida.* Tampa: University Presses of Florida.

Wunderlin, Richard P. 1998. *Guide to the Vascular Plants of Florida.* Gainesville, FL: University Press of Florida.

Yatskievych, George and Michael D. Windham. 1993. Pityrogramma. *Flora of North America, Vol 2, Pteridophytes and Gymnosperms.* New York: Oxford University Press.

INDEX

Note: This index contains both common and scientific names of every plant species mentioned in the text. Scientific names that appear in italics are those that are considered synonymous with the currently accepted name for a species. Those not in italics are considered valid for the species.

CP refers to color photos. Numbers in **bold** refer to pages that contain drawings or black-and-white photos.